GODS WITHIN
THE MACHINE

GODS WITHIN THE MACHINE

A History of the American Society
of Newspaper Editors, 1923–1993

PAUL ALFRED PRATTE

PRAEGER

Westport, Connecticut
London

Library of Congress Cataloging-in-Publication Data

Pratte, Paul Alfred.
    Gods within the machine : a history of the American Society of
Newspaper Editors, 1923–1993 / Paul Alfred Pratte.
        p.   cm.
    Includes bibliographical references and index.
    ISBN 0–275–94976–1 (alk. paper)
    1. American Society of Newspaper Editors.   I. Title.
PN4841.A1P73   1995
070.4′1′06073—dc20   94–24624

British Library Cataloguing in Publication Data is available.

Library of Congress Catalog Card Number: 94–24624
ISBN: 0–275–94976–1

First published in 1995

Praeger Publishers, 88 Post Road West, Westport, CT 06881
An imprint of Greenwood Publishing Group, Inc.

Printed in the United States of America

∞™

The paper used in this book complies with the
Permanent Paper Standard issued by the National
Information Standards Organization (Z39.48–1984).

10 9 8 7 6 5 4 3 2 1

Copyright Acknowledgment

The author and publisher gratefully acknowledge permission for use of the following material:

Quoted excerpts from *Read All About It! 50 Years of ASNE* by Alice Fox Pitts. Reston, Va.: ASNE, 1974. Reprinted with permission.

Every reasonable effort has been made to trace the owners of copyright materials in this book, but in some instances this has proven impossible. The author and publisher will be glad to receive information leading to more complete acknowledgments in subsequent printings of the book and in the meantime extend their apologies for any omissions.

Contents

Introduction

... The newspaper has become institutional, an entity in itself, and editors, however able, are but gods within the machine who serve and pass giving place to others of their kind. And yet there is no calling that commands higher qualities than ours, and none, I venture to say, that is pursued with such selfless devotion.

—Casper Yost, first president's address,
American Society of Newspaper Editors, April 27, 1923

Even in one of the most expensive cities in the United States, the JW Marriott Hotel in Washington, D.C., is an extravagant meeting place. The 773-room Marriott boasts that it is one of the great hotels of the world, "making reputation and reality come together." In 1987, it was the site of the summit meetings between President Ronald Reagan and Soviet leader Mikhail Gorbachev. Six thousand journalists were also there to cover the event.

Since 1986, the JW Marriott has also been the site each April of the annual $300,000 convention[1] of one of America's most prestigious and influential journalistic organizations, the American Society of Newspaper Editors (ASNE). With the exception of 15 conventions held in other locations[2] across the United States and Canada since its founding in 1922, the ASNE has always met in Washington at the largest and best hotels, including the Willard, the Statler, the Washington Hilton, and the Sheraton Park. Leo Bogart says that unlike the Associated Press Managing Editors (APME), who move around the country and attend programs filled with intense discussions of newspapers' workday problems, ASNE in its meetings features addresses on "cosmic" issues by cabinet members, the president and visiting heads of state.[3]

"This is the kind of group that just expects the President and his cabinet members to show up to meet with them," explains Everette E. Dennis of the Freedom Forum Center for Media Studies, who attends numerous other journalism meetings each year. "There is no question that ASNE members are the Brahmins of the newspaper business."[4]

Compared to earlier ASNE membership (illustrated in a 1950s photo on the cover of a 1974 ASNE history[5] in which dozens of male, white editors are holding up front pages of their newspapers), the members who attended conventions in the 1990s were more diverse, if not elite. A study showed that of the 700 attendees in 1990, about 10 percent were female and 3 percent were Hispanic, African American and Asian American. But the membership changes were far from satisfactory, according to ASNE's outgoing president Loren Ghiglione, editor of the Southbridge (Mass.) *News*.

One of only four small-town editors[6] among the 64 men and 1 woman to serve as ASNE president from 1922 to 1992, Ghiglione spent much of his year-long term crisscrossing the country at his own expense and meeting with other editors to encourage staff diversity. The only ASNE president with an Italian-American heritage, Ghiglione was particularly proud of the work of his human resources, disabilities and minorities committees. These committees reached out to historically black colleges and universities and persons with disabilities; they went public with employment figures on minorities, gay men, and lesbians.

Unlike his predecessors, who traditionally focused on press issues such as the First Amendment and restrictions at home and abroad, Ghiglione told the ASNE membership that rather than being "Davids" fighting the establishment, the public saw the editors instead as "status-quo Goliaths." He urged the members to become editors of action—"combating complacency and developing a higher level of commitment to diversity and other goals." Ghiglione recommended that newspapers make use of magazine-style fact checkers to increase accuracy, report about themselves with more candor, drop horoscopes and cease sponsorship of journalism events by tobacco companies.[7] He also underscored the need to support high school newspapers and prison publications. "Each of us could do worse than adopt an institution that makes us uncomfortable— a prison, a mental institution, a noisy, overcrowded, big city school, an AIDS hospital ward—and try to work in that world or at least understand it from the inside," Ghiglione told the editors. "If we can know it, maybe we can explain it better to our readers and even help change it."

The rhetoric and specific recommendations in the president's welcome to the newspaper editors were emphasized even more in the four-day convention agenda approved by Ghiglione. In addition to studies on newspapers of the future, ownership trends, and women's bylines, the results of a study of gays and lesbians in the newsroom were presented. This study culminated in a statement from the senior vice president of news at the Oakland *Tribune*, when he announced that he was gay.[8] "I, as an editor and a gay man, am proud of ASNE," Leroy Aarons said. Eighteen months after Aarons presented the landmark survey, he reported that membership in the National Gay and Lesbian Journalists Association, of which he was founder and president, was edging toward 500.[9]

ASNE emphasized diversity in the 1990s. Of the 89 speakers or participants at the 1990 convention, there were 18 females, 10 blacks and 7 Asian or Native Americans, along with 54 white males. A session which especially interested Ghiglione emphasized that the most important issues of the 1990s were the unfinished business of the 1960s. The panelists included 1960s icons Gloria Steinem, Jessica Mitford, Dick Gregory and retired General William Westmoreland. At the convention was President George Bush, who continued the tradition that each of the U.S. chief executives addresses ASNE at least once in his term of office. Other prestigious speakers who used ASNE meetings as a bully pulpit in the 1990s were President Bill Clinton and Vice President Al Gore, a former journalist. "ASNE conferences definitely attract the heavy hitter newsmakers," observed Ted Pease.[10]

Not everyone was enthusiastic about Ghiglione's presidency and the first convention agenda of the '90s. According to the New York *Times*, some editors characterized the convention as "a vast consciousness-raising effort," and many editors felt it was unnecessary. "I think I'm already sensitive," said Jerald A. Finch, managing editor of the Richmond *News Leader*. The hometown Washington *Post*, where Ghiglione had once worked as an intern,[11] also carped in an opinion piece by Ombudsman Richard Harwood on "our earnest but colorless trade association." The lackluster ASNE response to major challenges confronting the press, Harwood charged, was to follow the practice of former U.S. President Jimmy Carter's unsuccessful presidency—change the subject.[12]

"It was like going to a museum," said Paul Janesch, editor of the *Journal News* in West Nyack, New York, referring to the panel on the 1960s. He complained that panelists had mostly rehashed old issues.[13]

One museum that few editors complained about was the "American Journalist: Paradox of the Press" exhibit which opened at the Library of Congress in connection with the ASNE conference. Completed in part through Ghiglione's efforts and made possible by a $325,000 grant from the Gannett Foundation, the two-floor exhibit explored the 300-year history of American journalism, beginning in the colonial period. The second floor examined the American journalist in fact and fiction. This part of the exhibit focused on the journalist of fact (street reporter, persuader, crusader, investigator, exploiter, entertainer, war correspondent, broadcast journalist). It also examined the fictional archetype (editor, newspaper carrier, newswoman, scandalmonger, small-town editor, war correspondent, TV journalist, owner).

Conspicuous by their absence in the Library of Congress exhibit were references to ASNE, which despite criticism has been one of the leaders, if not the leader, in journalism. Although generally unknown except in journalism circles, ASNE has developed and promulgated journalism's major ethics code. The society has helped shape freedom of information legislation, press–bar guidelines and voluntary censorship practices during wartime. In addition, ASNE has produced a library of studies and books relating to the information, opinion, education and entertainment roles of journalism in the United States and around the world. Its *Proceedings* are primary resources in journalism departments. Yet ironically, despite its members' involvement in bringing government and business leaders to accountability, most citizens know little about ASNE.

This lack of knowledge of ASNE as well as other journalism professional groups and journalism in general may be one reason for a growing credibility gap between the press and the public. In his keynote address at the 1994 meeting in Washington, D.C., William Hilliard, editor of the Portland *Oregonian*, warned about what he called "a cancer of mean spiritedness festering in the journalistic gut today." Other speakers from within and without journalism, including President Bill Clinton, emphasized the mood of self-criticism.[14]

The purpose of this volume is to provide the general public, as well as ASNE members and journalists, with an interpretive, critical history of how the society and its individual members, especially its presidents, have functioned as leaders since the organization's beginnings in the 1920s. The title of this volume comes from a speech delivered by the society's first president, which referred to editors as "gods within the newspaper machine" who serve, then give place to others of their kind. This study places particular emphasis on the presidents as agenda setters, or causal agents in the movement of events. See Appendix A for a complete list of presidents and their newspapers. One of the major themes of this history is that the character and institutional history of ASNE have been influenced in great part by the individual presidents and committee chairpersons. Former president James S. Pope, in his opening address at the 1955 convention, emphasized the role of the committee chairs:

Our business is run largely by committees. The chairmen, particularly, are busy men who contribute a great deal to the society. Somehow under that system, the officers don't seem to have as much leisure time as they should have. I suppose we are rather like basketball referees who seem to run about as fast as players, trying to keep up with the ball.[15]

This history provides a general description of the ASNE organization, its staff, management, budget and means of communication (or bridge) for editors between the reporters and publisher/owners. The study provides the background of some key leaders in ASNE and describes the major issues they faced or overlooked. It also attempts to assess their leadership and their influence on journalism in light of the society's structure as a scattered group of individual editors who seldom come together. As noted by Russell Wiggins, a past president: "If ASNE was any looser it would fall apart. If it was more effectively organized it would be a menace." Wiggins praised the general looseness of the society as a form of check and balance against its abuse by any politically minded journalists who might attempt to use unanimity of society members for personal advantage.[16] ASNE's first president, Casper Yost, explained why this would be difficult:

If we expect this society to accomplish any great and immediate reform of, or advance in, newspaper conduct we are likely to be disappointed and discouraged. Such results are rarely brought about save through continuous and cumulative impressions acting upon an increasing consciousness. That consciousness, once made fully alive and active, through the influences we are setting in motion, will gradually effect the primary purposes of the organization.[17]

More specifically, this history attempts to evaluate the ASNE, its members and its leadership in consideration of what former ASNE president Michael J. O'Neill of the New York *Daily News* defined as the three major problems of American journalism:

1. Journalism concentrates heavily on effects rather than causes. Instead of probing ahead of today's events to discover the hissing fuses of tomorrow's disasters, journalists wait until they hear the explosions. By philosophy and practice, journalists focus on present action; they seldom search out the precursors of crisis in hopes of alerting the public in time to act in its own defense. From the race riots to the great savings and loan catastrophe, reporters were almost the last to catch up to the story. There is something profoundly wrong with a journalism that claims to be the public's sentry and doesn't even see the treasury being looted in broad daylight of untold billions in people's savings.[18]

2. Journalism's profound ethnocentricity projects the whole world onto American screens, looking at incoming images through the prism of American culture and translating issues into American stereotypes so that Americans do not see other societies as they see themselves and we do not see ourselves as others see us. From Vietnam to the dispatch of the Marines to Lebanon, U.S. history is littered with tragic miscalculations based on an ethnocentric view of the outside world. A tiny example in journalism was the overreaction of many American newspaper editors to the so-called New World Information Order championed by UNESCO. Their outrage was defined entirely by their own constricted view: there wasn't the slightest hint that some third world complaints were justified.[19]

3. The massive intrusion of television's oral-visual culture into society emphasizes impressionistic and existential communication. Emotion, immediacy, celebrity, entertainment, etc., now dominate the way people experience the world. TV politics have revolutionized the United States democratic system. Instant mass emotions create instant mass opinions even before leaders have

time to lead. All this has diminished rational deliberation. The result, according to Neil Postman, is that Americans are on the verge of amusing themselves to death.[20] Television has also diminished the role of newspapers. It has driven many newspapers out of business and created serious readership troubles for those that have survived.

To make these evaluations, the author has had complete access to all the ASNE official minutes from 1922 to 1992, as well as studied the official *Proceedings* of its annual meetings from 1923 to 1992 and the *Bulletin* from 1933. Earlier copies of the *Bulletin* were not available. Correspondence was exchanged or interviews occurred with most of the society's living presidents as well as relatives of deceased presidents.

Special thanks must go to Jay Ambrose of the *Rocky Mountain News* and Loren Ghiglione of the Southbridge (Mass.) *News*, who both served as chairs of ASNE's History and Newspaper Committee, which approved this project, as well as to Lee Stinnett and the full-time ASNE staff. Acknowledgments should also go to former ASNE executive director Gene Giancarlo, Philip Ault, Edward Adams, Linda Hunter Adams, George Chaplin, Everette E. Dennis, Howard H. (Tim) Hays, Lee Hills, Curtis and Suzanne Houghton, John Hughes, Norman Isaacs, David Jensen, Kenneth MacDonald, Felix McKnight, J. Edward Murray, Shelly Nicholls, Robert C. Notson, James Pope, Jr., Richard Schmidt, Richard Smyer, Donald Sterling, Jr., Leonard Teel, Jr., Patrick Washburn, Jeff Welch, Miles Wolff, Jr., and others who have reviewed drafts of this history.

Special thanks to more than a dozen students in media history and graduate classes at Brigham Young University who did term papers on ASNE-related topics, and to Martha Carlisle, whose master's thesis painted a portrait of ASNE presidents. Related topics by the author have previously been published in the *Journal of Radio Studies*, *Journal of Women's History*, *American Journalism*, the *ASNE Bulletin*, *Editor and Publisher* and other publications.

Gratitude is also expressed to numerous other professional colleagues who have reviewed drafts of these chapters and other related papers while attending conventions of the West Coast Journalists group of the Association for Educators in Journalism and Mass Communication (AEJMC) and the American Journalism Historians Association (AJHA).

Thanks also go to Jane Clayson, Richele Koenig, Annette Lyon, Heather Seferovich and Claire Verschoof of the Brigham Young University Humanities Publications Center for proofreading and production.

NOTES

1. Denise McVea, "Marriott ready for puttin' on the Ritz," ASNE *Reporter*, April 3, 1990, 1.

2. They include meetings in Atlantic City, 1924; New York City, 1942, 1979; San Francisco, 1957, 1970, 1987; New Orleans, 1962; Montreal, 1966; Atlanta, 1974; Honolulu, 1977; Chicago, 1982; Denver, 1983; Boston, 1991; and Baltimore, 1993.

3. Leo Bogart, *Preserving the Press: How Daily Newspapers Mobilized to Keep Their Readers*, New York: Columbia University Press, 1991, 9.

4. Everette Dennis, interview with author, Washington, D.C., April 5, 1990.

5. Alice Fox Pitts, *Read All About It! 50 Years of ASNE*, Reston, Va.: ASNE, 1974.

6. In addition to Ghiglione, the other small-town editors include William Allen White, Emporia *Gazette*, 1938; Dwight Marvin, Troy *Record*, 1941; and Richard Smyser, Oak Ridge *Oak Ridger*, 1984.

7. Loren Ghiglione, "The next decade in our society will require editors to work on the front line, not the sidelines," *ASNE Bulletin*, May–June 1990, 23.

8. Leroy Aarons, "Gay and lesbian journalists report most newsrooms are good places to work," *ASNE Bulletin*, May–June 1990, 30–31.

9. Leroy Aarons, "Membership is approaching 500 in new association for gay and lesbian journalists," *ASNE Bulletin*, January–February 1992, 20.

10. Ted Pease, interview, Washington, D.C., April 6, 1990.

11. In an August 28, 1990, letter to the author, Ghiglione said his internship at the Washington *Post* "felt like a large bureaucratic corporation with people climbing over each other to get ahead, also shaped my vision of where in journalism I wanted—and did not want—to work."

12. Richard Harwood, "Poor Editors," Washington *Post National Weekly Edition*, April 16–22, 1990, 28.

13. Alex S. Jones, "Newspaper Talk: Reappraisal and the 60s," New York *Times*, April 6, 1990, A13.

14. William Glaberson, "Editors Look at Themselves in Response to Criticism," New York *Times* (National), April 14, 1994, A12.

15. ASNE *Proceedings*, 1955, 11.

16. Russell Wiggins, telephone interview, December 5, 1990.

17. ASNE *Proceedings*, 1925, 21.

18. Michael O' Neill, letter to the author, August 3, 1990.

19. O'Neill, August 4, 1990.

20. Neil Postman, *Amusing Ourselves to Death: Public Discourse in the Age of Show Business*, New York: Penguin Books, 1985, 3–4.

GODS WITHIN
THE MACHINE

Chapter 1

" . . . what sort of teeth . . . and who is it to bite?"

It seems to me that, lacking teeth, we can substitute therefor [*sic*] a moral factor. If we don't, we have indulged in a beautiful gesture that is entirely meaningless, and I for one decline to participate further in such an empty motion.
—Herbert Bayard Swope, New York *World*, April 28, 1923

There are some amongst us who insist that we must have a code with teeth in it; but what sort of teeth, how is it to bite and who is it to bite? I cannot agree with this view. The enforcement of a code of ethics, applicable only to institutions by an organization having but a degree of control over these institutions is, in my opinion, impracticable.
—Casper Yost, St. Louis *Globe-Democrat*, January 15, 1926

The editor of the Philadelphia *Evening Bulletin*, Fred Fuller Shedd, was overjoyed. "The move for adoption is unanimous," he exclaimed to members of the American Society of Newspaper Editors (ASNE) who were meeting at the Willard Hotel in Washington, D.C., on April 22, 1932. "Thank God!"[1]

After six years of heated debate between editors—led by "die-hards"[2] such as Herbert Bayard Swope of the New York *World* and Willis Abbot of the *Christian Science Monitor*—seeking methods to enforce a code of ethics, and a group of more cautious editors—including Shedd and ASNE founder Casper Yost of the St. Louis *Globe-Democrat* (described at various times as "pussyfooting,"[3] "old fogies"[4] or "yellow bellies"[5])—ASNE had finally reached accord. Its members agreed on a compromise that was designed to give enforcement powers to a code of ethics conceived at ASNE's first meeting in April 1923.

The debate over ethics enforcement was the major divisive issue during the first decade of ASNE's existence. For a number of years it contributed to the society's perceived lack of credibility with the public, as well as with other journalists.[6] The remarks of Pulitzer Prize winner Paul Y. Anderson of the St. Louis

Post-Dispatch demonstrate how some journalists felt. Anderson denounced the ASNE as "cowardly and pusillanimous" for rejecting an amendment to its constitution that would allow censure, suspension or expulsion of its members for gross misconduct and violation of ethics.[7]

The steps leading to the passage of the code and the 1932 compromise, which omitted what some described as "the court character" of ASNE and replaced it with a "due process clause," are significant. They illuminate the environment, personalities and philosophical approaches toward ethics, as well as other major issues and controversies in the first decade of the society's existence. In particular, the ethics debate demonstrates the contention of scholars Wilbur Schramm and Robert Logan that the ASNE code seems to follow rather closely James Madison's libertarian thinking rather than Thomas Jefferson's social responsibility approach to ethics.[8]

Despite claims that the motivation for the organization came from a critical article appearing in *Harper's* magazine in 1922, Malcolm Bingay says the concept went even further back. Writing in his "Good Morning" column in the Detroit *Free Press* in 1946, Bingay traced the founding of ASNE to a summer night in the Rockies in 1912. A group of newspaper editors were enjoying a preview of Glacier National Park. As they sat around a campfire they heard Yost discuss an idea which possessed him. "His dream was the creation of an ethical organization of American newspaper editors. He wanted to see them banded together on the common ground of high purpose."[9]

Bingay recalls that although the seed had been planted, World War I intervened. In addition, he says, most editors were not receptive to an organization that promoted ethics: "No group of men are more self-conscious or more cynical as to their own activities than newspaper editors. That cynicism is born of too many years behind scenes where they see a different picture for the drama of life."[10]

Remarkably, the ethics code that caused so much contention in ASNE's early years and that covers issues that are still being debated in organizations such as the Society of Professional Journalists[11] was written primarily by one person, H. J. Wright of the New York *Globe*. It was adopted within a two-day period at ASNE's first conference in Washington, D.C., April 27–28, 1923.

Officially, the organization came into existence the previous year in Chicago when Yost, the editorial page editor of the St. Louis *Globe-Democrat*, and four others from midwestern states met at the Blackstone Hotel in February of 1922. They gathered to discuss collective action for the advancement of the news and editorial side, to develop a constitution and a code of ethics and to launch a recruiting campaign for the organization.[12]

PURPOSES OF ASNE

The first ASNE Constitution described the purposes of the new organization: "To promote acquaintance among members, to develop a stronger and professional esprit de corps, to maintain the dignity and rights of the profession, to consider and perhaps establish ethical standards of professional conduct, to interchange ideas for the advancement of professional ideals and for the more effective application of professional labors, and to work collectively for the solution of common problems."[13]

Among the founding fathers of the organization (along with Yost) who called for the ethics code were Erie C. Hopwood, Cleveland *Plain Dealer*; E. S. Beck, Chicago *Tribune*; Charles H. Dennis, Chicago *Daily News* and George E. Miller, Detroit *News*. By October, 49 charter members had been enlisted. Wright was assigned to draft a code of ethics to be presented at the first convention.

Yost, who dominated the society during its first decade, presided at that meeting. A studious man weighing scarcely a hundred pounds, Yost added much to the journalistic traditions of St. Louis by contributing to professional ethics before promulgating his philosophy on a national scale. He scrupulously practiced high standards in the conduct of his editorial page until his death in May 1941.[14] Little Casper, tagged "arsenic-and-old-lace" by his contemporaries, might more appropriately be remembered as creating the modern concept of the responsibility of the press, a concept often lost today in the more dramatic scuffles about press freedom.[15]

After assisting Yost in the early organization, Hopwood succeeded him as president in 1926–1927. Hopwood was the first of three Cleveland *Plain Dealer* editors elected to the ASNE presidency.[16] He served as secretary of the fledgling organization during its 1923 debate over the creation of an ethics grievance committee. It was Hopwood who suggested that a grievance committee was unnecessary, because an ethics committee could watch out for flagrant ethics violations.[17] While president, Hopwood recommended that the society hire a counsel to fight a growing number of contempt cases against reporters. Speaking at the University of Missouri, Hopwood also called for higher salaries for poorly paid journalists across the country.[18] Archer Shaw states in his history of the newspaper that "few men ever brought to the *Plain Dealer* greater gifts than Hopwood, and none ever made greater use of his gifts to the glory of newspapermaking in Ohio."[19] Grove Patterson of the Toledo *Blade* recalls that Hopwood's ideas were in no way better or finer than Yost's, but that Hopwood had "a strong, vigorous manner and personality, and he put an immense amount of constructive effort into the early days of the organization."[20]

The third founding father of ASNE was Edward Scott ("Teddy") Beck. Indiana-born and a graduate of the University of Michigan, Beck was described by one colleague as "a man of education and natural refinement, conservative, tactful, mild-mannered." Beck's only fault, in the opinion of a colleague, was that he had been beaten down too much by flamboyant managing editor James Kelley when Beck was city editor of the Chicago *Tribune*.[21] One of Beck's major contributions to the advancement of journalistic ethics was his presentation at the 1930 convention of a report on honesty and freedom from graft in sports reporting, prepared by Don Maxwell of the *Tribune* sports staff.[22] Recalling why 9 of 11 Chicago newspapers had failed from the time he started as a reporter in 1893, Beck said that the fate of newspapers was related to the integrity of their owners: "There was, of course, the irresistible modern tendency to consolidation as in all industries. But I want to make the point that the character of their ownership and control had a share in their ultimate fate."[23]

Personal correspondence between Beck and another early member of the pro tem board of directors, Arthur Krock of the Louisville *Times*, also illustrates Beck's desire for independence from publisher control of newspapers and for a strong professional organization: "At the outset I fell in with the idea but on the whole the organization developed feebly. In a basic sense, it seems to me that the trouble is that we are employees and are, to a degree, under inhibitions and cannot speak freely for our papers. I do not know that the association as it has evolved is of considerable value, but the acquaintanceship is pleasant and perhaps useful."[24]

Krock, who was in the process of moving to the New York *Times*, expressed similar concerns about the new organization in a 1951 letter to David Lawrence:

I had my doubts at the time of how much of consequence such an organization could accomplish because it was composed in the main of employees, and in those days editors rarely had the freedom which publishers now give them. My doubts were augmented at one of the early conventions of the society in which a majority declined to take any stand against journalistic practices then current in Denver, that had been brought to our attention. But I must say that in succeeding years these doubts have been resolved in considerable measure . . .

I helped to draw up the Constitution and the Bylaws, and was a member of the first Board of Directors. The prospect of an annual trip East with all expenses paid would doubtless have increased my enthusiasm for the project had it not been, that as a member of the Associated Press, I already had that privilege.[25]

Neither the *Proceedings* nor the minutes provide much information on the role of the other two founders, Charles H. Dennis of the Chicago *Daily News* and George E. Miller of the Detroit *News*. William Lutz records that Miller was a former Washington correspondent who helped Senator-elect Charles E. Townsend promote the idea of what was later to become the St. Lawrence Seaway.[26] Malcom Bingay recalled that Miller had a saying which had been drilled into the hearts and minds of every man on the *News* staff: "I would rather have the *Detroit News* beaten on the biggest story of the day than have a member of our staff do anything that would permit it to be said that a dishonorable thing had been done to get the information."[27]

Dennis took a more active role in the ethics debate in 1927 when he helped submit an amendment to strengthen the ethics code, only to have it turned down because of its courtlike character. Ted Smiley of the Philadelphia *Public Ledger* characterized the proposed process as similar to the American Bar Association's board of censors, "but lacking the backing of the courts and without similar processes to pursue."[28]

Dennis headed the program committee, which invited John W. Davis, president of the bar association, to be one of two major speakers. Dennis also helped establish a convention that reflected major journalism concerns of the early 1920s. These included the growing reliance on syndicates and press service copy, inadequate schools of journalism, truth and accuracy in the news, the reader's part in instructing the editor and the process of seeking and getting publicity.[29]

As noted by Frederick Allen in his informal history of the 1920s, the years from the end of World War I to the 1929 stock market crash included "ballyhoo years" for many newspapers, particularly those in major urban areas.[30] Fewer newspapers with larger circulations were being standardized to an unprecedented degree by the use of press association and syndicated material. Newspapers all over the country were also being gathered into chains under more or less centralized direction.[31]

In a discussion of the emergence of the modern media, the press of this period is described as a "leviathan" and as an oligopoly being challenged by magazines and radio. The significant marketing strategies of the period were interpretive reporting and the publication of tabloids.[32] As a result of growing negative criticism against newspapers, Dennis encouraged ASNE to deal exclusively with live issues in a frank and courageous manner. "Certainly this is not a mutual admiration society nor a medium to facilitate the production of pink platitudes for pale people," he asserted.[33]

One reporter who helped create the popular image of roughhouse Chicago-type journalism during this period was a member of Dennis's *Daily News* staff, Ben Hecht. Coauthor with Charles MacArthur of the Broadway play (and later film) *The Front Page*, Hecht wrote that Dennis, "despite being a world-thinker, righteous editorial writer and passionate grammarian, was not without a touch of newspaper larceny in his soul."[34]

ADOPTION OF THE CODE OF ETHICS

Aside from his Jeffersonian writing role as author of the first ethics code, little is known of H. John Wright. Speaking in 1947, Marvin Creager said he did not even know what the H stood for in Wright's name: "It might well have stood for Hippocrates, for Mr. Wright laid down a pattern that is to journalism what the Hippocratic oath is to medicine. The canons reflect well the sentiments of the early members, and I hope, of all who have joined in later years. So long as they are faithfully observed, we need not fear for the salvation of the press."[35]

In his autobiography, Lincoln Steffens refers to Henry John Wright, the city editor of the New York *Evening Post*, upon whom Steffens was forced for his first journalism job after returning from Europe. Both Wright and Steffens worked under the supervision of E. L. Godkin, who also edited the *Nation* magazine until his death in 1902. Wright later edited the *Commercial Advertiser*, the oldest newspaper in New York, before going to the New York *Globe*.[36] Wright appears in the 1923 *Proceedings* to introduce the seven-point code of ethics. He defends it, helps revise it and then disappears from the organization. Even the history of ASNE's first 50 years misidentifies Wright's newspaper as the New York *World* rather than the *Globe*.[37]

This confusion may occur in part because the best-known New York journalist defending the code, as well as methods of enforcing it during the 1923 debate, was Herbert Bayard Swope, who had been executive editor of Joseph Pulitzer's newspaper since 1920. Once referred to as "The *World*'s greatest reporter—New York *World* or the whole wide world,"[38] Swope was joined in the first-day discussion by, among others, Arthur Vandenberg, editor of the Grand Rapids *Herald*, who was to be appointed a U.S. senator in 1928 and served until his death in 1951. After further discussion, the code was unanimously adopted on the second day. Following an impressive preamble, the canons emphasized nine major points: responsibility, freedom of the press, independence, sincerity, truthfulness, accuracy, impartiality, fair play and decency (Appendix B).

GRIEVANCE COMMITTEE TO ENFORCE CODE

Adoption of the code was not sufficient for Wright and a number of others at the first conference. "If we are to give it any useful purpose, we must keep it alive and keep it up-to-date," he advised. To do this, he recommended appointment of a seven-person standing grievance committee similar to the grievance committee of the American Bar Association. The group would interpret the code, which could be changed from meeting to meeting.[39]

Such a grievance committee was opposed by Ted Smiley of the Philadelphia *Public Ledger* and James T. Williams of the Boston *Transcript*. The latter spoke for members of the New England Association, who felt that the newly formed organization was taking on more than it could handle. "I very much fear that we shall lose some of our members if we attempt too much," he warned.[40] The word *grievance* implies that you have power to correct the issue, Williams stated. "What power have we to correct it?"[41] Smiley said he did not believe that ASNE should set itself up as anything similar to the board of censors of the bar association.

Swope, diametrically opposed, urged the society to set forth a conception of what ought to be done. "Later we can discover how that can be done," he argued. "It seems to me that, lacking teeth, we can substitute therefor [*sic*] a moral factor. If we don't, we have indulged in a beautiful gesture that is entirely meaningless, and I for one decline to participate further in such an empty motion."[42]

The first debate ended after Hopwood, Willis Abbot and others observed that the ethics committee could serve the purpose of the grievance committee under consideration. Wright withdrew his motion. In his closing remarks, Yost called attention to the "extraordinary skill and intelligence" of Wright and his committee in creating the code. "It was a real task to have created a code of ethics of that kind in view of the fact that there was really nothing upon which to base a beginning," Yost said. "He had to make a start from nothing, from his own conceptions and the conceptions of journalists as to the ethical principles and their practice and make a definite Code that would appeal to this Society in general."[43]

Yost added that Wright had established a "guidestone for future journalism. Whatever may be developed from that, we have started it, we have done something concrete and definite toward the establishment of ethical principles."[44]

PRESIDENT HARDING'S OBSERVATIONS ON ETHICS

When U.S. President Warren Harding spoke that evening, he took note of Wright's work on the code. "There has never been a time, gentlemen, when a fitting code of ethics was so essential to the press of America," Harding said. He discussed three ethical concerns in his rambling remarks: responsibility, decency and the need to omit news at certain times.

"I believe that if I were to write the code and could write it for all other newspapers in America," the former Marion, Ohio, publisher told the editors, "I would ban everything of a vicious character except that which is necessary as a public warning. If I ran a newspaper to suit my own ideals, there would not be a police court reporter on the paper, never a police court column in the paper."[45] In conclusion, Harding said:

You know there is a fine bit of ethics sometimes in the omission of news as well as the publication of it. I think there are often times when the news ought to be suppressed. There are certainly times when news of international importance cannot be given to the public. Don't you see how important it is to tell the simple, comforting truth? And don't you see how important it is to omit the things that tend to destroy the faith in society? Don't you see how essential it is that you preach faith in the justice of the republic rather than a suspicion that justice cannot abide under our present social system?[46]

Harding's troubled state of mind before his sudden death in San Francisco shortly after the convention is described in "An American Tragedy," a chapter from William Allen White's autobiography. White met with Harding shortly before President Harding's speech to ASNE. The Kansas editor said he left the White House convinced that Harding "realized the conflict around him and that, so far as a man with his sordid background could, he was trying to line up with the righteous forces, striving to break away from the hands of the past drawing his administration down to shame."[47]

Hamilton Owens, editor-in-chief of the Baltimore *Sun* and the *Evening Sun*, stated that newspapers were already full of stories of the doings of the "Ohio gang." "Mr. Harding was not my idea of the perfect mentor for newspaper editors," Owens wrote. "Still he was an editor by courtesy and the society had granted him honorary membership."[48]

THE BONFILS AFFAIR

Notwithstanding the consensus at the first meeting and the pleasant words from President Harding,[49] ASNE was not to be spared the agony of the ongoing ethics debate which dominated its first decade of existence. At the 1924 convention the ethics debate was triggered by the Harding administration scandal over naval oil reserves at Teapot Dome, Wyoming, and Elk River, California. These reserves were leased to private parties without competitive bidding by Albert B. Fall, U.S. secretary of the interior. Denver *Post* publisher Frederick G. Bonfils allegedly had a conflict of interest after his newspaper initially wrote news stories and editorials challenging the actions, only to stop writing about the scandal after becoming involved in transactions with a landowner. Although never mentioned by name in the ASNE minutes or in its *Proceedings*,[50] the Bonfils affair haunted the society for the next two years and helped distort its position on ethics for much of its organizational life.

According to the colorful account of former Denver *Post* reporter Gene Fowler, Bonfils' connection with the Teapot Dome scandal of Harding's cash-and-carry administration was "incredibly weird." The *Post* was the first newspaper to report the malodorous deal; nevertheless, in the end Bonfils benefited handsomely.[51] Although the *Post* was not a part of the scandal itself, Bill Hosokawa says the paper became involved "in a curious indirect manner."[52]

Led by firebrand Willis John Abbot of the *Christian Science Monitor*, the society's membership instructed the board of directors "to investigate charges made against certain members and take action accordingly."[53] At an organizational meeting in Atlantic City on April 25, 1924, it was moved that the investigation of charges affecting "certain newspapermen," as provided in the resolution, be referred to the committee on ethical standards and that President Yost be empowered to give any necessary instruction.[54] Also speaking in favor of "enforcing the canons as they already stand" was Vandenberg: "I don't want to waive the opportunity of saying that after this society has dared for the first time in the history of American journalism to set down the bases of journalism, honest journalism, I don't want to waive the opportunity to say that we ought to equally dare to enforce them."[55]

In discussion on the floor, Vandenberg said that "a pretense of ethics would be a mere gesture if the glaring violation of the ethics isn't promptly and properly attended to in such a forum as this, and as far as I am concerned, I would prefer that the gesture were never made than that a glaring challenge to the ethics should be ignored." He went on to argue:

I suppose that in a small way, all of us, day in and day out, are violating some phase of this code. That is to be expected. We are human. But when the public attention is concentrated on what seems to be magnified offenses against decency and against what we assume to be the ethics of journalism, I don't see how a convention of this society can pass without taking notice of it.[56]

The following year Yost reported that the board had retained counsel to make the society's position fair and secure, as well as morally right. Unfortunately for the firebrands, the counsel advised that the society's position was valid under the constitution only in regard to expulsion for misconduct in an individual's personal, but not professional, life. The board invited Bonfils, his attorney, and E. D. Stacklebeck, a reporter who had much to do with the production of some *Post* stories that were never published, to appear before the board. Minutes of the meeting record that transcripts of the entire afternoon's discussion with the three were taken and arrangements made to mail them to members of the board who were unable to attend the meeting.[57]

At its 1926 meeting Yost discussed the question of enforcement in detail:

I am merely calling attention to the differences of opinion that prevail, and must prevail, as to abstract concepts of right. There are some amongst us who insist that we must have a code with teeth in it; but what sort of teeth, how is it to bite and who is it to bite? I cannot agree with this view. The enforcement of a code of ethics, applicable only to institutions, by an organization having but a limited degree of control over these institutions is, in my opinion, impractical.[58]

Although the society attempted to enforce the code through the creation of a "committee on the integrity of the press," the committee was not taken seriously. This can be seen in an exchange between secretary Hopwood and his friend Paul Bellamy, also of the *Plain Dealer*:

Mr. Hopwood: Mr. Chairman, not that I have any desire to oust my distinguished associate, Mr. Bellamy, from his position, but it is my honest opinion that this committee on the integrity of the press is the most asininely constituted committee that exists in this organization.

Mr. Bellamy: Amen![59]

At its 1926 fall meeting, the board adopted a report which censured and suspended Bonfils from the society.[60] But after further examination of the issue with attorneys, the board rescinded its action against Bonfils upon finding that it did not have the authority to discipline its members.[61]

THE ONGOING DEBATE

Rescinding the censure and suspension action against Bonfils, however, did not end the movement for ethics enforcement under the leadership of Abbot and Swope (before the latter left journalism in 1929). They continued to promote changes in the constitution to allow for censure and expulsion of members. About one-tenth of the 1927 *Proceedings* is devoted to discussion of ethics issues, including a six-page report by William Allen White, who succeeded Walter Lippmann of the New York *World* as head of the committee.[62] Among the other ethics-related topics on the program were "How Much Contact Shall the Editor Have with the Public?" and "Obligations of the Newspaper and Newspaper Editor to Its Public."

President Hopwood announced that a mere statement of facts from the ethics committee had been sufficient to show that the board of directors lacked authority to examine charges of unprofessional conduct that allegedly took place April 14, 1922, and September 25, 1922, before the adoption of the code of ethics. Instead, Hopwood introduced a resolution to amend the constitution and eliminate the word *perhaps* with reference to the establishment of ethical standards of professional conduct. The motion was carried.[63] This action during his introduction at the final banquet that same night was among the last Hopwood performed for the ASNE. He died on March 18, 1928.

The ethics issue again occupied much of ASNE's 1928 meeting. There was prolonged discussion concerning the committee's report on the revision of the constitution; the discussion focused on ethics enforcement. A split existed and was eventually resolved when a motion (made by Yost and amended by Abbot) to give the society "power to discipline, censure or expel members for unprofessional conduct" was passed by the membership by an 18–15 vote.[64] Another milestone in the ongoing ethics debate was reached when Paul Bellamy and Walter M. Harrison of the Oklahoma City *Oklahoman* took part in a hypothetical case history of John Goodman, a character originated by *Quill* magazine.[65]

In April 1929, ASNE secretary Marvin H. Creager read an amendment drawn up by John W. Davis, attorney for the Associated Press. It provided the board with authority to investigate violations of professional ethics and to censure, suspend or expel offending members.

Speaking against such an amendment was "Skipper" Harrison, the third ASNE president, and Samuel M. Williams, editor-in-chief of the St. Paul *Dispatch & Pioneer Press*. Harrison argued that "everything that could have been said, has been said on the subject."[66] Williams claimed that ASNE had no right to inflict upon a member a punishment that would extend beyond him individually:

You have the right to discipline the membership of your own voluntary association as long as the penalties fall upon that member, but when by inference or indirection the action of a small group, a handful of men, may result in irreparable damage to properties with which they may be connected, then I say we are going beyond our rights, our privileges, our duties toward the owners of the property which may be ourselves, or it may be others who employ us.[67]

Despite passionate arguments for the amendment, Willis John Abbot failed to gain support from the floor. A former writer for Hearst's New York *Journal*, Abbot had been named the third editor of the *Christian Science Monitor* in 1921. He took a particular interest in working with peace advocates after an earlier career in politics. He also found time to write more than 20 books.[68]

Speaking against the motion, Edward Scott Beck said that the amendment, if adopted, "instead of strengthening, it might be, or probably would be, weakening the society." Yost called the amendment neither practicable nor desirable:

Any violation of ethics is the work of an institution. We cannot convict a newspaper in this society, we have no right to do it. We cannot find any individual editor guilty of a violation of ethical conduct, because you cannot fix the responsibility of a single individual in an institution and hold that individual responsible for what it may do. I think the possibility of action by this society or by the board of directors on questions of ethical conduct would be likely to be destructive and bad for the society.[69]

The 1929 amendment was rejected 34–21. Harrison said he thought it would be "in the best interests of all of us, if for at least one year we put aside all discussion of the question."[70]

THE 1931 DEBATE

Despite the rebuff from both the leaders and members of the ASNE, Abbot did not give up. In 1931 he spoke on behalf of resurrecting the resolution drafted by Davis. He suggested that it be presented to the membership at the next annual meeting. He stressed the need for organizations to be able to expel a member for reasons other than "actually ushering him into the doors of a penitentiary."[71] Without mentioning the name of the ASNE villain, Abbot described him "as notorious, whose guilt was demonstrated not only in our hearing, but in official hearings of various kinds, and who was a scoff and byword in journalistic circles of the United States."[72]

This time, Abbot received support from Henry Watterson's protégé Tom Wallace of the Louisville *Times*. Wallace noted that ASNE had been excoriated by many respectable newspapers because it would not take action "that showed we have any backbone or any disposition to put out of the society, if he once gets in, any common crook, not an editor who is guilty of some indiscretion or unethical practice, but let us say a man who was put in the penitentiary."[73]

Yost disagreed with Wallace's assertion about the society's impotency in the Bonfils affair. "Every society in existence has an inherent and inalienable right, constitution or no constitution, to decide whom it shall take into its membership and whom it shall eject from that membership, for cause," he said. Later in the heated discussion, Yost said he didn't "enjoy a fight, although I was once red-headed, but Mr. Abbot has accused me of a lapse of memory."

Abbot replied in kind to Yost's remarks about his own memory of 1924:

My recollection is that what happened was that the gentleman whom we strove to discipline being a pugnacious person served notice on us that each one of us directors would be made the defendant in a suit of anywhere from ten to five-hundred thousand dollars apiece for having slandered him and there wasn't enough guts in the whole board of directors to be willing to stand that risk. I know I didn't have them.[74]

Subsequently, a motion was made for a subcommittee of the board of directors to investigate the matter and submit a report to the board; then the board would make a concrete proposal to the membership the following year. The motion passed unanimously.

Despite losing the ethics debate, Abbot was reelected to the board of directors. This caused Yost to comment: "I don't know of any more valuable member of the society from its beginning than Mr. Willis Abbot. He has been a valuable member of the board and it gratifies me greatly to see him reelected. I would regret it very much if he had been dropped out. We want him and we need him. We don't agree on anything, but he is a good fellow."[75]

THE 1932 DISCUSSION

The same good spirit that existed when the 1931 session ended seemed to prevail in the 1932 meeting. Because of an accident, it was in a "crippled condition" that Abbot appeared to move for adoption of a formal report, which was hammered out in the midyear meeting in Philadelphia. Abbot said that he and Yost had discovered that both were seeking the same thing for the good of the organization and for journalism: "We found, like the character in Molière who was astonished to discover that he had been speaking prose all his life and didn't know it, that the prosaic materialism of the *Globe-Democrat* as applied to this matter and the poetic idealism of the *Christian Science Monitor* had both for their aim the strengthening of the ethical standards of our society."[76]

Yost's remarks were less effusive. He noted simply that the board of directors had devised a formula that "like charity would cover a multitude of sins." The phrase "due cause," he said, was "sufficiently broad and comprehensive to apply to any conceivable contingency that may arise within the experience of the society."[77]

Abbot noted that there had been only two instances in the 10-year history of the association where some disciplinary methods might possibly have been applied to members who violated "distinctly ethical standards which the society should maintain."[78] Wallace, admitting that he had "produced part of the noise on behalf of the action," said that if the society had not united, it could not have looked forward to the growth and usefulness that it should have as the result of ending the controversy.[79] Wallace also revealed an interesting irony, that although indicted for a felony, one member of the first committee on ethics was still a member in good standing, insofar as the action of ASNE was concerned. "I think that illustrates the need of a means of disciplining members and removing them for due cause."[80] On the more positive side, William Allen White said he wanted to second the motion "with bells."[81]

Even more enthusiastic at the 1932 love fest was President Shedd, who ruled that the resolution was not retroactive. Shedd's reference to deity was followed by a round of applause before he noted: "I consider this the proudest thing, the best achievement of the two years I have been honored by the presidency of the society. I think it is the biggest thing that we could have accomplished. I think it means more for the welfare, the growth, the development of the society, and its general influence and power in the newspaper profession, than anything we could have done."[82]

SINCE 1932

Although unanimous passage of the "due process" resolution in 1932 helped resolve the postbirth struggle over enforcement, it did not end the ethics debate. Marvin Creager recalls that because of the criticism of Yost and the society, it was a long time before many prestigious papers would have much to do with the society. This was particularly true of the Pulitzer papers, the Hearst group, the Washington media and others who spurned the society, Creager said:

Time was when the Washington papers, with our meeting right in their town, barely mentioned us along with the obituary notices and our directors were constantly working on vain schemes to get the papers like the N.Y. *Times* and the Baltimore *Sun* really to take some part in our endeavors. Some felt that we must go hat in hand to the big names. In some cases memberships were taken out, but the holders did not get to the meetings all of which made us feel somewhat like poor relations. But that situation cured itself when we decided to be ourselves and go on about our society. If they wanted to join, well and good, if not, be damned to them.[83]

In a 1951 letter to David Lawrence, Creager wrote: "But we at least got over the idea of being policemen, turned in our clubs and stars, and settled down as an organization hoping to be of benefit if we could, but determined, meantime, to have a good time with each other and not lose perspective in our missionary zeal."[84]

The ethics debate has continued until today, however, in various forms. ASNE minutes show other times when ethical issues were raised:

- The society in 1928 directed President Harrison to inform the American Gas Association that he would not accept expense money for his trip to Atlantic City, New Jersey, to address the association. Instead, ASNE authorized the payment of travel expenses by the society.[85]

- A proposal was made to the 1934 ASNE president that he appoint a committee to consider publicizing newspaper ethics and the importance of freedom of the press.[86]

- Such issues as subsidies to sportswriters from organizations related to their specialties,[87] and contempt cases involving the St. Louis *Post-Dispatch* and Los Angeles *Times* were discussed during 1922–1949.[88]

- The society in 1945 approved John S. Knight's protest on temporary suspension of filing facilities in the European Theater of Operations because of alleged premature and unauthorized dispatches announcing the German surrender.[89]

The ethics issue was brought up again in 1947, after publication of the report by the Commission on Freedom of the Press headed by Chancellor Robert M. Hutchins of the University of Chicago. ASNE President Norman Isaacs later described the report as "the most important assessment made of modern communications and its obligations."[90] Herbert Brucker, another ASNE president, said the Hutchins document set the teeth of the editors and publishers on edge. Among other things, it reminded the editors that

at an early meeting the Society drew up and adopted a code of ethics which, if followed, would have made the newspapers responsible carriers of news and discussion. The only means of enforcement was expulsion from the Society. Shortly after the code was adopted, a case of gross malpractice on the part of one of the members was reported. After the Society had deliberated long and painfully the case was dropped. This settled the function of the code.[91]

The 1947 *Proceedings* reveal 24 pages of dispute over how the editors would pronounce an anathema upon the Hutchins report. Brucker recalled that there was to be no watchdog over journalism because ASNE believed the press was performing with increasing effectiveness and fairness the duties of keeping the American people the best-informed people in the world.[92] Harry Ashmore, then editor of the Arkansas *Gazette*, saw the august ASNE membership "huddle rumps together, horns out, in the immemorial manner, say of the National Association of Manufacturers faced by a threat of regulated prices."[93]

More than a decade later, in 1958, Erwin Canham, editor of the *Christian Science Monitor*, and ASNE president in 1948, reviewed arguments for and against code enforcement in a speech entitled "Organized Self-Control of the Press." Canham diverged from the tougher stance taken in the earlier debates by his *Monitor* predecessor Willis Abbot. He said the question of defining ethics violations had remained at the heart of the objection to punitive powers, or rather the chance that any possible definition could be abused tragically. "Dissent is a precious value. The right to be wrong is indispensable."

Canham believed it was the conviction of most American editors that organized self-control of the press should remain voluntary. "I conclude with the utmost earnestness that self-control is working among American newspapers through organized self-analysis, self-improvement and a voluntary sense of the accepted responsibility which means long-run survival."[94]

Taking an opposite approach during the next decade, Norman Isaacs succeeded in getting the directors to establish an ethics committee to respond to the complaints against daily newspapers and to study the legal ramifications of handling complaints against newspapers that were represented in ASNE.[95]

In 1969 Isaacs told President Vincent S. Jones, his immediate predecessor, that the society should sponsor an "overall, intelligent, unbiased study of the state of journalism." Isaacs added, "The more we examined, the more we agreed that desirable as the study might be, there was one necessary first step, and this was a good look at ASNE's own role." Isaacs went on to charge: "There are many who feel the society has never amounted to a great deal since the 'founding fathers' knuckled in to Fred Bonfils. Perhaps it is much too late to make ASNE into a really select group instead of dispensing automatic prestige on the basis of circulation and a cashable check."[96]

Jones himself added to the renaissance of ethics awareness by sending letters to representatives of syndicates, who for years had sponsored cocktail parties and entertainment during the convention, asking them to avoid providing the traditional commercial hospitality. Gene Giancarlo, former ASNE executive director, notes that the Hall Syndicate traditionally held its party immediately after the banquet and, in later years, had invited first-class names and entertainers. Ostensibly, the party was held to entertain those ASNE editors and their spouses who used Hall material. Other syndicates held cocktail parties for their clients.[97]

As pointed out by Isaacs, however, these parties had completely changed from the early-day small gatherings in hotel suites and had become quasi-official parts of the program. Objections to the parties had been voiced, and Isaacs had encouraged an *ASNE Bulletin* symposium which showed that opinion was divided among the general membership.[98] Despite the divided opinion among the directors and members, Jones took the initiative to stop the practice.

An announcement in the *Bulletin* of plans to establish the ethics committee triggered conflicting letters and articles, including one from former President A. H. Kirchhofer arguing that "the society was never intended to be a regulatory agency and should not be restructured so now." In rhetoric reminiscent of the 1920s, Kirchhofer evoked the memory of patron saint Yost. He concluded with a broadside at Isaacs and the board of directors: "This is leadership? No, it is reckless and irresponsible conduct on the part of the men honored by the society. It is counter to the interest of members and their newspapers, which are representative of the best in American journalism."[99]

In order to pass on the explosive issue of ethical enforcement once again, Isaacs' successor, Newbold Noyes of the Washington *Star*, appointed a new ethics committee of society senior statesmen, including five past presidents, to study the complicated question. They included Erwin Canham as chair, Kenneth MacDonald, Vermont Royster, Michael J. Ogden and Vincent S. Jones.[100] The following year, Canham said that after examining several ethical cases the committee had determined they were "beyond its capabilities." The committee advised the board to postpone a decision on establishing complaint procedures.[101] Additional nails in the coffin of ethics enforcement came from members: in response to a questionnaire, they opposed any action by a grievance committee to receive complaints alleging unethical newspaper practice and to pass judgment on them.

Isaacs later recalled that many of his ideas, which reflected his own generation of editors, were opposed by a number of "elder statesmen" editors such as Basil "Stuffy" Walters, who regarded Isaacs as one of the Young Turks: "Stuffy, Turner Catledge (New York *Times*) and Ben McKelway (Washington *Star*), in particular, had great influence on Noyes, and he moved to defuse the whole (grievance committee) process when he took over and succeeded in sidetracking it through a special committee."[102]

According to William B. Dickinson of the Philadelphia *Bulletin*, the committee sent out a six-question poll that revolved around the issue of a grievance committee. Members who replied opposed, by more than three to one, any action to set up a grievance committee. An even larger margin voted against establishing some organization other than ASNE to handle grievances.

A few years later, Noyes told an ASNE convention that he felt he had made a mistake and wanted to go on record as saying that Isaacs was right. Isaacs eventually got his "grievance committee" in the form of the National News Council, which lasted 10 years before being killed in 1983.[103]

In his charge to the new ethics committee in 1972, President J. Edward Murray concluded that a clear majority opinion had emerged. "It rejects the establishment by ASNE of grievance machinery, censure procedures or any other method of subjecting individual editors to group judgment concerning their professional ethics."[104]

Since then, the Society has moved even further away from efforts to enforce its code, preferring instead to use the term "Statement of Principles." The preamble of the principles, revised October 23, 1975, simply encourages society members to adhere to "the highest possible standards of ethical and professional performance." It also trims from nine to six the articles: responsibility, freedom of the press, independence, truth and accuracy, impartiality and fair play (see Appendix B).

The National News Council and other media councils established at the community and state levels were not greeted with enthusiasm. As noted by 1981 President Michael J. O'Neill, "The trouble was that it established a kind of judicial tribunal. Aside from the fact that no council had the staff, etc., to investigate grievances very well, it was quickly subverted into being a kind of quasi extension of our legal system. Lawyers used our ethical guidelines and council statements as evidence in courts, so what was supposed to be voluntary became coercive."[105]

The 1987 debate, before the board voted to take no position in a controversy that involved the codes of ethics of the Society of Professional Journalists/ Sigma Delta Chi (SPJ/SDX), reflected the gradual change in position in regard to ethics. SPJ's convention had instructed ASNE to provide guidelines for addressing complaints on ethics in light of the SPJ code provision that journalists "should actively censure" violations of its standards. In response, the board passed the following resolution:

The board of directors of ASNE takes no position on the current dispute inside SPJ/SDX. However, the board encourages its president to express the sense of the board that ASNE opposes censorship in any form, including license or censure. As former Chief Justice Warren Burger wrote in the 1974 *Miami Herald v. Tornillo* case: "A responsible press is an undoubtedly desirable goal, but press responsibility is not mandated by the Constitution and like many other virtues cannot be legislated."[106]

Executive director Lee Stinnett recalls that at the time SPJ was embroiled in an internal controversy. The leadership of the organization was firmly opposed to a vote of the membership during a convention to establish an enforcement procedure in SPJ's code of ethics. The controversy mirrored the debate that had occurred within ASNE several decades earlier. SPJ members asked SPJ, rather than ASNE, to take the action. Behind the scenes, the president of SPJ asked the ASNE board to support a motion in favor of "teeth" or enforcement. The language of the opening of the resolution was a matter of institutional politeness.

According to Stinnett, "There wasn't any sentiment on the ASNE board in favor of 'teeth' in any code of ethics." The ASNE board took a position in solidarity with the SPJ leadership. After their convention, SPJ members rescinded the "teeth" policy. ASNE's motion was an attempt at solidarity with the SPJ leadership, nothing more. The issue has long since been resolved within the ASNE that codes of ethics shouldn't be enforceable.

This resolution came after another "behind-closed-doors" debate by directors which was far less heated than ethics debates of previous years. David Lawrence of the Detroit *Free Press* argued that he knew of no instances in which ASNE was "strangled by [their] own principles." Raising new concerns, Michael Gartner said that even though the press is not homogenized, codes of ethics and statements of principles "set a standard for all of us." Such statements can be and frequently are used against the press in courts. ASNE counsel Richard Schmidt said a survey had unveiled seven instances in which the ASNE Statement of Principles was introduced to support the argument that journalists weren't reasonably prudent.[107]

In a letter to the author, Michael O'Neill noted the complexity of the ethics enforcement issue and stated that the question has no simple answer. But his declining to support the National News Council (which O'Neill was asked to head) "by no means suggests I think newspapers shouldn't be patrolled by the public."[108]

For legal reasons, Ted M. Natt, editor of the *Daily News* of Longview, Washington, and chairman of the 1990 Ethics Committee, said the ASNE avoids calling its document a code of ethics but that the society "clearly speaks to some standards which any newspaper ought to be practicing."[109] Writing in *Untended Gates*, Norman Isaacs concludes that no matter how important editors may be, the ultimate decisions are made by publishers, and most publishers have decided against enforcing press performance standards.[110]

THE LONG-TERM TREND

In the nearly 70 years since it was founded, therefore, ASNE has retreated from advocating strong censure and suspension for violation of its code of ethics to a less courtlike and strict character in which the society primarily displays a generalized statement of principles. This statement has been borrowed by other media organizations.

The general softening of its approach, from the method propounded by "diehard" enforcement editors to a more conciliatory "due process" tone articulated by Casper Yost and nearly all other ASNE leaders, can be seen most vividly in ASNE minutes and copies of the *Proceedings* from 1923 to 1932. It is also evident in the minutes and the committee structure of recent decades.

Consensus against the strong approach came about because ethics enforcement was not included in the original constitution, because the code was created separately, and because infractions involving F. G. Bonfils occurred before the code was passed. Even after a compromise allowed the board of directors to discipline members through due process, no infractions were reported. In ASNE, the libertarian approach to code enforcement (espoused by publishers) appears to have prevailed over a more socially responsible approach suggested by groups such as the Hutchins Commission. Most recently, use of ethics codes against journalists in the courts has meant even less support for any of these principles.

With a few exceptions, ASNE leaders follow the more moderate ethics enforcement advocated by leaders such as Yost, Shedd and B. M. McKelway. In 1950 McKelway called attention to the division among ASNE members as to the role of the society:

One group, distressed and at times understandably outraged over abuses of newspaper responsibility and other shenanigans associated with our craft, would have us move in the direction of unfrocking . . . those deemed guilty of malpractice. They have a zest, in other words, for disciplinary enforcement of the things they stand for. If that is an exaggerated description, others may express the same idea in more precise and moderate terms.[111]

The other group within the society, though it may sympathize fully with the sentiment of the honorable opposition, doubts the wisdom of applying this sort of prescription. It believes that our role as a society is more properly advocate than that of policeman, judge or jury. It believes that our hope of raising standards of performance is more securely based on demonstration, exemplification and discussion of the attainable ideal than upon the attempts to enforce acceptance of what some of us may think is the ideal. Certainly, this concept of our role conforms more closely to the concept of a free press.[112]

McKelway claimed that since 1932, ASNE has established "a unique record for universal virtue on the part of our members—a startling conclusion, but one in which all of us should take due pride."[113]

ASNE members who seek more accountability or have advocated a council-like or courtlike approach with censure and suspension have not prevailed. These members, with the exception of Wallace, Isaacs and Ghiglione, who support the concept of media councils, have not been elected to leadership positions. Leaders who support strong ethics enforcement have also become increasingly reluctant to promote their agendas. As noted by Vincent Jones: "Those of us in the ASNE leadership who have pushed the idea of an Ethics Committee have done so with the certain knowledge that its establishment might easily tear the society apart. This risk we have been willing to take because we believe that a smaller, more vigorous society could be of more use to the profession and to the public that we are trying to serve."[114]

Although not "entirely worthless" or completely toothless, as described by Herbert Bayard Swope in one of the earliest debates, the ASNE code of ethics does not appear to have reached the potential ascribed to it by Yost and the other founders. Yost's rhetorical questions about ethics teeth—what sort, how they are to bite, and whom they are to bite—have yet to be resolved.

NOTES

1. *Proceedings of the Annual Meeting of the American Society of Newspaper Editors*, 1932, 39. Hereafter referred to as ASNE *Proceedings*.

2. The term is used by Alice Fox Pitts in *Read All About It! 50 Years of ASNE*, Reston, Va.: ASNE, 1974, 35.

3. ASNE *Proceedings*, 1924, 78.

4. Term used by George A. Hough, Jr., of the Falmouth (Mass.) *Enterprise*. Quoted by Pitts, 32.

5. ASNE *Proceedings*, 1924, 79.

6. As an example, charter member Arthur Krock, of the New York *Times*, recalls that he lost interest in ASNE when members failed to pass a resolution against "certain perverters of responsible newspaper work—publishers" after some members argued that a group of employees should not commit themselves against their employers. Since that time, Krock said the ASNE had accepted greater responsibility. Quoted in *ASNE Bulletin*, December 1, 1947. The issue of a lack of enforcement of the ASNE ethics code is also mentioned in the 1947 Hutchins Commission Report on a Free and Responsible Press, 74–75.

7. Edmund B. Lambeth, *Dictionary of Literary Biography 29*, Detroit: Gale Research, 1984, 28.

8. See Wilbur Schramm, *Responsibility in Mass Communication*, New York: Harper & Brothers, 1957, 88, and Robert A. Logan, "Jefferson's and Madison's Legacy: The Death of the National News Council," *Journal of Mass Media Ethics*, Vol. 1, No. 1 (Fall–Winter 1985–86): 68–77.

9. Detroit *Free Press*, April 23, 1946. See also "Bingay traces growth of society from founder's dream to '46 meeting," *ASNE Bulletin*, June 1, 1946, 5.

10. Ibid.

11. For example, see Casey Bukro, "The SPJ Code's Double-Edged Sword: Accountability, Credibility," *Journal of Mass Media Ethics*, Vol. 1, No. 1 (Fall/Winter 1985–1986): 10–13.

12. See minutes of organizational meeting of ASNE, April 26, 1922, 4–5. A second organizational meeting held in Cleveland, October 10, 1922, shows that 93 members had enrolled in the society before the annual meeting scheduled for Washington in April 1923, 6–9.

13. ASNE *Proceedings*, 1923, 15.

14. Jim Allee Hart, *A History of the St. Louis* Globe-Democrat, Columbia: University of Missouri Press, 1961, 219.

15. Ibid., 248.

16. In addition to Hopwood, the other two editors from the *Plain Dealer* elected as ASNE presidents were Paul Bellamy (1933–1934) and Wright Bryan (1952–1953), who moved to Cleveland from the Atlanta *Journal*. A third president, Grove Patterson, was an editor at the *Plain Dealer* before going to the Toledo *Blade*. Archer H. Shaw, also an early ASNE member, discusses Hopwood and Bellamy in *The* Plain-Dealer: *One Hundred Years in Cleveland*. The family-owned publication was sold to the Newhouse group in 1967. In the 1970s, *More* magazine listed it among the "ten worst" newspapers in the country.

17. ASNE *Proceedings*, 1923, 123–124.

18. ASNE *Proceedings*, 1927, 17, 184.

19. Archer H. Shaw, *The* Plain Dealer: *One Hundred Years in Cleveland*, New York: Alfred A. Knopf, 1942, 339–340.

20. Grove Patterson, letter to David Lawrence, August 7, 1951 [ASNE archives, Reston, Va.].

21. Lloyd Wendt, *Chicago* Tribune: *The Rise of a Great American Newspaper*, Chicago: Rand McNally & Company, 1979, 599. See also "Death of E. S. Beck, Charter Member, Saddens Society," *ASNE Bulletin*, February 1, 1993, 3.

22. ASNE *Proceedings*, 1930, 175–179.

23. "Fate of Newspaper Hangs on Character, says Edward Beck," *ASNE Bulletin*, February 1, 1940, 3.

24. Pitts, 7.

25. Arthur Krock, letter to David Lawrence, June 23, 1951 [ASNE archives].

26. William Lutz, *The* News *of Detroit: How a Newspaper and City Grew Together*, Boston: Little, Brown and Co., 1973, 177–178.

27. ASNE *Proceedings*, 1927, 89.

28. ASNE *Proceedings*, 1923, 122.

29. ASNE *Proceedings*, 1923. The table of contents provides an overview of the entire two-day conference.

30. Frederick Lewis Allen, *Only Yesterday*, New York: Harper & Row, 1931, 155–187. A critical article by Allen, "Newspapers and the Truth," in *Atlantic Monthly*, January 1922, was said to be a major reason Yost decided to start an organization to combine forces that would combat attacks on newspapers (see Pitts, 3).

31. Ibid., 157.

32. Joseph P. McKerns, "The Emergence of the Modern Media (1900–1945)," in *The Media in America: A History*, edited by David Sloan, James G. Stovall, Worthington, Ohio: Publishing Horizons, 1989, 243–260.

33. ASNE *Proceedings*, 1923, 22.

34. Ben Hecht, *A Child of the Century*, New York: Donald I. Fine, 1954, 276.

35. ASNE *Proceedings*, 1947, 28.

36. *The Autobiography of Lincoln Steffens*, New York: Harcourt, Brace and Co., 1931, 660.

37. See Pitts, 5. Richard Kluger in *The Paper: The Life and Death of the New York Herald Tribune* (New York: Alfred A. Knopf, 1986, 210) says that after its founding in 1904 the *Globe* absorbed the *Commercial Advertiser* and became "a surprisingly fresh, liberal and independent voice in New York newspaperdom." In 1923, the same year

Wright helped author the ASNE code of ethics, Frank Munsey paid $2 million for the *Globe* and merged it into Munsey's evening *Sun* with positive results.

38. Christine M. Miller, *Biographical Dictionary of American Journalism*, New York: Greenwood Press, 1989, 687.

39. ASNE *Proceedings*, 1923, 121.

40. Ibid., 123. Additional information on Williams can be found in *The Boston Transcript: A History of the First Hundred Years*, Boston: Houghton Mifflin, 1930, by Joseph Edgar Chamberlin. The North Carolina native is described as "a distinctly one-hundred percent American." He went to work for Hearst in 1925.

41. ASNE *Proceedings*, 1923, 124.

42. Ibid., 122.

43. Ibid., 152.

44. Ibid.

45. Ibid., 164.

46. Ibid., 165.

47. William Allen White, *The Autobiography of William Allen White*, New York: Macmillan, 1946, 621.

48. Hamilton Owens, *ASNE Bulletin*, September 1955, 9.

49. In addition to the death of President Harding before the next convention, the ASNE lost one of its founders when Frank Cobb of the New York *World* died.

50. Although not mentioned by name in the ASNE *Proceedings*, Bonfils is included in the "confidential" index of the meetings of the board of directors, April 25, 1922–April 20, 1949, under the heading "Teapot Dome Investigation." Early references requesting the committee on ethical standards to conduct an investigation, or referring the issue to the committee, mention "certain newspapermen" or "certain members of the newspaper profession." It is only when Bonfils appears before the board of directors (31), when he is censured and suspended from membership (34–36), and when the board rescinds its action (38) that his name is mentioned in the minutes.

51. Gene Fowler, *Timberline: A Story of Bonfils and Tammen*, Garden City, N.Y.: Blue Ribbon Books, 1940, 405.

52. Bill Hosokawa, *Thunder in the Rockies: The Incredible Denver* Post, New York: William Morrow & Co., 1976, 138.

53. ASNE *Proceedings*, 1924, 67–77.

54. ASNE minutes, 1924, 23.

55. ASNE *Proceedings*, 1924, 69.

56. Ibid.

57. ASNE minutes, January 17, 1925, 31.

58. ASNE *Proceedings*, 1926, 22.

59. Quoted in ASNE *Proceedings*, 1950, 32.

60. ASNE minutes, February 9, 1926, 34–36.

61. ASNE minutes, October 5, 1926, 38.

62. ASNE minutes, October 5, 1926, 37. Other members of the 1927 committee on ethical standards included Tom Wallace, Louisville *Times*; Fred Fuller Shedd, Philadelphia *Evening Bulletin*; Col. Luke Lea, Nashville *Tennessean*, and Frank Knox, Manchester (N.H.) *Union and Leader*. An unsuccessful candidate for governor in New

Hampshire, Knox worked for the Hearst organization from 1927 to 1931 until he resigned over differences in business judgment.

63. ASNE *Proceedings*, 1927, 190–193.

64. ASNE *Proceedings*, 1928, 85–105.

65. Ibid., 134–148. Despite similarity of the two organization's goals, the ASNE board of directors turned down a proposal from the journalistic fraternity for joint issuance of the *Quill* and *The Bulletin of the American Society of Newspaper Editors*. See ASNE *Proceedings*, 1929, 14.

66. ASNE *Proceedings*, 1929, 156.

67. Ibid., 157.

68. Erwin Canham, *Commitment to Freedom*, Boston: Houghton Mifflin, 1958, 269. Additional information on Abbot's career can be seen in *Watching the World Go By*, New York: Beekman Publishers, 1974. Abbot also authored another 20 books, primarily "drum and trumpet" books for juveniles, leading with *Blue Jackets of '61*. His most widely circulated book was *Panama and the Canal in Picture and Prose*.

69. Ibid., 1929, 160.

70. Ibid.

71. ASNE *Proceedings*, 1931, 138.

72. Ibid.

73. Ibid., 137. A colleague of "firebrand" Arthur Krock, Wallace was chief of the editorial staff from 1923 until he was named editor in 1930. An admirer of "Marse Henry" Watterson, Wallace was the only one of the ethics firebrands ever to be elected ASNE president until Norman Isaacs. Wallace held the office from 1940 to 1941.

74. ASNE *Proceedings*, 1931, 141.

75. Ibid., 146.

76. ASNE *Proceedings*, 1932, 37.

77. Ibid., 38.

78. Ibid., 37.

79. Ibid., 38.

80. Ibid. Wallace was wrong when he said he was a member of the first committee on ethical standards. The 1923 *Proceedings* shows only the following members: Jas. T. Williams, H. R. Galt, Charles McD. Puckette, Donald Sterling and James Stuart.

81. Ibid., 39.

82. Ibid.

83. Marvin Creager, letter to David Lawrence, August 2, 1951, 2.

84. Ibid.

85. ASNE minutes, October 14, 1928, 49.

86. ASNE minutes, April 19, 1934, 93.

87. ASNE minutes, April 17, 1941, 162.

88. Ibid.

89. Ibid., 6.

90. Norman E. Isaacs, *Untended Gates: The Mismanaged Press*, New York: Columbia University Press, 1986, 100.

91. The Commission on Freedom of the Press, *A Free and Responsible Press*, Chicago: University of Chicago Press, 1947, 74–75.

92. ASNE *Proceedings*, 1947, 231–232. See also Herbert Brucker, "A Conscience for the Press," in *Communication Is Power: Unchanging Values in a Changing Journalism*, New York: Oxford University Press, 1973, 203–204.

93. *Columbia Journalism Review*, Summer 1967. Quoted by James Aronson, *The Press and the Cold War*, Indianapolis: Bobbs-Merrill Company, 1970, 266.

94. Quoted by Randy Block, "How effective is our code of ethics?" *ASNE Bulletin*, July 1968, 15.

95. ASNE minutes, February 24, 1970, 421–434. For a more detailed account of those "having the temerity to embrace a cause that challenge[s] the most sacred cow in journalism's holy credo—its self-proclaimed right to reject any type of examination of its performance," see chapter 6, "The Seed Bed of Heresy," in *Untended Gates*.

96. ASNE minutes, April 14, 1969, 390.

97. Gene Giancarlo, letter to the author, August 31, 1990, 2.

98. Ibid.

99. A. H. Kirchhofer, "The Ethics Committee Idea—A Negative Reaction," *ASNE Bulletin*, June 1970, 8–9.

100. ASNE minutes, October 2, 1970, 471–472.

101. ASNE minutes, October 4, 1971, 559.

102. Raymond Moscowitz, *Stuffy: The Life of Newspaper Pioneer Basil "Stuffy" Walters*, Ames: Iowa State University, 1982, 185.

103. Ibid.

104. ASNE minutes, April 22, 1972, 569.

105. Michael O'Neill, letter to the author, August 4, 1990, 3.

106. ASNE minutes, April 7, 1987, 1097.

107. Ibid., 1093.

108. O'Neill, 3.

109. Ted M. Natt, chair, ASNE ethics committee, 1990. Letter to the author, April 12, 1990.

110. Isaacs, 111.

111. ASNE *Proceedings*, 1950, 33. See also "Pres. McKelway's Address," *ASNE Bulletin*, May 1, 1950, 2.

112. Ibid.

113. ASNE *Proceedings*, 1950, 32.

114. Vincent Jones, paper for the Humdrum Club, March 2, 1970, 8.

Chapter 2

The 1930s: " . . . due to the persistence of the few . . . "

It was during the Thirties that some of us despaired of the Society; its critics were many and its apologists few. The discussion of syndicates and treatment of crime news as convention subjects had been wrung dry. But thank heaven, due to the persistence of the few the organization survived and soon began to thrive.

—Donald J. Sterling, 10th ASNE president, 1939

Three nationwide surveys and two scientific studies of the media which were conducted in the decade "From the Crash to the Blitz"[1] dramatize the declining credibility and influence of the print media during the 1930s. In October 1938 the American Institute of Public Opinion asked the American people: "In the European crisis, were you more interested in radio reports or newspaper reports?" Some 70 percent expressed a preference for the radio. In August 1939, *Fortune* magazine asked: "If you heard conflicting versions of the same story from these sources (radio/newspaper), which would you be most likely to believe?" The results again leaned heavily toward radio. A study by *Broadcasting* magazine supported the view that radio had displaced the newspaper as the public's primary source of news.[2]

Two milestone research projects underscore two significant trends: (1) the rise of competing entertainment-oriented media and the attempts by ASNE membership to cope with the economic threats, and (2) the cultural trauma of the 1930s that continues today as an "invisible scar"[3] in American life. The first study related to the panic of an estimated one of six million Americans who listened to Orson Welles and his Mercury Theater Playhouse actors' radio depiction of H. G. Wells' *War of the Worlds* on October 30, 1938. This study by Hadley Cantril emphasizes the confidence the American people had in radio—then two decades as a commercial medium—as their primary source of news. It also found that the economic uncertainty of the time and the threat of another world war contributed to the mass hysteria.[4] Other important factors in the national panic were the sheer technical brilliance of the radio show, particularly the on-the-spot reporting technique, the interviews with experts and the fact that persons who tuned in late missed the announcement that the presentation was fictitious.

A good contrast to the hypodermic needle, cause-and-effect selective perception relationships found in the radio hysteria incident is presented in a political study conducted in the Erie County of Cleveland *Plain Dealer* presidents Hopwood and Bellamy examined during the 1940 U.S. presidential elections. This study showed that media-promulgated propaganda had little direct impact on the minds of the public. What little influence the media had, according to *The People's Choice*, came primarily from interpersonal sources. Social scientists, including Paul Lazarsfeld, who spoke at the 1941 ASNE convention,[5] later described the communication process as a "two-step flow," the media having more influence on opinion leaders in a community and less direct effect on a mass audience.[6]

Actually, the sophisticated study only proved what Americans had demonstrated in the 1932 and 1936 presidential elections. The "power" of the so-called one party (print) press, at least as far as its editorial endorsements were concerned, was not being taken seriously. More important was the growing concern that press organizations such as ASNE and the older American Newspaper Publishers Association (ANPA) were not only out of touch with the American people and politics but abusing their positions for their own financial interests. Professor Peter Odegard referred to the trend at the 1941 ASNE annual meeting, quoting from an editorial in the St. Louis *Post-Dispatch* published just before the ANPA annual meeting. He likened the publishers trade group to the National Association of Manufacturers, the American Petroleum Institute or any other coalition of businessmen:

This comparison is borne out by the bylaws of the ANPA showing it was created to foster the business interests of the members, to procure uniformity of usage and settle differences, to protect members from irresponsible customers and so on. This is the language of business; it is not the language of the newspaper profession. It is the language of men engaged in manufacturing a product; it is not the language of men engaged in the high and responsible calling of writing, editing and interpreting the news.[7]

Donald J. Sterling, an ASNE charter member, was among many who called attention to the need for greater leadership by the ASNE: "It was during the Thirties that some of us despaired of the Society; its critics were many and its apologists few. The discussion of syndicates and treatment of crime news as convention subjects had been wrung dry. But thank heaven, due to the persistence of the few the organization survived and soon began to thrive."[8]

William Allen White, ASNE president in 1938, also spoke on the issue of independence of editors from publisher influence. Along with other external critics of the society, White noted that the press had become too commercial and was losing its influence because it was not keeping faith with the people.[9] White, a former muckraker and confidant of U.S. presidents, also said that in the conflict between labor and capital, capitalism had obtained control of the press.[10] In a letter to Kent Cooper of the Associated Press in 1932, White pointed out how easy it was for reporters, copyreaders, city editors and other staff members of prosperous papers to take the "country club" attitude, the boss's slant toward those who were whacking the established order.[11]

CRITICS CONDEMN NEWSPAPERS

Some critics argue that the post–World War I "country club" mind-set and the 1920s preoccupation with dramatic, sensational and episodic coverage caused newspaper editors to miss some of the major events of the first half of the 20th century. ASNE charter member Frank Cobb of the New York *World* charged that the nation's newspapers were not ready for the waves of discontent and unrest that spread across the country. "They were not prepared for the social ferment that followed the war. They were not prepared for the industrial upheavals that came."[12]

Critic George Seldes went even further. In his indictment of the press during the period leading up to World War II, he stated, "It is held by many people that the failure of our newspapers to inform us about the economic situation from 1927 to 1929, and the wish-fulfillment policy from 1929 on, constituted its greatest failure in modern times."[13] By 1933 corporate profits had fallen from a 1929 high of $10 billion to $1 billion, and the gross national product had dropped by half. In 1930, 4 million Americans were jobless, and by 1933 one-fourth of the labor force—13 million people—were unemployed.[14] In a 1940 report entitled "How Editors Deal with Administrative Problems," J. R. Wiggins, then of the St. Paul *Dispatch and Pioneer Press*, said that monthly editorial budgets of papers with circulation over 200,000 during the 1930s averaged only $20,000 and ranged from $7,000 to $28,000. As percentage of total costs, the budgets generally were distributed as follows: staff, 60 percent; state news, 5 percent; syndicates, 13 percent; telegraph news services, 20 percent. Although Wiggins could not obtain many estimates, he ventured that editorial budgets had increased by about 30 percent in the decade.[15]

In 1937 Irving Brant, editorial page director of the St. Louis *Star-Times*, accused the press of a sin greater than a failure to inform. An ardent champion of the New Deal, which was opposed editorially by a majority of the nation's editorial pages, Brant charged that "taken as a whole, the newspapers of America furnish no driving force for social reform. They are a positive handicap in economic reform. . . . It is impossible to point to one important constructive step in the last eight years which represents either the inventiveness, the initiative or the supporting activity of the American press."[16]

George Seldes helped indict the American "House of Lords" of the ANPA during the 1930s. In a series of hypercritical books, including *Freedom of the Press*[17] (1937) and *Lords of the Press*[18] (1938), the former foreign correspondent for the Chicago *Tribune* attacked many major media owners for legal and illegal actions against the American people. Among his main targets were Joseph Medill Patterson, "Lord of Tabloidia"; Colonel Robert McCormick, owner of the Chicago *Tribune*; Paul Block, "Little Lord Northcliffe"; "Lord (Roy) Howard and His Empire"; Abraham Canham, "A Jewish Press Lord"; Arthur Hays Sulzberger of the New York *Times*, "The American Thunderer"; Moses Annenberg; and William Randolph Hearst, "The Lord of San Simeon."[19]

Seldes and other critics charged that publishers and some editors had opposed all issues which threatened profits, led the attacks against the pure food and drug law, opposed the Wagner Act (the Magna Carta of labor), urged amendment of proposed social insurance legislation to put newspapers into a special class, proposed outlawing strikes to force arbitration of labor disputes, favored child labor and frowned at the Securities Act.[20]

Missing from Seldes' broad-brush criticism are the positive contributions of Chicago *Tribune* publisher and ASNE member Robert McCormick in challenging the Minnesota gag law, which the U.S. Supreme Court later declared unconstitutional in *Near* v. *Minnesota* (1931).[21] That case, along with others, including *Grossjean* v. *American Press* (1934), was a continuing part of the agenda of both the ANPA and ASNE in the 1930s. McCormick discussed the matter in detail at the 1931 ASNE convention as the chairman of the Committee on Freedom of the Press.[22]

Involvement in the Minnesota case also marks the formal entrance of ASNE into the fight for freedom of information, which had been cited as a major reason for founding the society. Joining McCormick on the committees that provided mostly rhetoric in the fight for freedom and against censorship were Edward S. Beck of McCormick's *Tribune* and Samuel Williams and R. J. Dunlap of the St. Paul *Pioneer Press*. Typical of the language used by ASNE was the wording of a resolution introduced by A. H. Kirchhofer of the Buffalo *Evening News* in 1929 when he called for the board to "throw the weight of the judgment and influence of this society upon the side of the freedom of the press, engaging counsel, if necessary and expedient, to the end that the voice of a united American press may be raised in the Supreme Court of the United States against a statute clearly breaking down the constitutional guarantees for a free press, which indeed are the bulwark of liberty."[23]

Ironically, despite this ringing rhetoric, his idea of freedom of the press was limited to the print media. McCormick said such freedom was not intended for broadcasting. "There is a matter quite contentious in it. I don't care to put it out to the public, and, on the other hand, I have no objection to it being published."[24]

The society also voted to allow the board of directors to censor the 1933 *Proceedings* before publication. According to the record, this was because members had spoken freely about financial conditions in various cities, naming banks and newspapers. Publication of this, said one member, would only cause a renewal of lack of confidence, "which we are trying to build up."

In her history, Alice Fox Pitts reported that according to some oldtimers, the directors made no deletions. They let stand the statement by Fred Fuller Shedd, who said: "We went through a period when banks were falling like dominoes, mostly smaller banks. Philadelphia editors met daily with a clearinghouse committee. We deliberately suppressed news, and I thank God we had the nerve to do it."[25]

In addition to such conflicts between the rhetoric of openness and actual practice, publishers and editors did not always provide enlightened leadership for their workers. They displayed reactionary attitudes against the mainstream population and mainstream politics, and even against their own employees. Evidence of this is seen in court cases in which ANPA was involved during the pre–World War II period and in their attempts to use the First Amendment to protect their business interests.[26] The most infamous case involved the efforts by the Associated Press to prevent reporter Morris Watson from organizing a unit of the American Newspaper Guild by contending that such action violated the First Amendment. The U.S. Supreme Court disagreed, however, and the newspaper union movement received a strong impetus in its infancy.[27]

NEWSPAPER GUILD ORGANIZED

In 1933, underpaid and overworked reporters around the country received a challenge from Heywood Broun of the New York *World-Telegram* to organize themselves. The first local guild began in Cleveland and guild units followed in Minneapolis–St. Paul, New York, Rockford (Ill.), Newark, Akron, Duluth–Superior, Cincinnati and Philadelphia.[28] ASNE, however, gave little support to the guild's proposal that financial rewards for editorial workers should coincide with their ability and effort.

Like publishers, editors were not quite ready to accept the important step of supporting guilds to help foster a reporter's self-respect. In his 1938 presidential address, Kirchhofer noted that although society members had listened to William Green of the American Federation of Labor in 1930, ASNE held no opinion of the guild. In resolutions it had passed in 1937, the society saw no impropriety in organizations of newspaper workers in editorial departments but felt it was unsuitable for journalists to affiliate with trade unionists.[29] Kirchhofer said this action, which came after several years of deliberation, still seemed sound. Minutes of the October 16, 1938, board meeting indicate that a resolution called for a study on the origin and causes of all strikes between editorial employees and newspapers during the previous five years.[30]

J. David Stern and William Allen White, both members of ASNE, were among the few owner/publishers who, Seldes said, wanted to publish free newspapers.

Stern was lauded for his fight for liberalism and White was heralded as an "Anti-Press Lord." Seldes also praised ASNE along with hundreds of organizations and thousands of men and women who, as "leaders of the intelligent minority," took a forthright stand against William Randolph Hearst: "There has been repudiation in the press, on the platform and from the pulpit. The episode is one of the most heartening in the history of American journalism."[31]

THE ROLE OF WILLIAM ALLEN WHITE

In contrast to the press lords such as Hearst, William Allen White emerges from this period as a hero of the ASNE and of American journalism. This Kansas-born editor, the first of four from a small town elected to the ASNE presidency, appears throughout the ASNE minutes and *Proceedings* as a major figure. In one meeting early in the Depression, in fact, he was invited by Fred Fuller Shedd simply to come to the rostrum and smile at his fellow members to cheer them up.[32]

Tributes from other ASNE presidents after White's death in 1944 endowed him with near-godlike characteristics. Paul Bellamy said, "There was always a quality of immortality about him; he was so much of the spirit and so little of the flesh." Don Sterling said White's "very humility inspired respect and generated a power which he chose to invest in the social good." Roy A. Roberts of the Kansas City *Star* said that from his early boyhood, he had looked up to White as "a constant guide and inspiration." Dwight Marvin of the Troy (N.Y.) *Record* said he knew of no editor who had influenced him so strongly or whose memory he would constantly revere. "In our society and in the hearts of its members he was always McGregor—at the head of the table."[33] Excerpts from White's 1939 presidential address typically call for greater journalistic leadership from ASNE members. He defended journalism against critics who claimed the media had reported inadequately the events leading up to the Depression. Comparing morals and ethics of journalists to those of doctors, lawyers and preachers, White intoned, "Stand any one of these callings or orders against the press, measure our leadership with theirs, their best against our best, their worst against our worst, and the common run of their ways and works with our daily outpourings, and no one would question that measured by integrity and intelligence, American journalism is worthy to hold up its head in the presence of any other estate of our American life."[34]

Editors as well as publishers were indicted for failing to report adequately on major social and cultural problems during this period. In their role as middlemen between the so-called liberal reporters and the conservative publishers, they also felt the wrath of critics. Gadflies such as H. L. Mencken,[35] educator Peter Odegard[36] and the youthful college president Robert Hutchins, who later received national notoriety as head of the Commission on the Freedom of the

Press, unleashed broad-brush diatribes against the media during the 1930s ASNE annual conventions.

Perhaps in a joking tone Hutchins criticized President Walter M. Harrison for making an error on the middle initial of Hutchins' name. The college president's opinion was that editors were in a position "to direct the course of empire and mould the form of public opinion." Described by Hutchins as being exceedingly prosperous so as to command respect, he also charged editors were "individuals weak in mind and low in character, and totally defective in the scientific spirit which should be the principal trait of all great men."[37] Quick on his feet, the managing editor from Oklahoma City reacted to Hutchins' remarks:

It seems to me that the good doctor made the mistake of weaving one blanket and throwing it over the entire press of the United States, for surely there is not an editor present who, if called upon, could not name a dozen newspapers which have devoted, this generation and the previous generation, under the same management, to the development of educational matters and the encouragement of greater and greater endowments for educational institutions.[38]

Hutchins was not invited back to ASNE for 25 years.

Another critic was Mencken. Paul Bellamy, famous for his spirited debates at ASNE conventions, responded to criticism from Mencken. Countering the Baltimore *Sun* writer's charges that the American newspaper was "venal, cowardly and stupid," Bellamy recounted instances of newspaper bravery, initiative and dependability and finished by exposing a number of Mencken's fallacies. The statements so impressed magazine and newspaper publisher Cyrus C. K. Curtis that he ordered Bellamy's entire speech to be reprinted in his Philadelphia and New York newspapers—perhaps, says N. R. Howard, "the fullest coverage of any ASNE speech by a newspaper person ever received."[39]

Paul Bellamy, son of Edward Bellamy,[40] a Springfield, Massachusetts, editor (author of the best seller *Looking Backward*), rendered the society a particular service during his 1933–1934 presidency. This was the year the Depression hit newspapers the hardest. Bellamy devised a convention program sufficiently alluring to draw members at their own expense when their newspapers felt too poor to send them.[41] Bellamy urged the 184 members in regard to what he described as "a great centralization of authority by constructive efforts, wherever we can [to keep an open mind] and beware of over-emphasizing the critical."[42]

As part of Bellamy's "open mind" approach, ASNE members met with Frances Perkins, the newly named Secretary of Labor, and President Franklin D. Roosevelt in a closed, off-the-record session. The following year, Bellamy said, the convention program was to include frank and open consideration of new problems of the press precipitated by the New Deal. "We have proceeded upon the theory that we would not be afraid to tackle hot pokers because they were hot. We have felt that the same policy, which makes an individual newspaper great, namely never flinching from a hard decision, would be that which you would wish followed by the society as a whole."[43]

No record is available of what the editors discussed in sessions with the newly elected president of the United States. Like his Republican predecessor Herbert Hoover, FDR maintained "not for attribution" sessions with editors at the White House during most of his meetings with ASNE. FDR's efforts at press control and acquiescence of editors were reinforced by photographers, who helped promulgate the healthy, confident image the crippled president maintained for his Depression-ridden country.[44] FDR's activist wife, Eleanor, added to the press access by holding regular news conferences for women only.[45]

The Roosevelt administration's program of manipulation, as well as FDR's verbal spanking of journalists and publishers who displeased him, culminated at the 1938 convention with incoming ASNE President William Allen White's criticism of Roosevelt's handling of an incident in which a newspaper played up a story which attacked the president. "Generally speaking I should say that as a matter of news it is vastly more important as news to play up a speech skewering a President than it is a speech defending a president—any president any time—and it is one of the burdens of the office if you will that a man in the presidency should know that and forget about it."[46]

White also pointed out how the Depression "class struggle" had placed editors and labor on opposing sides, "because [editors] represent property. In the nature of things we have to represent property, because it takes considerable capital to operate a newspaper," White said. "So we are placed by our position on the other side of those who are struggling for a fair adjustment of the matter of income for labor."[47] A major responsibility for the press during the Depression, White said, was to hold the confidence and respect of the American people:

It is going to be a hard job. In the nature of things it is thrust upon us by the organization of the modern world. We are businessmen, merchandising the news. We are in a way big business in our own towns. Our payrolls and our capitalizations are among at least the leading organizations. Our incomes are comparable with those of the bank or the manufacturer, and we are under the burden because of that to be more fair, to lean back, to report labor troubles if not with sympathy at least with accurate, scientific understanding, to so report a labor trouble that they will not say it is a capitalist report. It can be done. Intelligent reporters can be found, plenty of them. They are developing; I see new bylines every few weeks from men who are really intelligent, accurate reporters of the news. And the press associations must particularly seek out those men.[48]

Prior to the remarks of White and Bellamy at this 1938 convention, Shedd had called for greater leadership by ASNE in two speeches during his two-term presidency: "There is no agency or means other than the newspaper press by which discussion of such a national problem, its adequate exposition, the consideration of its various phases and angles, the differentiation between true and false remedies, can serve the public and aid in the formation of desirable sentiment and competent opinion."[49]

Noting that he might be overstepping proprieties, Shedd, described in biographical material as "a staunch Republican," urged his colleagues to assess the Depression responsibly:

It is not the function of this society to assume to dictate or even suggest editorial opinion, but it may properly be regarded within our function, as we gather here to discuss the matters of our newspaper service, to emphasize and distinctly to mark the existence of a problem concerning which each of us, in his individual view, must recognize as an obligatory part in encouraging and facilitating full and frank discussion.[50]

In 1932, before editors met with President Hoover in a closed session, Shedd continued to discuss the role of ASNE members: "We have an influence, a power, that is possessed by no other factor in our society at the present time, and that we can keep the heads of our people, our readers, fairly level, that we can influence them to think on these problems and to talk out these problems and to work out the solution of these problems in a sane and proper manner."[51]

Shedd concluded his presidential address by stressing that the whole program, as far as he had anything to do with it, had been inspired by the thought that "this was the crisis in which the American Society of Newspaper Editors ought to actually take and exercise leadership."[52]

EFFORTS TO STRENGTHEN JOURNALISM EDUCATION

In addition to nudging ASNE toward greater leadership in the nation's newsrooms, Shedd directed the society's efforts to strengthen journalism schools. ASNE's identification with this began as early as 1923, when Arthur M. Howe of the Brooklyn *Eagle* reported on the status of journalism schools. Very little was done to assist educators with general policies, programs or finances during the next 10 years. Throughout the 1920s ASNE promoted the teaching of practical skills in American colleges and universities. A major step in ASNE's attention to journalism education occurred in 1930, when S. M. Williams of the St. Paul *Pioneer Press* read a report by the committee on schools of journalism. This report recommended that schools pursue liberal arts teaching as opposed to technical skills training.[53]

President Shedd responded to the ASNE Committee report in *Journalism Quarterly*: "I cannot agree fully with the report of the committee of my own American Society of Newspaper Editors who, unfortunately to my mind, did not soften their sneer at the 'trade schools' operating as schools of journalism, and who would restrict such schools to the post-graduate field."[54]

In 1930, George Armstead of the Hartford *Courant*, head of the committee on education, mentioned in his report that a practical skills education was "too utilitarian, unconsciously too selfish, to be acceptable in this American Society of Newspaper Editors."[55] While not disagreeing with this statement, Shedd proposed a middle-of-the-road stance to incorporate practical skills and liberal arts training. In 1931 he led the movement to establish the Joint Committee of Schools of Journalism and Newspaper Groups and then served on it with such prominent educators as Willard G. Bleyer, University of Wisconsin; Frank L. Martin, University of Missouri, and John E. Drewerey, University of Georgia. By the end of Shedd's term, ASNE had defined its stand in favor of liberal arts education as part of the journalism curriculum.

Marvin H. Creager continued to emphasize ASNE's leadership role in his 1937 opening address. The Michigan-born, Kansas-educated reporter had helped turn the Milwaukee *Journal* into a more metropolitan publication after he left the Kansas City *Star*. As managing editor, he fostered a philosophy that a newspaper serves as an "attorney for the people"; he also advocated strict separation of the editorial function from the business department.[56] A former *ASNE Bulletin* editor, Creager said the society "does aspire to leadership through influence and example. It is the sole organization through which editors, independent of other affiliation, may be articulate and through articulation may be mutually helpful. We are in a field the limits of which none of us knows."[57]

Creager repeated a previous suggestion that the ASNE hire a full-time staff to work toward its goals between annual meetings. "It just does not seem possible that an organization that does nothing but have an annual meeting has any real purpose to its existence, and I cannot see how the ASNE is going to make a big imprint on journalism if that is all it proposes to do."

P. I. Reed, a journalism professor from West Virginia University, recalled Depression convention speaker Harry Hopkins expounding his tax-and-elect philosophy. A guild member embarrassed fellow ASNE members by saying that underpaid and overworked reporters wanted to live like members of other equally responsible professions. "We want to send our children to college; and if you don't make it possible, we will use the tactics of organized labor."[58] Reed also recalled a speech by Alexander Kerensky, head of the provisional Russian government: "If the countries of Europe had the freedom of expression found in the American press, the first World War would not have lasted three days."[59]

Another writer, Oswald Garrison Villard, referred to the failings of editors and reporters in the 1930s. Villard admitted to the bias of one who had belonged to the trade for more than 47 years, "who cannot witness its rapid decadence without sharp pain." He said the newspapers' loss of influence was also due in large measure to the belief that most local reporting is "one-sided, biased and inefficient."

I can come to no other conclusion, than that there has been a marked deterioration of the character and quality of average reporting. There are brilliant exceptions— dailies earnestly seeking to be accurate—but in the main the reliability of news accounts is far below what it was years ago, and the chance of misrepresentation through unintentional misquotation as well as carelessness is so great that it is frequently necessary for speakers to safeguard themselves by preserving a copy of their statements, or by preparing in advance a handout for the reporters.[60]

NEW STYLES IN JOURNALISM

While the majority of publishers sought to economize and fought against the spread of unionism, editors and reporters began to develop another form of reporting to supplement the objective style. Beginning in the 1920s with the development of the political column and continuing throughout the 1930s, journalists developed interpretive reporting in specialized areas such as labor, science, agriculture and even foreign affairs.[61] It also used more realism and photojournalism to depict the tragedy of the Depression and the exploitation of American workers. Political cartoonists such as Rollin Kirby, Ding Darling, Daniel Fitzpatrick and Edmund Duffy refined their art before millions of readers.

Henry Luce and his growing publishing empire pioneered this new form of interpretive journalism, which received extensive criticism from ASNE. For example, former ASNE President Walter M. Harrison wrote a letter to the editor of *Time* in which he pointed out inaccuracies in the weekly magazine.[62] Another blast at the magazine came from an unnamed ASNE member, who responded to a *Time* article, which charged that the editor threw his news yardstick out the window when it came to criticizing the press. Censorious *Time* was obviously flawed in its reasoning, the *Bulletin* claimed, "for if matters pertaining to the press were not interesting, presumably it would not devote as much space as it does to telling newspapers how to run their business. Belittling and muckraking in the modern manner, it evinces an attitude of superiority to the Fourth Estate, but nevertheless it gets nine-tenths of its material from the press it pretends to despise."[63]

In addition to *Time*, which started the year after ASNE was founded, Luce began *Fortune* magazine in 1930, selling it at the then surprising price of $1 per issue. In contrast, Luce's *Life,* first published in November 1936, sold for a dime. *Life* triggered a revolution in picture magazines, just as *Time* stimulated such replicas as *Newsweek* in 1933 and later *U.S. News & World Report*, founded by ASNE member David Lawrence in 1947. Coupled with the new interpretive magazines was the growing concern that syndicated columnists and syndicated material could be purchased for less than staff-written material could be produced. Commenting on this in 1938, President Kirchhofer said:

I have no quarrel with the important political commentators, whose work I respect and value, but to a degree they, by reason of their brilliance and competence, have usurped the function of the editorial writers. That is not going to be, ultimately, in the best interests of the country, the newspaper readers or the newspapers themselves. There is only one way to correct it. That is to revitalize editorial writing, and put the vital spark of life, understanding and the force of authority into it.[64]

Kirchhofer was one of several Republicans who dominated ASNE in the 1930s. Assistant director for President Hoover's 1928 campaign and publicity director for Alfred M. Landon's unsuccessful 1936 campaign, he was described by *Liberty* magazine editor John Wheeler as one of the three greatest managing editors Wheeler had ever known (along with Carr Van Anda of the New York *Times* and O. K. Bovard of the St. Louis *Post-Dispatch*). Casper Yost, E. C. Hopwood, Fred Fuller Shedd, Grove Patterson and William Allen White also identified themselves as Republicans. In contrast, three of the first ten presidents (Walter Harrison, Donald Sterling and Tom Wallace) considered themselves Democrats.

Another ASNE leader who expressed concern about commentators taking over the role of the editorial page was Tom Wallace of the Louisville *Times*. A protégé of the famous "Marse Henry" Watterson, Wallace was an editorial writer from 1923 to 1930, before becoming editor. Earlier he had examined postwar conditions in Europe and had written articles on Mexico and other countries which he felt were not getting the in-depth coverage they deserved.

FOREIGN REPORTING UNDER SCRUTINY

Some critics charge that the American media, partially as a result of neglect and inaccuracy in foreign reporting, particularly concerning revolutionary movements in Russia and Italy, did not prepare U.S. citizens for the Second World War. For example, ASNE members Walter Lippmann and Charles Merz studied Russian news as it appeared in the New York *Times* between 1917 and 1920 and discovered that even the most reputable American newspaper had misled the American public.[65]

Longtime ASNE member David Lawrence made similar charges against the American press in a 1950 address to the society: "I am convinced that had we had less secrecy in our diplomacy between 1919 and 1941 and a more vigilant press and a better understanding of what was going on in the Far East," Lawrence said, "Japan might have been our ally in World War II as she was in World War I."

The war in Europe would, therefore, have been shorter—perhaps the balance of power in the world would have been such that maybe World War II might not have been fought. So far as the Far East is concerned, we would have a better understanding today of what was going on there had we as a nation begun in the 20s and early 30s to familiarize ourselves with what our own government was doing.[66]

The *Christian Science Monitor*, founded in 1908 by Mary Baker Eddy as a remedy to the sensationalism and yellow journalism at the turn of the century,[67] was among a handful of newspapers to which ASNE gave credit for comprehensive foreign affairs reporting in the 1930s. After World War I, the *Monitor* led a group of elite newspapers in an attempt to communicate the changes in postwar Europe. Later the *Monitor* was the home newspaper for three ASNE presidents: Erwin Canham, John Hughes and Katherine Fanning.

It was Canham and Creager who in 1933 helped bring the question of illicit foreign correspondents or "ringers" with fake credentials to the attention of ASNE.[68] In the *ASNE Bulletin*, Canham cited examples of "peace zealots and irrational individuals" who had claimed to be members of the working press. The reform for the "ridiculous slight on the American press corps lies at home, on the desks of editors who write letters which might be construed as credentials and then forget all about them," Canham said. "If they don't tighten up on their amiable favor giving, some American fanatic may one day give our nation tragic cause for regret—and an international incident of that type is not easy to heal."[69]

At the ASNE convention White also helped focus attention on the international scene.[70] During World War I, he had visited the European front. In 1930 he was invited to report on his experiences in Haiti and again in 1933 he reported on extensive world travel that included a visit to Russia. Despite his differences with Roosevelt, whom he criticized in an ASNE speech, White assisted in the president's war-preparedness efforts, most notably as the chairman of the Committee to Defend America by Aiding the Allies.

The *Proceedings* show efforts to keep international issues on the ASNE agenda: Secretary of State Cordell Hull spoke on remedies for the depressed world situation, for example, and in 1935 commentators Raymond Gram Swing, Paul Scott Mowrer and Dorothy Thompson highlighted a session on "The Big News in Europe, What It Means, and How to Get It." The featured speakers at the annual banquet that year were Frank Simonds and Idaho Senator William Borah; guests included author Rebecca West and President and Mrs. Roosevelt. The following year, Dr. Franz Hoellering discussed his experiences as a former editor in Germany, and in 1937 Webb Miller spoke on "Covering the War in Spain." A. T. Steele reported to the Chicago *Daily News* the rape of Nanking in 1937 and Ernest Hemingway and Herbert L. Matthews reported on the Spanish Civil War.

Unfortunately, the reports given by such men and women were the exception to the rule. Much of what was happening in three wars—the 1931 Japanese invasion of Manchuria; the 1935–1936 Italian invasion of Ethiopia and the 1936–1939 Spanish Civil War—was relegated by the trivia of the period to back or inside pages. The most serious shortcoming of all was the neglect of the events leading to the genocide of nearly six million Jews. Discussion of these events were absent from the ASNE agenda and the pages of American newspapers.

Looking back on the 1930s and later, Evelyn Kennerly has charged that the American media committed serious ethical violations by allowing itself to be used as a tool of the German propaganda machine. The media's acceptance of

Nazi propaganda during the 1936 Olympic Games in Munich is an example of this: "Cynicism about Allied atrocity stories, seemingly the main factor influencing U.S. media responses to extermination news, also caused the media to assist Nazi propaganda. By burying Holocaust news and publishing relatively little of the available information, the media helped the Nazis cover up the truth until late in the war."[71]

Kennerly claims that the media committed another ethical violation by failing to inform the American people. Wyman writes, "Popular concern for Europe's Jews could not develop without widespread knowledge of what was happening to them." No one can prove that the outcome of the Holocaust would have been different if the media had responded differently, but, as Deborah Lipstadt says, media responses virtually assured that it would not.[72]

Foreign correspondents, ASNE editors and newspaper owners weren't the only ones being scrutinized in the 1930s. Radio, movies and newsreels were criticized at ASNE meetings for their economic impact on print and their superficiality and overemphasis on entertainment. In his 1940 presidential address, Donald J. Sterling of the Oregon *Journal* summarized innovations of particular importance to the newspaper that had occurred in the 27-year life of the society: "First came radio, which the newspaper snubbed at the outset to its subsequent chagrin. Then came the picture transmission by wire and wireless. And there are facsimile and television, among other things, each of which will rate in accordance with its ability to serve."[73]

Still another development which Sterling said helped promote accurate reporting, and which made the war in China "as intimate as the fire in the next block," was the motion picture newsreel. "The tempo ever increases. More and more we are geared to speed and paradoxically enough, speed begets accuracy."[74]

ASNE'S ATTITUDE TOWARD RADIO

Notwithstanding the popularity of the new medium of radio, the attitude of some ASNE members was negative toward its new competition. Unlike the 1980s, when print journalists and broadcasters joined forces, ASNE was not friendly to radio as it grew from an experiment to a fixture in 27 million of 32 million U.S. homes. Editors worried about the drain of advertising dollars away from print.

Rather than fight radio, as they had during much of the 1920s, many ASNE leaders decided in the 1930s that if you can't beat them, join them. Or at least buy them. Such pragmatism is seen in the remarks of President Harrison in 1930, who provided what Gordon Pates of the San Francisco *Chronicle* said were the three major themes of conventions for the society's early years of existence: press agentry in the news columns, low salaries for newspapermen and the resultant lure of public relations jobs. In addition, Harrison had some advice for editors who were puzzled by the treatment of radio: "The best out from the situation is to purchase a radio station and get on the line for a television permit. The radio and its little brother, television, constitute too serious a menace to fixed advertising methods and the dissemination of news to be in the hands of a unit unrelated to the newspaper business."[75]

Among the ASNE editors who followed this advice by buying into the broadcast industry was Kirchhofer. Through his association with the former secretary of commerce, who had helped design the public service oriented broadcast philosophy of the Federal Radio Act in 1927, Kirchhofer pioneered commercially successful plunges of newspaper into radio. In the late 1920s, his paper, like others belonging to ASNE members, sponsored regular broadcasts and printed program logs. Kirchhofer was also instrumental in establishing the *News'* WBEN, which rapidly became Buffalo's leader in both AM and FM.[76]

Stimulated by the 1927 Radio Act, the passage of the Communications Act of 1934 and a desire to maintain respect and dignity in the profession, ASNE also began to recognize radio at its meetings by inviting speakers favorable to that medium. Thus twin addresses by Merwin H. Aylesworth, "The Press and Radio," the radio viewpoint, and "Radio and Newspapers," by Paul B. Williams, in 1930 were given. They were followed by a report on cooperation among press, radio and the bar in 1938 and a discussion on radio by communications scholar Paul Lazarsfeld in 1941. Frank Mankiewicz' look at the 1940s reveals that 5 of the 10 most powerful opinion makers of the next decade were radio voices: Gabriel Heatter, H. V. Kaltenborn, Fulton Lewis, Jr., Paul Harvey and Edward R. Murrow.[77]

THE GROWING ROLE OF WOMEN

By contrast, the ten most influential voices in the 1930s were all print journalists, including the largest number of women ever to appear on such a list. These women—Dorothy Thompson, Eleanor Roosevelt and Emily Post— represented an increasing number of women in journalism and ASNE's interest in women's pages and so-called women's issues in order to increase readership. Of the ten conventions of the 1930s, nearly half included addresses or panels on women's subjects.[78] Some comments, by today's standards, appear patronizing. White referred to columnists Elizabeth M. Gilmer (Dorothy Dix), Inez Robb and Doris Fleeson in his introduction to "The Women's Hour" panel in 1939 as "these three lovely hellcats." He went on to say that he wished Doris Fleeson were "my own pet panther."[79]

When Anna Steese Richardson, director of the Good Citizenship Bureau of the *Woman's Home Companion*, addressed ASNE, President Grove Patterson quoted a female Toledo reader who criticized men for making a distinction between women and human beings: "We don't want any women's page. We are interested in the same features that men are interested in, and we don't like any kind of features that are set apart particularly for us."[80] "I thought that was rather an extreme position," Patterson concluded.

Despite this outward emphasis on "feminine"[81] and women's issues, the official records do not show any large influx of women into ASNE membership. The first female member was Mrs. Zell Hart Deming, publisher of the Warren (Ohio) *Tribune-Chronicle*, who attended the 1933 conference, took part in discussions and enjoyed the shop talks heartily.[82] According to a *Bulletin* account, Mrs. Deming was interested in the proceedings because she had progressed through the ranks and learned publishing on a small-town daily. She started as a young widow of 21. The *Tribune* was then a new and struggling daily. The *Bulletin* also described Mrs. Deming as the only female member of the ANPA and Associated Press.[83]

After the death of Mrs. Deming in April 1936, Eleanor Medill (Cissy) Patterson of the Washington *Herald and Times* was the only female member of the society before being joined by Oveta Culp Hobby, executive vice president of the Houston *Post*, in 1938. Amy Comstock of the Tulsa *Tribune* became the third female member in 1939. A graduate of the University of Wisconsin, Miss Comstock taught history before she became a secretary and began writing editorials. She gradually assumed other responsibilities and became an understudy to her boss.[84] Mrs. Hobby, wife of former Texas governor W. P. Hobby, was parliamentarian of the Texas legislature from 1925 to 1935 and author of *Mr. Chairman*, a textbook on parliamentary procedure. Mrs. Patterson and Mrs. Hobby were constantly photographed with male society members, presumably to give the appearance of a balanced organization. Mrs. Hobby was later named chief of the War Department's women's interest section in the bureau of public relations.[85]

Notwithstanding these well-known women, there was increasing criticism aimed at female editors. In his book *City Editor*, Stanley Walker vilified newspaperwomen in general, although he complimented those who had risen above the level of their sisters.[86] Walker later recommended that one of his reporters, Ishbel Ross, write about famous newspaperwomen of the 1930s. Her compilation was published as *Ladies of the Press* in 1936.

ASNE members were also learning to cope with movies, which were slowly nudging print media to provide greater doses of entertainment in the newspaper. The added attractions of sound and color increased the appeal of films. Helping Americans escape the Depression was a fantasy world of movie dancers including Fred Astaire and Ginger Rogers in the 1933 *Flying Down to Rio* and the high-stepping chorus girls choreographed by Busby Berkeley. This period also saw further developments of cartoon characters such as Mickey Mouse and improvements in the use of color; the climax came in 1937 with the first feature-length cartoon in Technicolor, *Snow White and the Seven Dwarfs*. The ultimate in entertainment pacifiers, however, was *The Wizard of Oz*. But the movie theaters also provided newsreels as well: *Time* magazine's famous "March of Time" started in 1935.

ASNE leaders did not appreciate Hollywood's depiction of the newspaper business. Ex-journalists Charles MacArthur and Ben Hecht may have established the mythical model of journalism in their Broadway production *Front Page*, but ASNE members were not pleased with what Hollywood was doing to an already tarnished image. In 1940, President Sterling referred to correspondence ASNE had with Will Hays of the movie industry on the "objectionable presentation of newspapermen in pictures," but no action was taken.[87]

EMPHASIS ON VIOLENCE

The ASNE board of directors also were concerned about the image of America that was being presented in the pages of its own dailies. But news of violence at home and abroad dominated entertainment and news media in the 1930s.

One example of this emphasis on crime and violence is Jack Lait's dramatic account of gangster John Dillinger's being killed by FBI agents in 1934. Another is the episode in which Walter Winchell, New York *Daily Mirror* columnist and radio newscaster, engineered the 1939 surrender of the "president" of Murder, Inc., Louis "Lepke" Buchalter. Buchalter had reportedly killed between 60 and 80 people before surrendering to the popular broadcaster. According to Louis Snyder, the fast-talking Winchell did more to rouse the conscience of America against intolerance and totalitarianism than any other journalist of his time.[88]

Although ASNE editors were adept at covering crime in their own streets after it happened, and even war overseas after it began, American newspapers did not accurately interpret the trends and events underlying such events. This was particularly true of the European situation, which reached its climax in 1939, following the rise of Adolf Hitler in 1933. Many editors and Americans never fully comprehended the portent of this situation, even after the Germans invaded Poland and bombed Britain. Broadcasters such as Ed Murrow brought the horror of the distant war into the minds of Americans. The shortcomings of the press, as well as of elected officials, in recognizing signs of the Japanese expansion in the Pacific culminated in the sneak attack on Pearl Harbor on December 7, 1941.

Overall, even though ASNE encouraged new methods of reporting and interpreting domestic and foreign affairs during the 1930s, the mainstream press focused on economic survival rather than on the emerging ethic of social responsibility suggested by Robert Hutchins. Irresponsibility can be seen in the sensational treatment of the Lindbergh trial and in publisher opposition to the unionization of reporters. Publishers and editors such as Robert McCormick provided leadership in supporting such legal cases as the *Near v. Minnesota* prior restraint dispute. But generally speaking, the lords of the press did not exert the leadership that was necessary for the task at home or abroad. They failed to provide adequate warning concerning the Depression and the concerning the attacks on the Jewish community in Europe.

The cry of the era, according to Oswald Garrison Villard, was that the period of great editors was gone. Although individual editors and institutions such as ASNE attempted to fill the vacuum created by the post–World War I changes in economics and culture, they could not overcome the publisher influence. Not only did the publishers dominate the boardrooms, but they also appeared as if they were becoming models for the editors, more than the editors served as exemplars for the front page reporters.

NOTES

1. Cabell Phillips, *From the Crash to the Blitz, 1929–39*, New York: Macmillan, 1969.

2. H. V. Kaltenborn, "The Role of Radio," *Journalism in Wartime*, Washington, D.C.: American Council on Public Affairs, 1943, 111–112.

3. Caroline Bird, *The Invisible Scar*, New York: Pocket Books, 1966.

4. Shearon Lowery and Melvin DeFleur, "The Invasion from Mars: Radio Panics America," in *Milestones in Mass Communication Research: Media Effects*, New York: Longman, 1983, 59–84.

5. "Radio, Help or Hindrance," ASNE *Proceedings*, 1941, 150.

6. Lowery and DeFleur, "The People's Choice: The Media in a Political Campaign," in *Milestones in Mass Communications Research*, 85–112.

7. ASNE *Proceedings*, 1941, 70.

8. Donald J. Sterling, *A Sterling Story*, Portland, Ore.: Privately printed by Arcady Press, 1952, 142–143.

9. George Seldes, *Lords of the Press*, New York: Julian Messner, 1938. See chapter 22, "William Allen White: Anti-Press Lord," 272–280.

10. Ibid.

11. William Allen White to Kent Cooper, August 29, 1932, in Walter Johnson, ed., *Selected Letters of William Allen White, 1899–1943* (New York, 1947), 326. Quoted in David Sloan, *The Media in America: A History*, Worthington, Ohio: Publishing Horizons, 1989, 294.

12. Frank I. Cobb, "The Press and Public Opinion," *New Republic*, December 31, 1919, 147. Quoted in Sloan, 292.

13. George Seldes, *Freedom of the Press*, Garden City, N.Y.: Garden City Publishing, 1935, 151. A modern version of the media's failure to anticipate the Crash of 1929 is the

$250 billion savings and loan collapse of the 1980s. According to U.S. House Banking Committee member Jim Leach, "It's the greatest single accounting misjudgment in this century. It's the largest lapse on the part of the press. It's the greatest regulatory lapse of this century." *Newsweek*, May 21, 1990, 27.

14. Jean Folkerts and Dwight Teeter, *Voices of a Nation*, New York: Macmillan, 1989, 404.

15. ASNE *Proceedings*, 1940, 142–143.

16. Quoted in Oswald Garrison Villard, *The Disappearing Daily: Chapters in American Newspaper Evolution*, New York: Knopf, 1944, 8.

17. Seldes, *Freedom of the Press*. In his introduction, Seldes says that no criticism in his 380-page book goes beyond that legitimately based on the 1923 ASNE code and that there are no strictures more severe than those written by the organized newspapermen (American Newspaper Guild), xiii.

18. Seldes, *Lords of the Press*.

19. Ibid., vii.

20. Ibid., chapter 1.

21. For a more balanced look at Robert McCormick and his role of defending freedom of the press, see Edwin Emery, *History of the American Newspaper Publishers Association*, Minneapolis: University of Minnesota Press, 1950, chapter 15. See also Fred Friendly, *Minnesota Rag*. In *Chicago* Tribune: *The Rise and Fall of a Great American Newspaper*, Chicago: Rand McNally Co., 1979, Lloyd Wendt estimates that the *Tribune* assumed the burden of legal costs in *Near* v. *Minnesota*, spending $35,000 while the ANPA spent a modest $5,000.

22. ASNE *Proceedings*, 1931, 99–105. McCormick is also described in a short feature entitled "As ASNE members appear to me" by Frank Parker Stockbridge in the September 5, 1935, *ASNE Bulletin*, 4.

23. ASNE *Proceedings*, 1929, 163–164.

24. ASNE *Proceedings*, 1931, 100.

25. Alice Fox Pitts, *Read All About It! 50 Years of ASNE*, Reston, Va.: ASNE, 1974, 50–51.

26. Even Arthur Hays Sulzberger, publisher of the New York *Times*, in a 1936 address, said that perhaps the ANPA was going too far in its campaign. Emery, 231.

27. Seldes, *Freedom of the Press*. See chapter 8.

28. One of the better books describing the growth of the guild is *A Union of Individuals: The Formation of the American Newspaper Guild 1933–1936*, New York: Columbia University Press, 1970.

29. ASNE *Proceedings*, 1938, 20.

30. ASNE minutes, October 16, 1938, 143.

31. Seldes, *Lords of the Press*, 227.

32. ASNE *Proceedings*, 1932, 104.

33. Such tributes to White and others are contained in *ASNE Bulletin*, February 1, 1944.

34. ASNE *Proceedings*, 1939, 15.

35. "Are Editors Effective?" ASNE *Proceedings*, 1937, 45–49.

36. "Educators or Agitators," ASNE *Proceedings*, 1941, 68–77.

37. ASNE *Proceedings*, 1930, 130.

38. Ibid., 135.

39. "He wore his *honor* as a badge as if to encourage honor in all he met," *ASNE Bulletin*, May 1956, 9.

40. Robert Downs says that of all the many utopias, the most successful, by all odds, is Edward Bellamy's *Looking Backward, 2000–1887*. In his *Books That Changed America*, Downs says that within a decade after its publication in 1888, a million copies had been published and translations appeared in virtually every language. "Over the past 80 years, Downs claimed in 1970, the social and political influence of *Looking Backward* has been incalculable."

41. *ASNE Bulletin*, May 1956, 9.

42. ASNE *Proceedings*, 1933, 13.

43. ASNE *Proceedings*, 1934, 15.

44. Betty Houchin Winfield, "FDR's Pictorial Image, Rules and Boundaries," *Journalism History*, Vol. 5, No. 4 (Winter 1978–1979): 110–114, 136.

45. Lewis Gould, "First Ladies and the Press: Bess Truman to Lady Bird Johnson," *American Journalism* (Summer 1983): 47.

46. ASNE *Proceedings*, 1938, 132.

47. Ibid., 133.

48. Ibid., 134.

49. ASNE *Proceedings*, 1931, 29.

50. Ibid., 21.

51. ASNE *Proceedings*, 1932, 107.

52. Ibid.

53. ASNE *Proceedings*, 1930, 43–45. See also Alf Pratte and Ed Adams, "At the Crossroads: The Unsettling Role of ASNE on American Journalism Education," paper presented at Western Journalism Historians Conference, San Francisco, February 27–28, 1992.

54. Fred Fuller Shedd, "The Newspaper Heritage," *Journalism Quarterly*, 1931, 45–58.

55. ASNE *Proceedings*, 1930, 42–47.

56. Will C. Conrad, Kathleen F. Wilson and Dale Wilson, *The Milwaukee* Journal: *The First Eighty Years*, Madison: University of Wisconsin Press, 1964, 110–111. See also "Milwaukee Journal Reflects Its Editor's Character," *ASNE Bulletin*, September 15, 1936, and "Defeatist Point of View Decried by Creager," *ASNE Bulletin*, November 1, 1938.

57. ASNE *Proceedings*, 1937, 20.

58. P. I. Reed, "ASNE in Depression Years," *ASNE Bulletin*, date unknown. Mr. Reed may have been referring to a speech by Allen Raymond, president of the American Newspaper Guild, ASNE *Proceedings*, 1934, 82–99.

59. Ibid.

60. Villard, 10.

61. For discussions on the growth of interpretive reporting in the 1930s, see Emery and Emery, 363–364; Folkerts and Teeter, 409–412.

62. "Mr. Harrison corrects *Time*," *ASNE Bulletin*, Second May Issue, 1933, #50, 5.

63. "Magazine Belittles News Yardstick," *ASNE Bulletin*, Second February Issue, 1933, #44, 1.

64. ASNE *Proceedings*, 1938, 17.

65. Walter Lippmann and Charles Merz, "A Test of the News," *New Republic*, August 4, 1920, 1–4. *New Republic* editor Bruce Bliven spoke on "The Future of Free Speech" at the 1934 ASNE convention. See ASNE *Proceedings*, 1934, 124.

66. ASNE *Proceedings*, 1950, 168.

67. See *Commitment to Freedom: The Story of the* Christian Science Monitor, by Erwin D. Canham (Boston: Houghton Mifflin, 1958). Canham served as the 18th president of the ASNE in 1948.

68. "Illicit Representation Abroad," *ASNE Bulletin*, First October Issue, #59, 1933, 1–2.

69. Ibid., 2.

70. This is illustrated in a picture and cutline on page 1 of the *ASNE Bulletin*, November 1, 1937. Titled "Most publicized," the cutline said, "Pick up a newspaper or magazine almost any day and you will find a story about member William Allen White—or a picture of him. This one is from *Editor & Publisher*."

71. Evelyn Kennerly, "Mass Media and Mass Murder: American Coverage of the Holocaust," *Journal of Mass Media Ethics*, Vol. 2, No. 1 (Fall/Winter 1986–1987): 68.

72. Ibid., 69.

73. ASNE *Proceedings*, 1940, 17.

74. Ibid.

75. ASNE *Proceedings*, 1930, 17. For a detailed account of print and radio, see Alf Pratte, "Going Along for the Ride on the Prosperity Bandwagon: Peaceful Annexation Not War between the Editors" and "Radio: 1923–1941," *Journal of Radio Studies*, 2 (1993–1994): 123–139.

76. Millard Browne, "A. H. Kirchhofer, Editor," in *Gentlemen of the Press*, edited by Loren Ghiglione, Indianapolis: R. J. Berg & Co., 1984, 194–198.

77. Frank Mankiewicz, "From Lippmann to Letterman: The Ten Most Powerful Voices," *Gannett Center Journal* (Spring 1989): 85.

78. For example, see "The Woman's Page," by Julia Coburn with discussion by John S. Knight, ASNE *Proceedings*, 1935, 79–89; "What I Think Women Want in a Newspaper," by Anna Steese Richardson, ASNE *Proceedings*, 1936, 20–30; "Streamlining the Women's Pages," by Marvin Lindsay, Washington *Post*; "The Woman's Page Changes Its Mind," by Mary Stow, Newark *News*; "What the Advertiser Wants to Know about Women's Pages," by Alice Couler, the Norwich Pharmaceutical Company, Norwich, N.Y., ASNE *Proceedings*, 1938, 139–154; " 'The Women's Hour': Mrs. Elizabeth M. Gilmer (Dorothy Dix), Mrs. Inez Robb, Miss Doris Fleeson," ASNE *Proceedings*, 1939, 77–95.

79. ASNE *Proceedings*, 1939, 89.

80. ASNE *Proceedings*, 1936, 30.

81. The word *feminine* is used in relation to women in early stories in the *ASNE Bulletin*. For example, see "Feminine Representation," #53, July 1933, 5, and "What Are the Feminine Interests?" #71, March, 1934, 5. Beginning with the August 18, 1934, issue of the *ASNE Bulletin*, the term changes to *women*: "What Are the Women's Interests?"

82. "Feminine Representation," *ASNE Bulletin*, #53, July 1933, 5.

83. *ASNE Bulletin*, May 4, 121, 1936.

84. "Miss Amy Comstock understudies boss to become editor," *ASNE Bulletin*, July 1, 1939, 3.

85. "Mrs. Hobby gives woman's slant to army news," *ASNE Bulletin*, September 1, 1941.

86. "How's the woman problem in your office?" *ASNE Bulletin*, #85, November 3, 1934, 2–3.

87. ASNE minutes, April 17, 1940, 161–162.

88. Louis L. Snyder and Richard B. Morris, *A Treasury of Great Reporting*, New York: Simon and Schuster, 1962, 549.

Chapter 3

Keeping the Faith in World War II

The propaganda interests of any government in war or peace are incompatible with the complete freedom of news and opinion which editors should maintain. The time will come when you will have to make a choice between government propaganda and the freedom of news. As president of the ASNE your judgment and your opinion should be above the influence of official pressure or the subtle effect of confidential information which cannot be shared with editors or the public.

> —ASNE member Carl Ackerman, Columbia University,
> in a letter asking ASNE President Roy A. Roberts to resign
> from a government wartime advisory board, July 1943

If the war isn't won, there won't be any free press or independent journalism. That's our first job. The war will be won and a free press maintained, but it won't be by everyone's locking himself up in an ivory tower and refusing to cooperate.

> —Mr. Roberts' reply to Mr. Ackerman, July 1943

A free press means a responsible press. A militant press means one that leads, not merely sits with a pad and records. Out of these sessions of the American society may we be stimulated to serve better our nation and our communities. Out of these sessions may we send the word to the hundreds of newsmen on every battlefront, on every sea, men doing the greatest job of reporting the world has ever known, the words, "Good luck! May you return home safely to us, but home to a press that has kept the faith."

> —Roy A. Roberts, Kansas City *Star*, April 21, 1944

In mid-July 1943, the wire services and other media carried accounts of an exchange of telegrams between two prominent members of the American Society of Newspaper Editors concerning the propriety of the ASNE president's sitting on a government advisory board.[1] Defending his appointment to the Office of War Information advisory board was ASNE President Roy A. Roberts, managing editor of the Kansas City *Star*. Questioning Roberts' as well as six other ASNE members' appointment[2] to the nine-member board, was Carl W. Ackerman, a former journalist–public relations practitioner and dean of the Columbia University Graduate School of Journalism. Ackerman told Roberts:

As president of the ASNE your judgment and your opinion should be above the influence of official pressure or the subtle effect of confidential information which cannot be shared with editors or the public . . . . I believe that the officers of the ASNE should maintain complete independence with respect to the government. Their allegiance should be restricted exclusively to free and independent journalism.[3]

Ackerman found an additional conflict of interest in the fact that the society president would serve on the government advisory board at a time when ASNE had just announced its intent to provide leadership in advocating worldwide freedom of the press. "Suppose the government decided on a policy of excluding the press at the peace conferences, or suppose it opposed freedom of international communications, how would you as president of ASNE serve both the government and press?" Ackerman also charged that as a war advisory board member, Roberts would help determine government policy: "The propaganda interests of any government in war or peace are incompatible with the complete freedom of news and opinion which editors should maintain. The time will come when you will have to make a choice between government propaganda and the freedom of news."[4]

The discussion of the alleged impropriety of the membership of one whom Ackerman called "the head of one of the most important journalistic trusteeships in the world" on a government board soon disappeared from the press. But the public debate was important for a number of reasons. First, it exposed the feeling of some that newspaper editors were not carrying out their societal responsibility as independent observers and critics during World War II. Ackerman and a handful of editors questioned the unquestioning support of the war effort by ASNE. Roberts defended himself in a stinging reply to his ASNE colleague: "If the war isn't won, there won't be any free press or independent journalism. That's our first job. The war will be won and a free press maintained, but it won't be by everyone's locking himself up in an ivory tower and refusing to cooperate. Nor can we go on a sit-down strike because we don't like the way things are run in Washington."[5]

Roberts had spent much of his journalistic career fighting corruption and helping promote Kansas City in the tradition of *Star* founder William Rockhill Nelson.[6] He stated that he hadn't been intimidated by those in government positions and had spoken out when he felt a need to do so. Acting in an advisory capacity and not an administrative one, or working hand in hand with the Office of Censorship (headed by former reporter and AP executive Byron Price), he argued, should not limit independence of action.

Frankly I do not believe that you can criticize and demand that the government do this or that and then, when asked merely to give advice or suggestions on how to achieve objectives, decline to do so on the grounds you might be improperly influenced. Presidents and past presidents of ASNE have served on the advisory committee on censorship from the outset of the war without stultification of the aims and purposes of the society. In fact Byron Price will tell you that their counsel has helped make censorship work.[7]

Roberts also indirectly alluded to Ackerman's comments in his presidential report at the 22nd annual ASNE meeting in April 1944. The report defended the "extraordinary cooperation" of ASNE in the war effort. Referring to those sitting in "ivory towers," Roberts said that editors could still contribute to victory without surrendering freedom of expression:

Naturally, as newspapermen our first concern has been that newspapers should make their full contribution, and more, to winning the war. We have kept the faith. Officers and directors of the ASNE have sat with Censorship, in which Byron Price has done such a magnificent job, with the OWI, on national loan sales committees, on scrap drive committees, with the Army, and with the Navy as specific problems came up. At the same time we have sought to protect zealously a free press within the bounds of legitimate military security that is necessary in war times.[8]

THE PRESS IN WORLD WAR II

Roberts' rhetoric, more than that of any other ASNE leader or journalist, capsulizes the story of ASNE and of mainstream American journalism during World War II. The son of a Congregational minister and an adjutant in World War I, he used religious imagery during his parting presidential remarks in 1944: "Good luck! May you return home safely to us, but home to a press that has kept the faith." From the morning when ASNE member Riley Allen mobilized the staff of the Honolulu *Star-Bulletin* to report the attack on Pearl Harbor, putting copies on the streets even before enemy planes had returned to their carriers,[9] to the time when General Dwight D. Eisenhower invited ASNE members to view Jewish death camps in 1945,[10] the American press worked closely with the government. It was one of the most remarkable examples of cooperation between media and military in the history of the free world.

ASNE President John Knight recollected that there was "not a single positive deliberate violation of the censorship code, and yet the code had no teeth in it whatsoever."[11] ASNE President Dwight Marvin described editors as "balladists" for democracy.[12] Patrick Washburn claims that journalists generally accepted censorship "cavalierly."[13] Not only did the editors sit on government advisory boards and take part in voluntary censorship, but they also used their papers to promote war loan campaigns and scrap drives, to save fat and to provide news clippings to soldiers in the field. Beginning in 1940, Eugene Meyer of the Washington *Post* cared for 16 child refugees from England on an estate he equipped for the purpose near Warrenton, Virginia.[14] Dozens of other examples were reported by ASNE members.

Although the ASNE membership may have kept the faith with the military and government in unifying the nation and boosting up morale, some historians, including Deborah Lipstadt,[15] Peter Irons,[16] Patrick Washburn,[17] and James D. Startt,[18] argue that the media record was less than impressive. They contend that the press may have breached its journalistic faith with minority groups while cooperating with the government. As Washburn suggests in his analysis of the federal government's investigations of the black press during World War II, there was a strong undercurrent of "antilibertarianism." The libertarian press was replaced by one which Roberts later described as more responsible and that helped pave the way for the social responsibility in the post–World War II era.

Ironically, the nearly unquestioned acceptance of federal censorship came within two years after the ASNE membership, at the 1940 convention, heard James M. Thomson denounce government control. Thomson, of the New Orleans *Item-Tribune*, described how Louisiana newspapers had fought to stop the legislature—controlled by Huey Long—from imposing an advertising tax on newspapers with circulation above 20,000. Thomson claimed that in the "old, conservative, civilized state of Louisiana, this strange man [Long] was moving steadily and effectively to build a dictatorship as iron-clad and air-tight as those of Stalin, Hitler or Mussolini." Long had solved every problem related to establishing a dictatorship, Thomson said, "except press control," which was struck down by the Supreme Court. The Court affirmed that "a free press stands as one of the great interpreters between the government and the people. To allow it to be fettered is to fetter ourselves."[19]

Press critic Oswald Garrison Villard used the world's largest cooperative press association as an example of how the media could fail to provide a true picture of government by withholding information from the public in the period before Pearl Harbor: "Once more the Associated Press felt that its first loyalty was not to the American people but to the government itself, and it cheerfully accepted the voluntary censorship the government asked the newspapers to impose and thereby established a precedent fraught with grave danger to the American press."[20]

At the ASNE annual convention in April 1941, Ackerman warned his fellow members about the dangers of government centralization as a prelude to censorship:

While I recognize that our government in time of war should establish and maintain censorship at the source of all military and naval information that is of advantage to an enemy for military purpose, we have the experience of all belligerent countries to prove that the centralization of power is followed by censorship or restrictions and official intimidations which suppress freedom of public expression or compel uniformity of public opinion.[21]

Ackerman sought support for an amendment to President Roosevelt's Lend-Lease Bill. The amendment would prohibit "the government censorship of the press, radio, forum, pulpit, classroom or any other facility or instrumentality of communication which will interfere with the free discussion of the issues of war or peace." Without the amendment, Ackerman claimed, American journalists were no longer free agents as far as certain war news was concerned. "Our future course of action must, under the law, be adjusted to our commitments of our government to those foreign powers we are obliged to aid under the Lend-Lease Act."

Ackerman also noted that Washington correspondents were not as free to obtain information and to report it as they were in time of peace: "News in Washington is supervised at the source of news releases and off-the-record conferences. Factually all Washington news relating to foreign affairs and to national defense is essentially the same, every day, in all newspapers. The variations appear in volume, interpretation, emphasis and timing."[22]

Ackerman suggested that governments gained great power over the press because many editors and publishers had long considered their editorial pronouncements as having the effect of law on public opinion. In fact, however, the government had used law to control the press: "Today, the free press is actually encircled by laws, regulations, and requests."

Other members in the *ASNE Bulletin* raised their voices about censorship three months before the attack on Pearl Harbor. A. H. Kirchhofer argued that "no self-respecting editor" would print anything to aid forces that the nation is attempting to overthrow, "but neither should editors lightly cast aside their responsibilities to preserve press freedom and maintain the essential reliability of their newspaper." A future war correspondent and ASNE president, Wright Bryan of the Atlanta *Journal,* argued that Secretary of the Navy Frank Knox, a fellow society member, should be free to determine what constitutes a military secret. "But suppression of facts already known to Berlin, Rome and Tokyo can only serve to embitter readers, first against the newspaper and later against the government."[23]

Tom Hanes, managing editor of the Norfolk *Ledger-Dispatch*, also joined the fight against the government's tendency to cover up legitimate news. He argued that "voluntary censorship" was less than it should be because the rules were made by the government and not by the press. Hanes expressed concern that citizens would lose confidence in the media because the "newspapers did not print news everyone could see was happening around them." Similar feelings were expressed by Julian S. Miller of the Charlotte *Observer*; he noted that his city was full of soldiers and sailors mingling freely with civilians and talking without restraint about what was happening within their sphere. "Naturally, the public, hearing of so many activities and seeing that nothing appears in the newspaper about them, begins its skeptical attitude toward the press."

From before the war until mid-1945, however, recommendations for an ASNE committee to explore the censorship problem attracted only lukewarm response.[24] With the exception of Ackerman's 1943 telegram and an ASNE resolution against President Roosevelt for banning the press from a food conference in Hot Springs, Virginia, the issue was never a prominent part of the agenda of the ASNE or of the public. As World War II drew to a conclusion, a nationwide survey of 154 ASNE members in 34 states indicated that most members did not believe the federal government had encroached on constitutional guarantees. According to the survey, 118 of the 154 members checked "no encroachment," while 36 believed there had been some.

Comments of William J. Pape of the Waterbury (Conn.) *Republican and American* and Kirchhofer of the Buffalo *Evening News* typified those editors who were concerned about an encroachment after World War II. Pape gave an unequivocal "no" to the survey question but added that the government manifestly intended to censor the press. "When a tough looking bulldog follows me for 50 yards growling and snapping at my heels, experience tells me that he will bite as soon as he dares." Kirchhofer said that if a categorical answer was required, it might be "no"; but that does not tell the story, he added. "There have been direct and indirect pressures." If a pending legal case were decided adversely, Kirchhofer said he would change his answer to "yes."

Frank Ahlgren of the Memphis *Commercial-Appeal*, Charles J. Lewin of the New Bedford (Mass.) *Standard-Times*, and Dwight Marvin of the Troy (N.Y.) *Record*, answered an unqalified "yes" to the question of government encroachment. Ahlgren referred to the government's actions in ordering union maintenance and encouraging CIO maintenance of unionization of newsrooms through biased and partial union agents as examples. Lewin said that censorship may have been voluntary at the start of the war, but it evolved into something far from voluntary: "We have experienced numerous cases in which we knew of incidents the publication of which would not have affected military security but which we did not publish for weeks after they were known to us and to entire communities, or did not publish at all, because of the military censorship rules against publication."[25]

Marvin referred to Attorney General Francis Biddle's attempts to get a bill through Congress which would make it criminal to divulge anything on departmental papers marked "confidential": "The OWI (Office of War Information) has sought to control, and has controlled, publicity passing from certain channels, thereby using its machinery for propaganda and to prevent propaganda it opposes. There is a prevalent disposition to confine news to handouts, if we may—and we can—trust our representatives in Washington."[26]

Notwithstanding such frank comments, as the war ended in Europe and ground to a conclusion in the Pacific, ASNE and the American media cooperated almost entirely with President Roosevelt, the military and the censors in a spirit of unity to try to end the war. One example of this is the society's long-standing practice of allowing off-the-record comments at its annual meetings. This was pointed out as early as July 1941 by Wilbur Forrest in planning for the annual meeting, when he called for fewer speeches and more discussion among members: "It is my personal feeling also that off-the-record sessions with government officials are illusory and that these gentlemen should be encouraged next year to give the public more important facts under ASNE auspices."[27]

In recalling the 1943 conference, Malcolm W. Bingay of the Detroit *Free Press* made similar comments: "From early morning till dewy night we listened to speeches. All off-the-record. Even in a few feeble question-and-answer periods— now almost extinct—nothing new was added. Not one of the dozen or more leaders in government who talked to us 'off the record' told us a thing we could not have found out by reading our newspapers and current magazines. 'Off the record' has been a synonym for run-around."[28]

The obvious rationale for off-the-record comments, self-censorship and propaganda was to end the war quickly and save lives, a concern realized dramatically with the loss of more than 2,000 American servicemen at Pearl Harbor. During the six-year conflict, which a divided America entered after two years, the Allies mobilized 62 million persons, and the Axis about half as many. An estimated 16 million Allies, including 49 members of the media, died.

ASNE MEMBERS AT WAR

Among those who lost their lives were children of ASNE members and staff. Articles such as "Sons in Service" were added to the *ASNE Bulletin*, which increased the number of pages to communicate better on a monthly basis.[29] It reported 86 children of ASNE members in the armed forces.[30] The in-house publication also reported the deaths of both sons of ASNE member Roger M. Blood of the Manchester (N.H.) *Union Leader*.[31] Also killed in action were the sons of ASNE's Freddy and Alice Pitts, J. N. Heiskell of the *Arkansas Gazette* and John Knight, Sr. The announcement of Knight's death in a German ambush near Muenster had been withheld from publication because the 22-year-old officer's wife was expecting a child. The baby, born two weeks after his father's death, was named John Knight III. In a moving editorial about "Johnny, the lovable, kindly kid who never had a vicious thought in his life," Knight revealed the anguish of every parent who is similarly hurt.

Nearly 300,000 Johnnys are gone. We must make an appointment with those gallant boys and give them a solemn pledge that we shall never again shirk the task of achieving a peaceful world. We must guarantee them further, that their returning comrades will be given the chance at life which was denied to them; that no one of them shall ever suffer through selfishness and greed; that our high-sounding promises will never re-echo as hollow mockery of words. We have made an obligation to those who have made the brave and gallant fight, a covenant with the dead.[32]

In addition to their family members, statistics show the involvement of ASNE members in the U.S. Armed Forces. Twenty-one[33] of nearly 250 ASNE members were allowed to waive payment of membership dues because they were in the service.[34] One headline in the *Bulletin* indicated "One in Twenty Members Working for Uncle Sam."[35]

The highest military rank of any ASNE member was held by Secretary of the Navy Frank Knox of the Chicago *Daily News*. He held the office during the Pearl Harbor attack and for the first three years of U.S. involvement.[36] In World War I, member Josephus Daniels, editor of the Raleigh *News and Observer*, had served as secretary of the Navy through Wilson's two terms, as well as ambassador to Mexico.[37]

Further evidence of ASNE members' service in the armed forces can be seen in a study of the lives of the society's 65 presidents from 1922 through 1992. It shows that 33 presidents, or more than half, served either actively in the military or in related duties, including as war correspondents, in World Wars I and II. Such firsthand involvement in the armed forces by ASNE members and presidents-to-be seriously counters charges that journalists are not loyal. An inside look at military life and mind may also contribute to a long-lived "patriotism" and support for involvement in other wars. On the other hand, such familiarity, triggered by an over-enthusiastic, cheerleading press, may have also planted the seeds of additional skepticism and responsibility in regard to possible involvement in any future wars in Korea and Vietnam (carefully disguised by the umbrella of security).

As the youngest bureau chief in United Press wire service history, Wilbur Forrest earned plaudits with the first interviews of the survivors of the *Lusitania* on the Irish coast: "He reported the mad butchery at Verdun, where a correspondent next to him stood up to see the action and lost an eye to a bullet. Bill Forrest was not a man who tempted fate. No lover of combat, he found covering the war to be mostly 'the glorified dissemination of government propaganda.'"[38]

Richard Kluger says that Forrest's later work with the New York *Tribune*— including the Lindbergh landing, an interview with Mussolini on his conquest of Rome, politics in Washington and the Seabury investigations—"was generally reliable and almost never better or worse than competent."[39] Basil "Stuffy" Walters enlisted with the Indiana University ambulance unit and later became editor of the *Ambulance Center News*. According to Raymond Moscowitz, "The United States Ambulance Corps—the embodiment of Walters' patriotism— became embedded in his life. Long before World War I ended, Walters kept in contact with survivors. He continued to be the USAC's 'designated editor' and was the first editor of the *USAC Bulletin*."[40]

Knight, who served two terms as ASNE president, left Cornell to join the army in World War I. His typing ability won him a job as company clerk, but he managed to transfer from the infantry to motor training. After serving on the Western Front, he returned home as a lieutenant with an estimated $6,000 won playing craps.[41] Like his publisher-father, who had opposed American entrance into World War I, Knight was an outspoken critic of Roosevelt's determination to get the United States involved in World War II. On June 1, 1941, after Roosevelt told the nation that the United States was involved in an undeclared war against Germany and her allies, Knight reluctantly switched from critic to supporter. Biographer Nixon Smiley says it was "one of the most significant decisions Jack Knight would make in his lifetime—and one of the most difficult."

In an editorial for his Miami newspaper, Knight wrote, "The *Herald* has opposed every step leading to involvement in the war which was not of our making but NOW the die is cast. We are in this war quite as though our Congress had made a formal declaration of hostilities. There is no turning back."[42] True to his word, Knight jumped into the war effort with both feet, working through the London blitz as chief U.S. censorship liaison officer. He covered the war's final phase in the Pacific for his expanding group of newspapers.[43]

Lt. Col. Walter M. Harrison was among the first of the 18 ASNE presidents to volunteer in World War II, enlisting in the Army in 1940 with Oklahoma's 45th Division. "While I may wear the uniform of the Army of the United States for a brief period of time," Harrison said, "I could never be anything but a newspaperman. I yield to no man in my conception of freedom of the press. I will expend my service here attempting to be of service to the newspapers of the United States."[44]

In remarks in the *Bulletin*, Harrison noted that he had been unable to enlist in World War I because he had a young family, but because of his desire to participate, World War II would be a "swell break." The son of an English horse breeder, Harrison also claimed to be a "raving Anglophile": "I have been for an alliance between Britain and the United States, lo, these many years. Sometimes I think I have made a local nuisance of myself . . . . In recent years I have seen the light going out in Europe, and the awful complacency of my friends and neighbors as Britain, alone, fights our battles, has shaken my belief in the power of the printed word."[45]

In addition to Harrison, another ASNE president served in the Army during World War II: Newbold Noyes of the Washington *Star*. Although he was ruled fit for only limited military service, Norman Isaacs says that Noyes reacted in the "No Sir, by God!" pattern, refusing not to serve.[46] Like Walters, Noyes joined up as a volunteer driver with the American Field Service and served in the Middle East and Italy. After a year's duty, Noyes wrote to editor Ben McKelway requesting a chance at war correspondence.

Among the ASNE future presidents serving in the Army were Eugene Patterson, Creed Black, William Hornby, Richard Smyser, Robert Clark and Ed Cony. Patterson served as a tank commander and then as a tank platoon leader in General George Patton's charge across Europe—he won a Silver Star and a Bronze Star with Oak Leaf cluster before transferring into the Air Corps to become a pilot. Black also earned a Bronze Star for heroism as an infantry-man with the 100th Division in Germany. Hornby served in the U.S. Army Signal Corps, where he learned Chinese. Smyser served in the Army from 1943 to 1945, studying languages (Dutch and Malay) under the specialized training program at Stanford University. He was then assigned to the Office of Strategic Services communications division in Washington, D.C., Algeria and Italy.[47] Clark was an Army captain in the southwest Pacific, while Cony served in the Army in France, Luxembourg and Germany from 1943 to 1946.

Other presidents-to-be served in the U.S. Navy: Kenneth MacDonald, Jenkin Lloyd Jones, Michael Ogden, Russell Wiggins, Thomas Winship and Vermont Royster. Ogden was in the Army Air Corps from 1942 to 1946 and Wiggins was in the Air Combat Intelligence. James S. Pope says the exact nature of Wiggins' exploits is still classified.[48] Winship served in the U.S. Coast Guard. After being activated from the Naval Reserve, MacDonald was an air combat intelligence officer from 1943 to 1946. Jones became a lieutenant commander from 1944 to 1946 after leaving the Naval Reserve. Royster served as an ensign.

Among the correspondents who became ASNE presidents were C. A. (Pete) McKnight, Lee Hills, J. Edward Murray, Warren Phillips, George Chaplin, Michael O'Neill and Wright Bryan. McKnight was twice rejected for military service because he was missing an eye. In December 1942, he became managing editor of the *World Journal*, an English language daily in San Juan, Puerto Rico. There he also became an accredited war correspondent for the Associated Press.

Hills and Murray, both of whom ended up working for the Knight newspaper group, served as European war correspondents; Murray worked in the London, Paris and Rome bureaus for United Press. Phillips and Chaplin worked for *Stars and Stripes*. O' Neill was a war correspondent for the 91st Division of the Fifth Army in Italy under General Mark W. Clark; he wrote hometown news-paper releases.[49] Wright Bryan left his job as editor of the Atlanta *Journal* only to be captured and interned as a prisoner of war. He reported later that while in prisoner of war camps and in American hospitals, he observed a grave danger of schism among the servicemen, the remainder of the population[50] and prisoners of war in Germany.

Other ASNE members played important roles during the war. Donald J. Sterling of the Oregon *Journal* served as consultant on the printing and publish-ing industries to Chairman Donald M. Nelson of the War Production Board.

Sterling's assignment to encourage publishers to decrease newsprint use was made easier by the cooperation of editors and publishers across the country. "If publishers will observe the spirit and letter of the limitation order, there will be no further curtailment of the use of newsprint," Sterling said after leaving his post in June 1943. "If they do not, an amended order may be necessary."[51]

Also serving the government were Gardner Cowles of the Des Moines *Register and Tribune* and Palmer Hoyt of the Portland *Oregonian*, who succeeded Cowles as domestic director of the OWI.[52] According to Bill Hosokawa, Hoyt proved his ability as an administrator by eliminating duplication, ending pamphleteering, reducing the number of regional offices and giving news directly to the media for distribution rather than trying to do tunnel news through OWI itself.[53] Before the United States entered the conflict, Hoyt had gained attention by telling readers how to read war news and detect the propaganda in it. "Take it with the same grain of salt ordinarily applied to statements made by football coaches on the eve of games," he advised. "Take the source of the article into consideration and make allowances for it." He added: "The general theories have been that America's confidence in its plan is well founded and that the press is fully aware of the dangers of wartime propaganda. However, I have discounted the value of front page warnings against war stories as I believe people of the United States are competent to make their own judgments."[54]

Such judgments, Hoyt argued, were better than those in World War I. National awareness of propaganda methods had been a factor in the United States' determination to keep out of the early European conflict, he said. But events in early 1940, which in 1920 would have whipped Americans into war fervor, were not considered an excuse for war because the public was better informed.[55]

THE CHALLENGE OF VOLUNTARY CENSORSHIP

George William Healy, Jr., served as director of the domestic branch of the U.S. Office of War Information. Before taking over the position, Healy described himself as a "missionary" for the Office of Censorship. He recalled that when code provisions were explained, no editor with whom he was acquainted questioned a single clause: "So widespread and wholehearted were acceptance and compliance that tens of thousands of mail censors who read publications leaving the country found few instances of code violations."[56]

In his autobiography, Healy says that no intentional violations were discovered in his territory in the deep south. Most provisions of the code were clear. As an example, Healy said it would be hard to find anyone who would question reports of ship movements in wartime. "Security involved in other types of publications was less obvious, and it was the responsibility of the Office of Censorship missionaries to explain it."[57]

As assistant to Byron Price, director of the U.S. Office of Censorship, Nathaniel R. Howard of the Cleveland *News* helped persuade the government and newspapers to accept voluntary censorship. Howard's assistant was another ASNE member, John H. Sorrells of the Scripps-Howard newspapers.[58] When Howard resigned in order to edit the *News*, Price said he had obtained the cooperation and concurrence of both American editors and publishers on one hand, and of the armed forces on the other. "I doubt whether very many on either side realize what a difficult accomplishment that was or how much we owe Nat Howard," Price said.

A former Associated Press executive who served in France in World War I, Price spoke at the 1942 ASNE meeting. Price described censorship as "a necessary evil" in wartime and gave the editors three factors to consider:

- The first of these is that you will never like censorship;

- Second, voluntary censorship will never be an exact science;

- Third, some censorship will seem nonsensical to the individual, particularly if he is among the censored.

"It is human nature to agree to a restriction in the abstract, but to become resentful when it strikes home," he added. "Censorship is therefore highly vulnerable; it is often unable to defend itself without disclosing the very information it is trying to withhold. In short, censorship is God's gift to the dyspeptic editor and the lackadaisical columnist. Whenever all other inspiration fails, it takes no effort to attack censorship."

Price briefed ASNE editors on the Code of Wartime Practices and suggested that they ask themselves whether the enemy would benefit from what they printed. Any editor who desired to do so could outwit the censor, he said, because there were many ways to evade the spirit of the code while living the letter of the law: "This is not, however, a contest between the government and the editor; it is a contest where the government and the editor are on the same team. The results are what count; and in the results, each of you has as large a stake as any of your fellow citizens who happen to be serving in official capacities."[59]

Colonel Ernest Dupuy, the second in command in the department of public relations, referred specifically to an unnamed reporter who had "irresponsibly published" a fanciful story on a mighty armada of American ships traversing the South Pacific.[60] "History is full of instances of battles lost, campaigns wrecked, nations shattered, because of the disclosure of information by the press," Dupuy charged. "I have given you but a fragmentary sketch." ASNE *Proceedings* and minutes do not indicate what incident the military leaders were referring to.

Within weeks of Dupuy's charges, McCormick's Chicago *Tribune* broke the story of the Midway battle, indicating indirectly that military intelligence had deciphered the Japanese code. A federal grand jury refused to indict the *Tribune* on charges of violating the Espionage Act.[61]

Military censors had little reason to fear such disclosures by most ASNE members or other journalists. As noted in his remarks in New York City in April 1942, shortly after the attack on Pearl Harbor, ASNE President Marvin had met with military officials and those from the ANPA to help establish a system of censorship. The result, according to Marvin, "was a plan for military censorship in the field and voluntary censorship at home which is now virtually in operation—a plan which with your help, may prove a reasonably workable solution of our problem."

At a meeting at the University Club in Chicago on October 25, 1942, newly elected ASNE President W. S. Gilmore of the Detroit *News* introduced a motion, later seconded by William Allen White, for the appointment of a special committee. This five member committee, to be known as the Committee on Government of the Press, was to act on behalf of the board on any exigencies of the war emergency. Members included Gilmore, Wilbur Forrest, Roy Roberts, Dwight Marvin and Erwin Canham.[62] At its February 1943 session before the annual meeting, the board voted to retain the committee. Its assignment was to act on any problem the president submitted and to advise him on the propriety of any government request for ASNE cooperation. The president was authorized to notify all government agencies that the society had appointed a committee which they could consult.[63] Two other committees were created to deal with war matters—one to open news channels to American press services so that they would be on equal terms with other nations, and the other a special Washington panel to expedite affairs when prompt cooperation between the administration and newspapers was necessary.

As president, Marvin had urged the growing ASNE membership to support him in efforts to establish closer ties with the ANPA. "I want to cement, if possible, with the publishers' associations of the country, particularly with the ANPA, a relationship of cooperative equality and comradeship," he said. However, Gilmore was less enthused about embracing the publishers. After 21 years, he said, it was time for ASNE to have a permanent executive officer. This official could be a spokesman throughout the year. That way ASNE instead of ANPA would be considered the voice of the principal newspapers. Marvin stated:

We who are primarily concerned with reporting the news and commenting editorially thereon; and with the ethics of our business (or profession, if you prefer) are the ones who should be carrying the flag for a free and untrammelled press. We are the society to which the government should have appealed when it wanted the newspapers to clean up the scrap. We are the organization that should take the lead in every movement involving the press as a medium of information.[64]

Not until the administration of Roberts, a Republican,[65] however, did ASNE decide to challenge the Roosevelt administration for misusing censorship. The issue reached a climax when Roosevelt excluded reporters from the May 8, 1943, United Nations food problems meeting in Hot Springs, Virginia. The directors passed a resolution chastising Roosevelt for denying reasonable access to original sources of information; they warned that he was establishing a policy which, if continued, would stifle the right of free inquiry and prevent a coninuous flow of complete information to the public. They charged that "the government should not use voluntary censorship to serve its convenience and interest."[66]

This bold ASNE action was greeted with enthusiasm by editors across the country and quoted in *Editor & Publisher*. In particular, E. Robert Stevenson of the Waterbury (Conn.) *Republican American* warned: "As follows night the day, inevitably a government that uses necessary war restrictions on military news next tries further press controls to suit its convenience. The food conference is only one. The peace conference will be next. Failure in what it would achieve in food and peace problems shadows the future."[67]

This criticism of government was followed the next month by Ackerman's challenge to Roberts and other ASNE members who were serving on government boards. But the questions and debate did not continue to any great extent. ASNE members such as Nelson Poynter, editor of the St. Petersburg *Times*, applauded Roberts' participation on the advisory council: "For two and a half years I have done what I could to contribute toward keeping communications free—even during war they are either free or not free—we can't be 'a little bit pregnant.' No other country is so fully committed to a policy of free communications. Keep on pitching."[68]

Others, including A. M. Piper of the Council Bluffs (Iowa) *Nonpareil*, however, agreed with Ackerman; Piper said that he was disturbed to note that Roberts had accepted the advisory post: "Whether it wants to or not, said advisory council will inevitably support the OWI, which has pretty much lost the confidence of American editors, because it has been a propaganda agency for the administration. If Mr. Roberts desires to promote the freedom of the press the first thing he should do is to resign from the OWI advisory committee."[69]

Ironically, the government agency which was described by some editors as a propaganda agency was not only advised by ASNE members; it was also providing editors around the country with information that truly depicted the brutality of war. This is evident in the "horror pictures" that the OWI provided editors. Unlike the World War I Committee of Public Information under George Creel, who controlled both censorship and propaganda, the OWI had been started on June 13, 1942, by President Roosevelt, to consolidate the activities of several highly criticized publicity agencies. Former foreign correspondent, broadcaster and New York *Times* reporter Elmer Davis headed the new agency. Palmer Hoyt of the Portland *Oregonian* joined Davis for a short time.

Hoyt found himself in the unusual position of defending the policy of sending graphic war pictures to editors for them to select for use according to community standards. The agency's obligation was to submit all news and pictures, no matter how unpleasant. Hoyt reminded editors that in World War I no pitures of American dead had been permitted: "Fifteen years after that fateful November 11, 1918, the country was flooded with war pictures that had been turned from war to horror pictures because they were no longer news . . . . The result was that pictures that might have put the war into perspective while it was being fought were used to throw it out of perspective when the war was finished."[70]

Letters to the *ASNE Bulletin* and to trade publications such as *Editor & Publisher* argued that such pictures were more shocking than effective. "We think that the OWI did wrong in releasing that type of picture," Milton Tabor of the Topeka *Daily Capital* wrote. "They do not inspire patriotic Americans to harder work. Indeed, fathers and mothers in war production plants may be seriously hampered by seeing pictures of soldiers lying dead—their imaginations may well picture their own sons in the same plight."

Many editors chose to run more acceptable pictures and stories of victory to accompany the propaganda movies and radio of the period. An illustration of the two different approaches can be seen in the photographs of Dorothea Lange and Ansel Adams, both of whom photographed California's Manzanar Relocation Center, one of ten camps in which the government placed a total of 110,000 West Coast Japanese-Americans. A study by Karin Becker Ohrn shows how the photographs produced two distinct points of view. The Adams pictures focused on the small businesses that grew up in the camp, with smiling people and serene landscapes. In contrast, Lange showed oppressive conditions and attempted to depict the internment as an injustice.[71]

Few editors noted the serious violations against the Japanese-Americans and other minorities, including blacks. According to a content analysis conducted by Vincent F. Arraya, a great deal of significant information that might have created favorable attitudes toward the Japanese-Americans was omitted from newspapers. Of the papers examined, Arraya says that only one interpretive writer, former ASNE President Paul Bellamy of the Cleveland *Plain Dealer*, challenged the military when Japanese-Americans were being evacuated, protesting the evacuation and internment. Only one writer, of the Idaho *Daily Statesman*, expressed a belief in the loyalty and morality of Japanese-Americans. In addition to the Cleveland and Idaho papers, the other publications sampled were the Los Angeles *Examiner*, Sioux Falls (S.D.) *Argus-Leader*, Fargo (N.D.) *Forum*, Salt Lake City *Tribune*, Oklahoma City *Daily Oklahoman*, Ft. Worth *Star-Telegram*, Atlanta *Journal*, Chicago *Tribune*, New York *Journal-American*, New York *Times* and the *Christian Science Monitor*.[72]

The ASNE interest in the issue is revealed to some extent in the remarks of Frank Jenkins (editor of the Klamath Falls [Ore.] *Herald and News*) in an *ASNE Bulletin*. The article supported the Army's takeover of a War Relocation Authorities camp at Tule Lake, California: "The Pacific Coast is glad to see the Army in charge at Tule Lake. It had come to have little faith in the ability of the WRA, with its social-worker complexes, to handle the situation presented by a community of 16,000 Japs, all loyal to Japan by their own signed statements."[73]

Similar to neglecting the civil rights of Japanese-Americans was the lack of concern by the mainstream press and ASNE indifference concerning suppression of the black media by government officials. In a book based on thousands of documents obtained through the Freedom of Information Act, Patrick Washburn describes the efforts of Roosevelt and J. Edgar Hoover to silence the black press. He reports that charges against the Japanese-Americans were made by Walter Lippmann, Westbrook Pegler and the Hearst press.[74]

A handful of ASNE members urged their colleagues to be more forthright, bold and imaginative as well as objective and fair in handling news of black Americans. Virginius Dabney, editor of the Richmond *Times-Dispatch*, wrote in the *ASNE Bulletin* that remedies that smoothed over points of friction could be found in the use of courtesy titles and capitalization of the word *Negro*. The author of *Below the Potomac: A Book about the New South*, Dabney said that ASNE editors could also play up the worthwhile achievements of Negro citizens rather than their derelictions. He urged editors to highlight the noteworthy feats of such black fighting men as Dorie Miller, the cook's helper who grabbed a machine gun at Pearl Harbor and won the Navy Cross for heroism: "The role of Negro men and women in the war effort is described regularly by such Southern papers as the Mobile (Ala.) *Register* and the Shelby (N.C.) *Star*. It gives Negro readers the feeling that their work in defense of democracy is appreciated."[75]

As might be expected, the voluntary censorship that dominated the thinking of editors at home was also prevalent on the battlefield, where some reporting was described as more sports reporting than foreign correspondence. One reporter described his colleagues as "cheerleaders": "I suppose there wasn't an alternative at the time. It was total war. But for God's sake, let's not glorify our role. It wasn't good journalism. It wasn't journalism at all!"[76]

Such reporting was challenged by at least one military officer in 1945, when the war was almost over. In the *Bulletin*, Lt. Col. Joseph C. Stehlin said he was increasingly dismayed by the way the nation's newspapers reported war news.

The war out here is treated as some sort of a football game or other circus sideshow. Victories are played up and difficulties played down to such an extent by most newspapers that the folks at home would suppose it is all very simple and easy. I cannot feel that this is the right propaganda for the homefront. If the ruthless maniacal fanaticism, the inhuman beastly torture and atrocities perpetrated on our lads by the Japs would be forcefully brought to the attention of the American people, they would rise as one—

increasing war production, stimulating enlistments, buying more war bonds, making sac-
rifices cheerfully, complain less, with fewer cocktail parties, as their answer to these
cowardly slant-eyed beasts: a people inculcated from birth with a barbaric determination
to destroy the American individuality as a nation.[77]

Reporting by the press about the government's plan to develop the atomic
bomb was more open than generally believed. According to Washburn, the
myth promulgated by William L. Laurence of the New York *Times* and others
that the creation of a superbomb was kept secret is simply not true. In fact, as
hundreds of documents in the National Archives indicate, the press referred to
the bomb numerous times during World War II. Even more important was the
way it was mentioned. As Washburn's study shows, the press revealed virtually
no technical details of the bomb, and few stories connected its development
within the three principal project sites in Tennessee, Washington and New
Mexico: "What was run on almost every occasion was simply that the United
States or Germany or both, were working on the bomb. That, of course, was no
secret, as the journalists quickly pointed out a number of times, occasionally
with flashes of anger, when criticized for mentioning the bomb."[78]

Washburn gives two reasons for keeping the story of the atomic bomb
"reasonably quiet." He refers to the threat posed by the Espionage Act, which
gave the Justice Department power to prosecute journalists who reported information that hurt the war effort. But an even greater reason for cooperation was
the editors' patriotism and overwhelming support for winning the war.

In an appeal that went beyond these basics, Roberts used a phrase that would
be borrowed later by the Hutchins Commission. In his 1944 ASNE presidential
speech, Roberts said that the word *responsibility* was connected with practically
every topic in the program. It was not just a happenstance, but the direct out-
growth of sessions of the directors:

In the hours of discussion of the problems confronting American newspapers the directors
were of the same mind as your president, that we have been talking entirely too much
about freedom of the press, without the public understanding what we meant, and we
have dwelt entirely too little upon the responsibilities of the free press. It is my firm
belief we will keep a free press as long as we deserve it—no longer. Hence our general
theme of this morning: "Responsible Journalism."[79]

FOCUS ON THE INTERNATIONAL SCENE

Notwithstanding Ackerman's comments about the contradiction of editors
supporting worldwide freedom of the press while associating with government
groups that might oppose freedom of international communications, the ASNE
turned its focus from problems in the United States to the international scene. In

1944, as the war moved slowly toward a conclusion, Roberts and the other directors held a special meeting in Washington. According to Dwight Young, "two major decisions, closely related, were made by the board in this historic two-day meeting."[80]

The first was a resolution calling for the postwar removal of all political, economic and military barriers to freedom of world information after the war. Such freedom everywhere, the resolution declared, was vital to world peace. The board invited reciprocal statements by the governments, press, radio and other media of the United States and other countries which embraced the right of the people to read and hear news without hindrance.[81]

The second resolution, in Young's account, "implemented the first resolution." It authorized ASNE President Knight (1944–1946) to appoint a committee of society members to visit various world capitals. The group's mission was to discuss the society's aims with governmental bodies, press associations and newspaper and radio executives and to learn their views on postwar freedom of information.[82] In its historic switch of focus from the United States to the world, the board pledged that ASNE would not relax its campaign for removal of all barriers to the free interchange of news "until freedom of information becomes a living reality everywhere in the world." The two resolutions, offered by David Lawrence and seconded by Dwight Marvin, were unanimously adopted.

Knight quickly named Wilbur Forrest, the first ASNE vice president, to lead the committee, with Ralph McGill, editor of the Atlanta *Journal* and chair of the society's Committee of World Freedom of Information, and Ackerman as members. Seven members of McGill's group also talked with the board in its initial meeting: Nelson Poynter, Sevellon Brown, Ralph Coglan, Lawrence L. Winship, Raymond McCaw, John Sorrells and Ackerman.

The board also approved Knight's protest against the temporary suspension of Associated Press filing facilities in the European theater of operations, which followed publication of premature and unauthorized dispatches of correspondent Edward Kennedy which announced the German surrender.[83] Articles in the *Bulletin* also showed more courage. In August 1945, W. G. Vorpe of the Cleveland *Plain Dealer* urged a general ban on off-the-record statements after the Kennedy incident. "It is a problem that is just as worthy of consideration to most editors and newspaper publishers as the other very important subjects of a free press for the world and the doing away with political censorship in the conquered countries of Europe."

Other brave talk about standing up to the government and its censorship followed in the *Bulletin*, the ASNE minutes and *Proceedings*, although in 1945 the annual session of the society was postponed for the first time. This newly discovered tough talk continued throughout the postwar years until the outbreak of the Korean War. The correspondents in the field had a brief period without censorship. It was a voluntary code of war reporting aimed at preserving military secrecy. But this openness was gone within a month. According to Phillip

Knightley, the Army extended the voluntary code to rule out any criticism of decisions made by the United Nations commander in the field or conduct by Allied soldiers. But this was not enough. Correspondents soon implored military authorities to introduce full, official and compulsory censorship.[84]

Such surprising action was followed by appointment of a Wartime Censorship Study Committee. It recommended that both editors and broadcasters in future wars follow the same principles that governed World War II censorship:

1. Censorship should be operated by an independent agency which is directly responsible to the president of the United States.

2. This committee should be headed by a civilian who has experience in the communications media.

3. Censorship should be voluntary.

The seven-man committee was headed by former government censor Jack H. Lockart and included Nathaniel Howard, Virginius Dabney, Jenkin Lloyd Jones, Edward R. Lindsey, James R. Wiggins and Walter Lippmann. This group asked for assistance from the 1951 program committee "to obtain a responsible civilian government speaker on the subject 'Plans for Censorship of News in the Next War' or something similar." Such support for the World War II censorship model did little to provide the American public with a realistic picture of America's "Forgotten War" in Korea and its accompanying problems, ranging from corruption to low morale. Knightley notes, "This willingness on the part of correspondents to write what they believed their editors and readers would find acceptable about the POW issue instead of the harsh but vital truth helped delay for years a proper examination of the reasons for collapse of morale unprecedented in American military history."[85]

Although Washburn believes World War II was significant because it was "the last war of the 20th century for which censorship would be generally accepted so cavalierly by U.S. journalists," the same was not necessarily true of the editors. The social responsibility model that replaced the libertarian approach and the important role of providing nondoctored information and even criticism in World War II was to continue for the ASNE throughout the Korean War and the Cold War until the Vietnam conflict brought challenges from a new breed of reporters and editors.

NOTES

1. "Roy Roberts refuses to resign from OWI group," *Editor & Publisher*, July 17, 1943, 12.

2. In addition to Roberts, the six other ASNE members on the OWI advisory board headed by Palmer Hoyt, domestic director of OWI and publisher of the Portland *Oregonian*, were Lawrence L. Winship, Boston *Globe*; George W. Healy, Jr., New Orleans *Times-Picayune*; Paul Bellamy, Cleveland *Plain Dealer*; Gardner Cowles, Jr., Des Moines *Register & Tribune*, and Wilbur Forrest, New York *Herald-Tribune*.

3. Complete texts of both Ackerman's protest and Roberts' defense can be seen in the *ASNE Bulletin*, #240, August 1, 1943, 5–6.

4. Ibid.

5. Ibid.

6. For example, see O. K. Armstrong, "Kansas City's Boss-Busting Editor," *Progressive*, January 27, 1947; and "K.C.'s *Star*," *Time*, April 12, 1948.

7 *ASNE Bulletin*, #240, August 1, 1943, 6.

8. ASNE *Proceedings*, 1944, 14.

9. See the author's account of "The Honolulu *Star-Bulletin* and the 'Day of Infamy,'" in *American Journalism*, Vol. 5, No. I (1988): 5–13.

10. Gideon Seymour, "Reflections on Atrocities," *ASNE Bulletin*, #264, July 1945, 1–2.

11. ASNE *Proceedings*, 1947, 209.

12. "President Marvin urges editors to be 'balladists' for democracy," *ASNE Bulletin*, #212, June 1, 1941, 1. Robert L. Bishop and S. LaMar McKay also evoke a musical chord in their accounts of military censorship in World War II in "Mysterious Silence, Lyrical Scream: Government Information in World War II," *Journalism Monographs*, #19, May 1971.

13. Patrick Washburn, *A Question of Sedition: The Federal Government's Investigation of the Black Press during World War II*, New York: Oxford University Press, 1986, 33.

14. *ASNE Bulletin*, #203, September 1, 1940, 1.

15. Deborah E. Lipstadt, "Pious Sympathies and Sincere Regrets: The American News Media and the Holocaust from Krystalnacht to Bermuda, 1938–1943," *Modern Judaism* 2 (1982): 53–72.

16. Peter Irons, *Justice at War: The Story of the Japanese Internment Cases,* New York: Oxford University Press, 1983.

17. Washburn, *A Question of Sedition.*

18. See James D. Startt, "The Media and National Crisis" in *The Media in America: A History*, Worthington, Ohio: Publishing Horizons, 1989, 305.

19. ASNE *Proceedings*, 1940, 112. See also *Grosjean* v. *American Press* Co., 297 U.S. 233 (1936).

20. Oswald Garrison Villard, *The Disappearing Daily*, New York: Alfred A. Knopf, 1944, 44–45. Villard was one of the 25 or 30 authors described "as those who in recent years have elected to needle the press," by Wilbur Forrest in an assessment of critics including the Hutchins Commission at the annual meeting in 1947, 22–23. Also criticized by Forrest was Morris L. Ernst, author of *The First Freedom*.

21. ASNE *Proceedings*, 1941, 135.

22. Ibid., 137.

23. "'Who'll Ante Up?' asks Wright Bryan," *ASNE Bulletin*, #215, September 1, 1941, 3.

24. "News Integrity—and the Defense Effort," *ASNE Bulletin*, #215, September 1, 1941, 2.

25. "How free is our press?" *ASNE Bulletin*, #259, February 1, 1945, 2–3.

26. Ibid.

27. "Off-record sessions often illusory, says chairman," *ASNE Bulletin*, July 1, 1941, 1.

28. *ASNE Bulletin*, October 1, 1943, 3.

29. In addition to "sons" in the service, at least one *Bulletin* article refers to a daughter. Commander James G. Stahlman, president of the Nashville *Banner* and an ASNE member, swore in his daughter an apprentice seaman in the Women's Reserve of the Navy. *ASNE Bulletin*, #237, May 1, 1943, 4.

30. "Still more sons of ASNE members reported in service," *ASNE Bulletin*, November 1, 1943, 3.

31. "Robert Blood loses two sons in war," *ASNE Bulletin*, #250, May 1, 1944, 12.

32. "John Knight's Son Killed in Action," *ASNE Bulletin*, date unknown. Knight's poignant thoughts are reminiscent of the comments of William Allen White, another ASNE president, who wrote an editorial about his 17-year-old daughter, Mary, after her death in a horseback-riding accident in 1921.

33. "Hoyt succeeds Cowles in OWI; Harwell in Army," *ASNE Bulletin*, #238, June 1, 1943, 1.

34. Complete discussions of the special exemptions for ASNE members in the armed services can be seen in ASNE minutes, October 19, 1941, 180; April 15, 1942, 185, and October 25, 1943, 191.

35. Among those referred to in the *Bulletin* or ASNE minutes were Lieutenant Barry Bingham, Louisville *Courier-Journal*; Lieutenant Commander William J. Connors, Buffalo *Courier Express*; Gardner Cowles, Des Moines *Register and Tribune*; Jonathan Daniels, Raleigh *News and Observer*; Lieutenant Colonel Walter M. Harrison, *Daily Oklahoman and Times*; Ovetta Culp Hobby, Houston *Post*; Nathaniel Howard, Cleveland *News*; Major Irving Hart, Boise *Statesman*; Palmer Hoyt, Portland *Oregonian*; Coleman Harwell, Nashville *Tennessean*; Frank Knox, Chicago *Daily News*; Major J. Noel Macy, Westchester; Talbot Patrick, Goldsboro *News-Argus*; Nelson Poynter, St. Petersburg *Times*; Lieutenant George R. Shoals, Rochester *Democrat and Chronicle*; Lieutenant Commander Paul Smith, San Francisco *Chronicle*; Major Rex Smith, Chicago *Sun*; John Sorrells, Memphis *Commercial Appeal*; Commander James G. Stahlman, Nashville *Banner*; Captain J. R. Wiggins, St. Paul *Dispatch and Pioneer Press*.

36. "In Memoriam: Colonel Frank Knox," *ASNE Bulletin*, May, 1944. See also Norman Beasley, *Frank Knox: American*, Garden City, N.Y.: Doubleday, Doran & Co., 1936.

37. See *Tar Heel Editor,* Chapel Hill: University of North Carolina, 1939, and *The Wilson Era: Years of War and After*, Chapel Hill: University of North Carolina Press, 1946.

38. Richard Kluger, *The Paper: The Life and Death of the New York* Herald Tribune, New York: Alfred A. Knopf, 1986, 282.

39. Ibid.

40. Raymond Moscowitz, *"Stuffy": The Life of Newspaper Pioneer Basil "Stuffy" Walters*, Ames: Iowa State University Press, 1983, 23.

41. Charles Whited, *Knight: A Publisher in the Tumultuous Century,* New York: E. P. Dutton, 1988, 16–17. See also Nixon Smiley, *Knights of the Fourth Estate: The Story of the Miami* Herald, Miami: Seemann Publishing, 1974.

42. Smiley, 179.

43. Loren Ghiglione, ed., *Gentlemen of the Press,* Indianapolis: R. J. Berg & Co., 1984, 206.

44. ASNE *Proceedings,* 1941, 141.

45. Lt. Col. Walter M. Harrison, "Service to Country No Sacrifice, but a 'Swell Break' to Harrison," *ASNE Bulletin,* October 1, 1940, 2.

46. Norman Isaacs, "Newbold Noyes, Editor," in *Gentlemen of the Press,* 301.

47. Letter to the author, June 4, 1990.

48. James S. Pope, in *Gentlemen of the Press,* 413.

49. Telephone interview, July 1990.

50. "Bryan urges tolerance to fuse ex-servicemen and civilian population," *ASNE Bulletin,* date unknown.

51. "Supply, Not Wishful Thinking, Governs Newsprint—D. J. Sterling," *ASNE Bulletin,* #238, June 1, 1943, 1.

52. "Hoyt Succeeds Cowles in OWI; Harwell in Army," *ASNE Bulletin,* #238, June 1, 1943, 1.

53. Bill Hosokawa, *Thunder in the Rockies: The Incredible Denver* Post, New York: William Morrow & Co., 1976, 225.

54. "War Propaganda Like Football Predictions, Hoyt Tells Audiences," *ASNE Bulletin,* July 1, 1940, 4.

55. Ibid.

56. George Healy, *A Lifetime on Deadline: Self-Portrait of a Southern Journalist,* Gretna, La.: Pelican Publishing Co., 1976, 105.

57. Ibid.

58. "Howard Appointed to Office of Censor," *ASNE Bulletin,* February 1, 1942, 1.

59. ASNE *Proceedings,* 1942, 28.

60. Ibid., 38.

61. For a discussion of the Midway story see Lloyd Wendt, *Chicago* Tribune: *The Rise of a Great American Newspaper,* Chicago: Rand McNally, 1979, 627–636; Jim Martin, "Did the *Tribune* Spill the (Navy) Beans?" American Journalism Historians' Association, Atlanta, October 7, 1989.

62. ASNE minutes, October 5, 1942, 193.

63. ASNE minutes, February 11, 1943, 199.

64. ASNE *Proceedings,* 1943, 15.

65. Although his friendships knew no label, Roberts' political objectivity was questioned at times because of his role as a Republican insider who helped Dwight Eisenhower become President and three others (Alf Landon, Wendell L. Willkie and Thomas Dewey) become presidential candidates. William Allen White, another ASNE president who also served in the Landon campaign against Roosevelt, described Roberts as "the core of the [Landon] organization" (Associated Press Biographical Sketch, 4246, September 1, 1965).

66. ASNE minutes, April 18, 1943, 201.

67. *Editor & Publisher*, April 23, 1943, 20.

68. *ASNE Bulletin*, #240, August 1, 1943, 4.

69. Ibid.

70. "Ban Lifting on Horror Pictures of Our Men at War," *ASNE Bulletin*, June 1945, 6.

71. Karin Becker Ohrn, "What You See Is What You Get: Dorothea Lange and Ansel Adams at Manzanar," *Journalism History* (Spring 1977): 14–22, 32.

72. Vincent F. Arraya, "An Analysis of the Media Coverage of the Internment of the American Japanese during the Second World War," thesis presented to the Department of Communications, Brigham Young University, Provo, Utah, August 1991.

73. Frank Jenkins, "Tule Lake—Still a Problem: Member Who Broke Story Gives Background, Views on Future Handling of Jap Center," *ASNE Bulletin*, #246, January 1, 1944, 1.

74. Washburn, *A Question of Sedition*, 72.

75. Virginius Dabney, "The Press and the Interracial Crisis," *ASNE Bulletin*, #242, September 1, 1943, 1.

76. More, November, 1974, quoted in Phillip Knightley, *The First Casuality*, New York: Harcourt Brace Jovanovich, 1975, 333.

77. *ASNE Bulletin*, June 1, 1945, 8.

78. Patrick S. Washburn, "The Office of Censorship's Attempt to Control Press Coverage of the Atomic Bomb during World War II," *Journalism Monographs*, April 1990, 33.

79. ASNE *Proceedings*, 1944, 14.

80. ASNE minutes, November 27–28, 1944, 220.

81. Ibid.

82. Ibid.

83. ASNE minutes, June 9–10, 1945, 230.

84. Knightley, 337.

85. Ibid., 353.

Chapter 4

Putting Mother Hubbards on
the Heathen

Universal press freedom is easier said than done. Our initial job is to cinch it in our own bailiwick before we go off on evangelical excursions and try to put Mother Hubbards on the heathen.

—Wilbur Forrest, New York *Herald-Tribune*, 1943

The American Society of Newspaper Editors has, I believe, attained an international stature. We have also gained the prestige of being asked to assist in the writing of the provisions of an instrument which may have significance in the postwar world.

—Wilbur Forrest, 1946

There is one fact which I am forced to admit and that is the failure of the World Tour of 1945 to sell freedom of the press. My opinion is that our tour only accomplished for foreign editors and some government officials an introduction to the American Society of Newspaper Editors and its zeal to promote press freedom . . . our report was merely a recitation of experiences which proved nothing except that freedom existed only by permission of a prevailing government.

—Wilbur Forrest, 1972

From the closing months of World War II to the beginning of the Korean War, ASNE reached beyond its own important but parochial interests to promote freedom of the press on a global level. Initiated by Roy A. Roberts and John S. Knight and pursued by other globally minded presidents including Wilbur Forrest and Erwin Canham, the new international focus demonstrated the growing maturity of ASNE and its desire to extend its influence. The five years between the end of World War II and the beginning of the Korean War also may be viewed as a time of once again delaying important accountability issues raised by the Hutchins Commission during the same postwar period. ASNE used its influence to help highlight the concept of freedom of information at home in the planks of both political parties and abroad through the insertion of rhetoric in the United Nations charter. But the quick trips and instant analysis of the world by some members using American models may have caused some minor mischief as well.

ASNE's growing international outlook was due in part to the global perspective and the distaste for authoritarianism acquired by society presidents, directors and members who had supervised censorship activities or been associated with federal propaganda groups. Knight's military service and his direction of U.S. censorship in London provided him with insights into other governments and supplied material for editorial page columns.[1] Similarly, Nathaniel R. Howard gained perspectives on freedom of information as assistant director of the Office of Censorship. Erwin Canham had covered the League of Nations and the London Naval Conference in the 1930s and became deputy chair of the U.S. delegation to the United Nations Conference on Freedom of Information in 1948. B. M. McKelway of the Washington *Star* had served in the U.S. Army in Europe in World War I. Early in 1948, he led an eight-member press censorship subcommittee which was created at the request of Secretary of Defense James V. Forrestal to work out a plan for "voluntary safeguarding of vital defense secrets."[2]

As a former foreign correspondent, Wilbur Forrest recalled that covering World War I was mostly "the glorified dissemination of government propaganda."[3] In a Round Table of the Air discussion in February 1946, he said: "There are certain barren areas without news coverage or sources and these should be covered by government news broadcasting . . . however, such news should not be re-processed by the government and it should be identified as agency material."[4]

But in a May 1946 appearance before the House Foreign Affairs Committee, Forrest reiterated his support for the State Department's international information program. Josephus Daniels, secretary of the Navy during Wilson's two terms and former ambassador to Mexico, questioned them during a debate at the 1946 ASNE annual meeting: "There never was an administration, there never will be an administration that will not think the policies they are carrying out are wise and they ought to disseminate them. If we make the mistake of going back upon a free press and free information without a government censor, some day will come that men will be in office who will send out news to suit the party or the policies they believe in."[5]

ASNE President Canham, whose *Christian Science Monitor* had long been identified with world information,[6] sought to lift restrictions on foreign news. Together Roberts, Knight, Forrest, Howard and Canham made 1944 to 1950 ASNE's golden age of globalism. In his report of the world trip and ASNE plans to assist U.N. committees to spread freedom worldwide, Forrest claimed: "The American Society of Newspaper Editors has, I believe, attained an international stature. We have also gained the prestige of being asked to assist in the writing of the provisions of an instrument which may have vast significance in this postwar world."[7]

ASNE had been involved in international efforts since the 1920s, when it granted $1,000 to the University of Peking in China,[8] and sent President Casper Yost to Geneva to represent the ASNE at the International Press Conference.[9] But the society had generated only limited interest in foreign affiliations, until near the end of World War II. After its initial support for the fledgling Inter-American Press Association (IAPA),[10] ASNE helped reorganize the group in 1950. ASNE also supported the International Press Institute and the International Federation of Newspaper Editors and Publishers.[11] Still another round-the-world ASNE delegation maintained that the Western model of the free press was essential to world peace. This group, which included Wilbur Forrest, Ralph McGill of the Atlanta *Constitution* and Dean Carl W. Ackerman of Columbia's Graduate School of Journalism, in 1945 completed what Alice Pitts described as more than a year of "ASNE restlessness about doing something global." Historian Leonard Teel says the committee's fundamental belief was

that freedom of the press and the free flow of news across borders should be advertised widely as a preventative against fascism, Nazism, and other strains of totalitarianism. In that scheme, an unrestricted and uncensored flow of news within nations and across national boundaries would serve to protect the vitality of dissent within nations and communications among nations. In so doing, world freedom of information ideally would foster democratic institutions and prevent the rise of dictators.[12]

Knight's remarks at the 1946 convention[13] typified the enthusiasm of ASNE leaders in this outreach era. Summarizing the 40,000-mile trip during which the ASNE Committee on World Freedom visited 22 cities in 11 major countries, Knight stated: "In my humble estimation, this was one of the finest achievements in the history of American journalism, and Messrs. Forrest, McGill, and Ackerman did more to advance the cause of freedom of information than a thousand newspaper editorials or speeches could have accomplished in the United States."[14]

Forrest gave an even more enthusiastic report:

Time will tell what this mission has accomplished. But even before the statesmen of the world sit down to negotiate the instruments of peace, it is patent that freedom of the press internationally is an important part of an enduring peace in the kind of world we live in; that there are editors all over the world who understand this and who will fight with words to accomplish it; that many statesmen from the heads of government down, who are already convinced of it and will lend their influence for it; that there are others who have given mere lip service and will seek to avoid it.[15]

"Perhaps the seeds sown by your committee will grow and flourish, some more rapidly than others," Forrest added. "But in the end the peoples of all nations will know each other better and the problems of nations may be more readily understood through a truer, freer flow of news." Forrest concluded by saying that the principle of free flow of news in the interest of postwar peace had not been rejected anywhere, even in the Soviet Union.[16]

Notwithstanding goodwill efforts funded by ASNE, Forrest, Ackerman and McGill did not agree on all the complex issues in their global survey. Dissent arose particularly between Ackerman and McGill. McGill's editorial efforts at the Atlanta *Constitution*, which helped defeat Georgia gubernatorial candidate Eugene Talmadge, had vaulted him into the national arena as a prominent liberal spokesman. The protection of human freedoms became a frequent topic in his columns and articles, which were published nationwide.[17] Teel says that because McGill was the most energetic member and the only practicing writer on the touring committee, he was the key figure in drafting the ASNE delegation's final report on world press freedom. Indeed, some sections of the report came directly from McGill's *Constitution* columns. Nathaniel Howard believes that although the reports did not say so, "their trip was hopeless." The futility became apparent after searching for persons to interview in Rome.[18]

McGill later claimed that his disagreements with Ackerman, who was also secretary to the Pulitzer Prize advisory board, prevented him from being awarded a prize until 1959. Intimately involved in the selection process, ASNE members had served as judges in all newspaper categories since 1925. In 1946, however, editors began to complain about being "used" to eliminate dozens of entries, only to have the advisory board overrule their decisions. In the *American Mercury*, Carroll Binder, ASNE member from the Minneapolis *Tribune*, charged the board with nepotism after seven of nine prizes went to organizations that were represented on the advisory board.[19] A number of lively debates followed in the pages of the *Bulletin*. Editors such as Tom Wallace of the Louisville *Times* called attention to the imperfections of the jury system, but the majority of ASNE members favored continued cooperation.[20] Melville Ferguson of the Philadelphia *Bulletin* urged ASNE to award its own prizes.[21]

In 1949 ASNE directors named a committee to consult with the Pulitzer board to develop a basis of "cooperation for the future."[22] A resolution which invited members to serve on Pulitzer screening committees but to make their recommendations public was presented to the Pulitzer board in October of 1949.[23] The recommendations failed to gain the Pulitzer board approval, and in 1950 ASNE directors voted to end its relationship with the Pulitzer advisory organization.[24] The issue of favoritism referred to by McGill and Binder did not end in the postwar period, however; it continued to be debated in the *Proceedings* and *Bulletin*.[25]

Teel suggests that McGill's friendship with two wartime allies, the Soviet Union and China, helped compromise his perspective. "The further east McGill journeyed, the more tangled he became in political conundrums. His fundamental error was in using western models to evaluate the dynamics of non-western systems." Teel concludes that McGill was too optimistic for insecure and unstable countries which were regrouping and trying to survive in the postwar world: "Within a few years, the Soviet Union would extinguish any semblance of a free press and democratic government in Eastern Europe. The coming of the Cold War led many nations to justify various means of control of the news media. The Soviets adopted some of the same controls of news dissemination that had been pioneered by the totalitarians."[26]

Margaret Blanchard says that years after the mission, Forrest recanted the committee's optimistic proclamations, calling its final report "merely a recitation of experiences which proved nothing except that freedom existed only by permission of a prevailing government."[27]

Speaking with 25 years' hindsight, Forrest conceded the committee's impotence. "There was one fact I am forced to admit and that is the failure of the World Tour of 1945 to sell freedom of the press. My opinion is that the tour only accomplished for foreign editors and some government officials an introduction to the American Society of Newspaper Editors and its zeal to promote press freedom."[28]

In time, Teel says, McGill realized the communists had deceived him. "He had embraced Mao's promises too naively, and taken the Russian enigma too lightly. In Moscow and Chungking, he had charged into the maze, a southern liberal in western ideals matching wits with the descendants of czars and khans."[29] By the end of the war, McGill and other ASNE members had become instant judges of Russian and Chinese character. "Such is the prerogative of the daily columnist, who can change his mind another day," Teel reminds us.

Canham also admitted the failure of efforts to promote freedom of information through the United Nations and UNESCO. Despite his own efforts and those of Richard J. Finnegan of the Chicago *Daily News*, Sevellon Brown of the Providence *Journal and Bulletin* and Oveta Culp Hobby of the Houston *Post*, Canham says that after 1948 there was little hope for improving freedom of information through diplomatic channels. ASNE-sponsored treaties were virtually worthless. "They lived in the half-world of the United Nations diplomatic bureaucracy for many years, but have never been of any effect good or bad in the cause of freedom of information," Canham said. "Thus the society's attention turned toward international cooperation between newspapermen themselves—an encouraging development."

Canham concluded that no lasting treaties, binding commitments or official guarantees evolved from the postwar period, despite the emergence of international organizations. "They [the treaties] are of some value in supporting aspirations to a free press, seeking sometimes to rescue an editor in distress, and whacking away at continuing barriers through private professional action."[30]

HUTCHINS REPORT STIRS DEBATE

In light of the ASNE commitment to what Margaret Blanchard describes as "exporting the First Amendment," the society's inaction on recommendations given by the Hutchins Commission puzzled a handful of editors, including Norman Isaacs and Herbert Brucker. The major problem referred to in the *Proceedings* and the ASNE minutes focused on the recommendations from the distinguished group headed by Robert M. Hutchins of the University of Chicago. Although nearly all the recommendations concerned general principles, at least two appeared to be directed at the newspaper publishers, who were fighting to survive in the postwar era, a period in which newspapers were threatened by television as well as radio. The committee referred to the growing concentration of ownership, saying that if the newspaper chains did not regulate themselves, they would have to be regulated.

One other recommendation called for self-regulation of the press; it was suggested that a new independent agency be formed to appraise performance. Worse, from a public relations point of view, the commission brought up the skeleton in ASNE's closet: its inability to penalize Fred Bonfils in the Teapot Dome scandal meaningfully.

Brucker, an educator who became editor of the Hartford *Courant*, says he never forgot ASNE's reaction to the report at the 1947 convention: "As a new member I sat on the back benches as my betters howled and growled at the commission and all its works."[31]

Forrest challenged the Hutchins Commission as part of his 1947 presidential address, charging that the "eleven-thirteenths percent pedagogic panel" had erred in its blanket indictment of the media. As the heart of his challenge, Forrest disputed two errors in the commissions's findings:

1. Instead of the ASNE doing nothing about the Bonfils scandal, ASNE had encouraged "Mr. Blank's" resignation from the society.

2. In 1932 the ASNE membership changed the constitution, empowering the board of directors to suspend or expel any society member for due cause; this gave the society full legal protection.

In a passionate defense of press freedom, Forrest also challenged "the more conservative critics of the press," those who charged undue advertiser influence.

He said, "The charge that the advertiser controls the policy of the newspaper or that anyone controls it in the long run except the daily reader is just so much outmoded claptrap."[32] What the critics and the Hutchins Commission overlooked, Forrest asserted, was that most editors were not newspaper owners: "These men are not, as the commission indicates, a type that join the country club and lose touch with the human side. Editors, I am sure most of us believe, are ever on the alert for the human side, and if they were not, they would not earn their editorial salaries or have a job."[33]

In contrast to Forrest's defensive remarks, a handful of ASNE members agreed in part with the criticisms of the commission. One of the best known, Josephus Daniels, supported Hutchins in an editorial entitled "Bias and the Press" (published in the Raleigh *News and Observer* two weeks before the 1947 convention): "The report truly points out that 'the bias of owners' who have large incomes, is responsible for the loss of the influence of the press . . . [and] endangers the position of the press as 'the tocsin of the people.'"[34]

Isaacs, who became ASNE president in 1969, wrote that the Hutchins recommendations caused problems because the commission had the temerity to challenge the most sacred cow in journalism's holy credo—its self-proclaimed right to reject any examination of its performance. With few exceptions, those in the press shuddered over the heresy.[35] Like the publishers, who opposed the commission's recommendations even more violently, the editors debated the report at length before coming up with an innocuous resolution.

"This society has long recognized the need for self-improvement of newspapers and believes our press is performing with increasing effectiveness and fairness the duty of keeping the American people the best informed people in the world," the amended resolution stated. The resolution then quoted another society patron saint, Thomas Jefferson:

These abuses of an institution so important to freedom and science are deeply to be regretted, inasmuch as they tend to lessen its usefulness and to sap its safety. . . . The public judgment will correct false reasonings and opinions in a full hearing of all parties, and no other definite line can be drawn between the inestimable liberty of the press and its demoralizing licentiousness. If there still be improprieties which this rule would not restrain, its supplement must be sought in the censorship of public opinion.[36]

Chair of the resolutions committee, Richard J. Finnegan noted that it was almost impossible to represent a consensus of 300 editors in one resolution. "We had a hard time coming up with this one, and I might say that no one on the committee was particularly proud of it."[37]

It was not until 1955—eight years later—that Robert M. Hutchins was invited to speak to the editors. It was the second and final time that the controversial University of Chicago president would speak to the ASNE. He publicly censored them more than any other critic. In 1930, Hutchins had accused the editors of being more interested in their own prosperity than in the educational needs of society. Newspapers, he said, ought to have "tremendous educational force." He also raised the question which appeared in the Hutchins report of whether or not foundations ought to endow some newspapers to give them greater social perspective.

In his 1955 address, Hutchins rebuked the editors for paying no attention to his 1930 recommendations. He also chastised ASNE members for their "neurotic sensitivity" to criticism, for being "furious" over the 1947 report and for being a one-party press. "Your own efforts to act as a critical agency have come to nothing," Hutchins charged. Condemning resolutions passed by ASNE to serve as a committee on self-examination as sounding as though they were written by a public relations man, he said, "In those sonorous sentences we hear the cadence of the psalms."[38]

The Hutchins Commission recommendations and a new foreign emphasis were not the only agenda subjects as ASNE membership neared 500 after World War II.[39] A. M. Piper, editor of the Council Bluffs (Iowa) *Nonpareil,* even suggested a membership limit of 500.[40] The education committee, dormant during the war years, discussed accreditation, licensing, internships[41] and debated a skills versus a liberal arts education. New York *Times* publisher Arthur Hays Sulzberger's comment that he was not in favor of chain ownership was challenged by John S. Knight as the type of generalization one might expect from critic Morris Ernst or any of the numerous other "self-appointed saviors of the press."[42] Knight also encouraged support for a 10-point ASNE program he had introduced in his first term in office.

1. Reread and practice the Code of Ethics.

2. Reestablish the three-day convention duration, so that one day, at least, could be devoted to discussion of editorial problems.

3. Give the editorial page a prominent place on the program.

4. Hold a roundtable discussion on the responsibility and integrity of syndicated columnists and on their influence, good and bad, on modern journalism.

5. Discuss deficiencies in newspaper readability.

6. See that the society does not get into the habit of renominating and re-electing the same members as directors year after year.

7. Welcome spirited and controversial resolutions from the committee and floor but insist that they be presented well in advance of the discussion period.

8. Demonstrate to reporters and photographers that the editors know something about public relations by providing them with proper facilities at the annual meeting.

9. Personalize the *Bulletin*.

10. Make the society an international organization.

Knight once again brought up the idea of establishing a year-round office or secretariat in Washington.[43] Earlier, a committee consisting of David Lawrence, Dwight Marvin and W. S. Gilmore had not recommended the full-time office, which could cost $15,000 a year,[44] but Knight said that it should be a goal. "Our membership has now reached a point where it is virtually impossible for your officers, located in various parts of the country, to conduct the affairs of the society on as efficient and thoroughgoing basis as I would like to see. We should find a way to overcome the financial obstacles and establish a Washington office."[45]

THE WORK OF FREDDY AND ALICE FOX PITTS

Freddy and Alice Fox Pitts provided ASNE part-time key professional help. Presidents, officers and directors did all the other work, the presidents operating from their own offices across the country. Because of the officers' increasing workload, including writing and editing a mimeographed *Bulletin*, A. H. Kirchhofer of the Buffalo *Evening News* hired Mrs. Pitts, who was his picture and feature editor. She attended her first convention in 1933, and she and her husband, Freddy, became an important part of the organization until they retired in the 1960s.[46]

In her 1963 valedictory at an ASNE luncheon, Mrs. Pitts recalled that only when Jack Knight became president was she able to "come into her own" after a decade of work for ASNE. "Jack evidently saw that the society needed somebody to take over and do things for them, and he not only encouraged me to make decisions but actually forced me to."[47] She later edited *Read All About It! Fifty Years of the American Society of Newspaper Editors* for the society's 50th anniversary in 1972.

Freddy Pitts was also a colorful Buffalo journalist who devoted most of his energy to coordinating the writing for the *ASNE Bulletin*. Like his wife, Pitts was a graduate of the Columbia School of Journalism; before beginning his "flywheel" association with ASNE, he had worked for newspapers in New York, Canada and Delaware. He became the Sunday editor of the Washington *Post*, a job which he said had provided good experience for editing the *Bulletin*. "The goddamn thing speaks for itself," was Pitts' retort when

ASNE's *Bulletin* editorial chairman, Michael Ogden, asked what he could tell the assembled editors about the publication.[48]

ASNE BULLETIN

Although the *Bulletin* was started shortly after the society's inception as a means of keeping members up to date, not all copies were available in the society's headquarters in 1992. However, the publication's importance can be seen as early as 1926. After the first three issues, Secretary E. C. Hopwood said, "The *Bulletin* will not be an effective publication, it will not satisfy the want felt by many members of the society unless every member makes it a part of his responsibility to read it, criticize it and contribute to it."[49]

The following year, Secretary Marvin Creager complained that the *Bulletin* was a great idea in abstract but that it was getting little support from editors. "If it is to be continued, the editor would strongly urge that each member assign himself to write a piece for the *Bulletin* and see that the assignment is covered. In short, write something for the *Bulletin*, even if it is no earthly good."[50]

In 1932, the year before recruiting Mrs. Pitts, Kirchhofer noted that although members were cooperating with suggestions and assistance, the *Bulletin* would be more valuable if it were made a prime source of information for editors. Numbers 41–75 (from January 1933 to May 1934) were written and mimeographed out of Kirchhofer's Buffalo *Evening News* office. Beginning with number 76 on June 18, 1934, the *Bulletin* was issued on a slightly changed schedule: the beginning and middle of each month. It was published from the Post Building in Washington, D.C., under editor M. V. Atwood of the Rochester *Times-Union*. Freddy Pitts was the assistant editor. Issues 112–166 were published in Rockville, Maryland, before the Pittses moved to Delaware.

To give the *Bulletin* new direction, the directors established an editorial board that would provide Pitts creative impetus. In July 1944 Knight appointed E. Z. Dittman of the Chicago *Sun*, Louis B. Selzer of the Cleveland *Press*, Waldo Arnold of the Milwaukee *Journal* and Harry Boyd of the Cedar Rapids *Gazette* to the board. Another advisory member, Carl Lindstrom, later wrote, "We don't need a house organ." The *Bulletin* had become a major forum for receiving complaints as well as being the object of complaints. Lindstrom's vision was to have an official medium that would rank in prestige and authority with the *American Bar Association Journal*, the *Journal of the American Medical Association* and *Christian Century*.[51] This concept was slow in evolving.

One of a number of articles to appear in the *Bulletin* in the postwar period related to the beginning of the American Press Institute on September 26, 1946. As noted in a resolution adopted at the 1947 convention, the seminars designed to raise the standards of operative journalism in the United States were established under the leadership of ASNE member Sevellon Brown, editor and publisher of the Providence *Journal & Evening Bulletin* at Columbia University.[52] By the 1970s, at least 80 percent of ASNE members had been through at least one, and frequently two, seminars.

An era reaching back into the 1920s ended at the April 20, 1950, society meeting with an announcement that David L. Lawrence had ended his 20 consecutive years of service on the board of directors. He had been elected into the society in 1927 when he was editor of the *United States Daily*. Along with Frank Kent and Mark Sullivan, he pioneered modern American newspaper political columns. Later, in 1948, he founded *U.S. News & World Report*. Despite his diligent work behind the scenes as chair of numerous committees and as developer of the index of ASNE minutes, Lawrence refused to be considered for the presidency, which he consistently maintained should be reserved exclusively for working editors of daily newspapers.[53]

For ASNE to remain a professional organization, Lawrence urged continuation of the practice of allowing members of the board of directors to elect the society officers. "My theory is that the work of members on the board itself and on its committees affords ample opportunity for a judgment to be made as to who will make the best officers."[54]

In his farewell as a director, Lawrence advised his colleagues not to use their meetings to disseminate propaganda. There is always the temptation for program chairpersons to invite government officials to speak of current news issues, he said. While it is interesting for ASNE members to see prominent government officials, their appearances should be incidental rather than primary: "Our real job, as I see it, is to consider and discuss the ethics of journalism and usefulness of the press as an institution. We should, moreover, in the society, never be the instruments for distribution of general news, as such. If anybody has a cause to advocate or if anybody has news to give out, he can deal directly with the press associations and the newspapers."[55]

NOTES

1. For a more detailed look at Knight's service in World War I and struggle to accept the appointment as a censor in London, see Charles Whited's *Knight: A Publisher in the Tumultuous Century*, New York: E. P. Dutton, 1988, 14–17, chapter 9, "The World Turned Upside Down."

2. New York *Herald-Tribune*, March 12, 1948. Also *Current Biography*, 1958, 264.

3. Richard Kluger, *The Paper: The Life and Death of the New York* Herald-Tribune, New York: Knopf, 1986, 282.

4. *Current Biography*, 1948, 222.

5. ASNE *Proceedings*, 1946, 203. See also Joseph L. Morrison, *Josephus Daniels: The Small-d Democrat*, Chapel Hill: University of North Carolina Press, 1966, 239.

6. Erwin Canham, *Commitment to Freedom: The Story of the* Christian Science Monitor, Boston: Houghton Mifflin, 1958.

7. ASNE *Proceedings*, 1946, 119.

8. See ASNE minutes, April 21, 1928, 45, and December 10, 1932, 71, when the funds were discontinued.

9. ASNE minutes, February 9, 1924, 33.

10. ASNE minutes, April 1944, 211.

11. See ASNE minutes, April 17, 1948, 281, 285, 294.

12. Leonard Teel, "The Shaping of a Southern Opinion Leader: Ralph McGill and Freedom of Information," *American Journalism*, Vol. 5, No. 1 (1988): 17.

13. The 1945 annual meeting was not held because of the war efforts in Germany and the Pacific. It was the only time the ASNE did not hold an annual meeting.

14. ASNE *Proceedings*, 1946, 13.

15. Ibid., 121.

16. Ibid., 118.

17. For more information on McGill and on Virginius Dabney of the Richmond *Times-Dispatch*, who became the 27th president of ASNE in 1957–1958, see *Southern Liberal Journalists and the Issue of Race, 1920–1944,* by John T. Kneebone, Chapel Hill: University of North Carolina Press, 1985. The other three leading liberal journalists of the South, according to Kneebone, were Gerald W. Johnson, George Fort Milton of the Chattanooga *News* and Hodding Carter of the Greenville (Miss.) *Delta Democrat-Times*.

18. Alice Fox Pitts, *Read All About It! 50 Years of ASNE*, Reston, Va.: ASNE, 1974, 177.

19. Herbert Brucker, "The Pulitzer Prizes no longer need an advisory board," *ASNE Bulletin*, #510, July 1, 1967, 2.

20. "Editors consider Pulitzer jury system imperfect, but majority favors continuing cooperation," *ASNE Bulletin*, #288, August 1, 1947, 4–6.

21. Melville E. Ferguson, "ASNE is urged to award own annual prizes," *ASNE Bulletin*, September 1, 1947, 2.

22. ASNE minutes, April 1949, 295.

23. ASNE minutes, October 10, 1949, 304–305. See also "Revised Basis for Participation in Pulitzer Prize Judging Proposed," *ASNE Bulletin*, #314, November 1, 1949, 1.

24. "ASNE Quits Pulitzer Juries," *ASNE Bulletin*, #320, May 1, 1950, 6.

25. See, for example, Herbert Brucker, "The Ambitious Future of Joseph Pulitzer's Brainchild," *ASNE Bulletin*, March 1966, 6–7; Brucker, "The Pulitzer Prizes no longer need an advisory board," *ASNE Bulletin*, #510, July 1, 1967, 1–2, 16; John Hohenberg, "Politics of the Pulitzers," *ASNE Bulletin*, October 1974, 8–12.

26. Teel, 26.

27. Margaret A. Blanchard, *Exporting the First Amendment: The Press Government Crusade of 1945–1952*, New York: Longman, 1986, 26.

28. Pitts, 181.

29. Ibid., 27.

30. Ibid., 184–185. See also Canham's more cheery presidential remarks in the ASNE *Proceedings*, 1949, 11–21.

31. Herbert Brucker, *Communication Is Power: Unchanging Values in a Changing Journalism*, New York: Oxford University Press, 1973, 203.

32. ASNE *Proceedings*, 1947, 22.

33. Ibid.

34. *News and Observer*, April 7, 1947. Quoted by Morrison, 258.

35. Norman Isaacs, *Untended Gates: The Mismanaged Press*, New York: Columbia University Press, 1986, 98.

36. ASNE *Proceedings*, 1947, 212–213. As is the case with most publishers, ASNE presidents and members quote Jefferson as though he is a libertarian like James Madison. In reality, as Robert Logan points out, Jefferson was closer to the social responsibility philosophy articulated by the Hutchins Commission.

37. Ibid.

38. ASNE *Proceedings*, 1955, 18–26.

39. For example, see "Society has no members in Idaho, New Hampshire or Wyoming," out of 444 members, *ASNE Bulletin*, September 1, 1947, 1.

40. A. M. Piper, "Membership Limit Suggested," *ASNE Bulletin*, September 1, 1947, 1.

41. See *ASNE Bulletin*, #265, #267, #288, #312, #313, #320.

42. John S. Knight, "Sulzberger Challenged on Chain Ownership," *ASNE Bulletin*, June 1, 1947, 1–2.

43. For a discussion of the establishment of a permanent ASNE secretariat from November 30, 1930, see the ASNE minutes, 55, 57, 138, 144, 150, 227, 234, 243–244.

44. ASNE minutes, April 21, 1946, 243–244.

45. ASNE *Proceedings*, 1946, 17.

46. Vermont C. Royster, "Alice and Freddy," *ASNE Bulletin*, April 1963, 8–9. See also Michael Ogden, "Alice Fox Pitts, 1896–1978," *ASNE Bulletin*, July–August 1978.

47. Ogden, "Alice Fox Pitts, 1896–1978," 19.

48. Michael J. Ogden, "Freddy Remembered," *ASNE Bulletin*, December 1973, 24.

49. ASNE *Proceedings*, 1926, 15–16.

50. ASNE *Proceedings*, 1927, 14. To contrast with the criticism of Creager and others concerning the *Bulletin*, see Alf Pratte, "We should stop hashing the *Bulletin*," *ASNE Bulletin*, April 1991, 44–45.

51. According to Loren Ghiglione, Lindstrom spearheaded the creation of another magazine, *The American Editor,* that was closer to what he envisioned.

52. Resolution #1, *ASNE Bulletin*, May 1, 1947, 3. See also, "Hope Welch Found Press Institute Exciting Venture," *ASNE Bulletin*, December 1, 1947, 1, and "Discussion Leaders Drawn from ASNE," *ASNE Bulletin*, December 1, 1947, 3. Other prominent ASNE members who contributed to the development of API included Grove Patterson, the first API chair; A. H. Kirchhofer, Ben McKelway, Vincent Jones, Turner Catledge, Alexander Jones, Felix McKnight, Newbold Noyes, Howard H. (Tim) Hays and Burl Osborne. For a detailed account of the API and the role of ASNE in its founding, see Don E. Carter and Malcolm F. Mallette, *Seminar: The Story of the American Press Institute,* Reston, Va.: API, 1992.

53. ASNE *Proceedings*, 1950, 159.

54. Ibid.

55. Ibid., 164.

Chapter 5

The Corporate Idea

The individual editor has given way to the corporate idea . . . . I think the loss of the personal editor may have tended to make newspapers follow rather than lead.
　　　　　　　　　　　　　　—Dwight Marvin, *ASNE Bulletin*, October 1957

Let a congressman from Podunk try to intimidate a publisher from Squedunk and the boards of the American Society of Newspaper Editors and the American Newspaper Publishers Association will rise up in emergency protest. Let a newspaper be suppressed in Batavia, and the alarms are loud. But let Mr. Hoover engage in the crudest sort of pressure, as he did in this instance, and suddenly the nation's editorial pages find themselves absorbed with censorship of the press in Turkey.
　　　　　　　　　—James A. Wechsler, *Reflections of an Angry Middle-Aged Editor*

Many Americans still recall the 1950s with nostalgia. David Schoenbrun recollects: "We were the greatest military power in the world, the leading industrial power, with a surplus of trade, and the envy of the world for our free, growing society. Our children did not smoke crack or swallow Quaaludes. We had never heard of AIDS. Homosexuals stayed in the closet, not on our front pages."[1]

Beneath the glitter of the "technological"[2] or "affluent"[3] society, built in part by the "organization man"[4] and governed by the "power elite,"[5] some growing problems were observed but often overlooked by ASNE members. This may have been due to a gradual replacement of ASNE's early editors by a new type of editor, who was described by former President Dwight Marvin as one who had "given way to the corporate idea" and was becoming more a follower than a leader. Also, as Russell Wiggins warned at the end of the decade, ASNE editors were in the midst of changes more profound than those of previous generations, "and I am afraid we have not adjusted our own perceptions to the new age rapidly enough."[6]

The inescapable reality, however, was that nuclear war was a heavier threat in the 1950s than in the last decades of the century; with this threat came an obsession with national security and a fear of those not devoted to the same goals. After the A-bomb became a vivid fact of life, an even deadlier form of destruction was unleashed: the H-bomb. These bombs literally changed night to day for the reporters and photographers in the western Pacific. But less diligently covered by the press was how government and scientists altered or totally suppressed evidence in their continuing tests in Nevada—which had deadly results on future Americans.[7]

THE CENSORSHIP PROBLEM AGAIN

The Korean War, which began June 25, 1950, when North Korean communists invaded South Korea, was covered extensively by the wire services and a handful of prestigious papers which practiced a form of voluntary censorship. By the time the armistice was signed on July 27, 1953, nearly 50,000 Americans had been killed and 100,000 wounded. Today most Americans' view of the Korean War is heavily influenced by the movie and television series *M*A*S*H*, a popularized version of some aspects of the struggle.

The ambiguous objectives of the American and other United Nations forces in Korea served as the prelude to the ideological conflict, brinkmanship and high international tension that characterized the decade of the 1950s as a period of cold war. Coincidentally, it was ASNE member Herbert Bayard Swope who coined the phrase "cold war" in a statement he presented before the Senate War Investigating Committee on October 24, 1948.[8]

At their 1951 convention ASNE members heard addresses by Keyes Beech of the Chicago *Daily News* and Marguerite Higgins of the New York *Herald-Tribune*, both Pulitzer Prize winners for their Korean coverage. General George C. Marshall (secretary of defense), General Omar Bradley (chairman of the Joint Chiefs of Staff) and assistant secretary Mrs. Anna Rosenberg appeared at an unusual off-the-record briefing. No word of what they said is preserved in the *Proceedings*. Another convention highlight was an appearance by General Douglas MacArthur only hours after his "Old Soldiers Never Die" telecast speech to Congress. MacArthur had just returned to Washington after President Harry Truman dismissed him from his command in Japan and Korea.[9]

During the Korean War the ASNE board of directors approved a resolution composed by a seven-person committee on censorship.[10] The report recommended the same three points that the World War II Wartime Censorship Committee called for.

1. Administration of censorship should be assigned to an independent agency, which is established for that purpose alone, and is responsible only to the president of the United States.

2. The director of the agency should be a civilian whose standing and experience make him acceptable to the communications media, especially radio and the press.

3. The censorship, as applied to radio and the press, should be voluntary, modeled after the voluntary censorship system of World War II.[11]

Also during the 1951 convention, James S. Pope, chairman of the World Information Committee, emphasized the distinction between censorship and withholding of information. He defined a censor as an official "empowered to take away from you something you've already got." Pope, who would become ASNE president in 1954, said there was no censorship as such in the Korean War, because no framework of censorship control had been set up by the government or the military. The only statute that carried penalties for publishing information, he said, concerned coverage of atomic energy.

As head of a special subcommittee on atomic information, Paul Block of the Toledo *Blade*[12] introduced the startling notion that the Atomic Energy Commission (AEC) was in some respects "a spoiled brat, hugging public information to its breast far beyond the call of security."[13] After Block's subcommittee traveled thousands of miles and interviewed 38 scientists and officials, Pope presented the following conclusions:

1. Secrecy is intrinsically a dangerous and corrupting thing. It is highly probable that it has already hampered research and development, and that it has wasted millions. While the press must recognize the necessity for some military secrecy, it also must constantly review and question the validity of AEC's decisions on what is to be withheld.

2. Reporting purely scientific aspects of atomic energy constitutes a comparatively minor part of a newspaper's problem. The public is little inclined to grapple with highly technical matters, and points of general scientific information are being covered adequately by science writers.

3. The press has reported inadequately many aspects of the atomic energy program which are not considered confidential. This appears to be due to a sense of awe, amounting almost to superstition, regarding nuclear fission. As a speaker told the 1950 convention, we have been "bamboozled by the atom." Pope concluded, "A touch of robust skepticism and the ruthless persistence of a police reporter are badly needed."[14]

McCARTHYISM AS A THREAT TO PRESS FREEDOM

Many ASNE members failed to be skeptical of charges made by U.S. Senator Joseph McCarthy that individuals and organizations were influenced by communism. Much of McCarthy's ability to manipulate the press came from his skill at feeding sensational accusations to the wire services and to other "objective" news reporters working under deadline pressure. These reporters' stories aided McCarthy's plan to capture headlines and air time across the country. Support and opposition to McCarthy became intertwined in the debate in both the ASNE and Associated Press Managing Editors Association. Some news-papers, editors and columnists aggressively challenged the senator. These included Drew Pearson and Jack Anderson,[15] Hank Greenspun of the Las Vegas *Sun*, the *Christian Science Monitor*, the Milwaukee *Journal*, and the Washington *Post* under Wiggins.

ASNE as an organization was far less aggressive than such individual members in challenging McCarthy. It failed to investigate charges. McKelway of the Washington *Star*, president in 1950, recalled that when McCarthy spoke to a capacity audience on "Communists in Government," he defended his inconsistent numbers on disloyal employees. Questions from the floor drew evasive answers, but to one question about the much maligned Secretary of State Dean Acheson, McCarthy answered directly: "I have never accused Acheson. I have not accused Acheson of being a communist or anything of the kind. I have said that the best thing you can say about Acheson is that he was not in the Marshall category . . . . The best you can say for Acheson is that he is incompetent, that he is completely incompetent because he has failed."[16]

McKelway said that because of the late hour, the speech and questions from ASNE members received little coverage. Acheson's cutting response to McCarthy's barb two nights later was only lightly reported also. After his fourth ASNE address in five years, Acheson spoke off the record, with McCarthy a few feet from him. In a searing conclusion based in part on Robert Browning's *Caliban upon Seetebas*, Acheson said he wasn't asking for the editors' sympathy or even their help: "You are in a worse situation than I am. I and my associates are the intended victims of this mad and vicious operation. But you, unhappily—you by reason of your calling—are participants. You are unwilling participants, disgusted participants, but, nevertheless participants and your position is far more serious than mine."[17]

The secretary of state said that as he left "this filthy business," which he hoped "never to speak of . . . again," he wanted to remind the editors of the words of John Donne: "Any man's death diminishes me, because I am involved in mankind. And therefore do not send to know for whom the bell tolls; it tolls for thee."[18]

McKelway recalled that as Acheson sat down, the applause was like a clap of thunder. Pitts concluded that this speech was "the beginning of both ends" for McCarthy, who was condemned in a Senate resolution in 1954.

The ASNE board also failed to act on a report by a committee President Basil Walters had appointed to consider McCarthy's misuse of the power of government "to probe into a newspaper's conscience and challenge its right to criticize government." The situation involved James A. Wechsler, editor of the New York *Post,* about whom McCarthy had held hearings on April 24 and May 5, 1953.[19] As noted in the statement to Walters, which was signed by Chairman Russell Wiggins[20] and the committee, the ASNE did not speak for its members on political matters:

These members are of every sort of political persuasion. We are, in politics, not a committee of several hundred persons, and required as such to reach agreement. We are, in effect, several hundred committees, free to differ with each other and to express these differences as we choose. In commenting on the Wechsler hearings, newspapers with members in the society did disagree on whether they constituted a threat to freedom of the press; and members of this committee disagree also as to the extent to which this threat existed.[21]

Wiggins commented in a later interview, "If ASNE was any looser as an organization it would have fallen apart. If it were more effectively organized it would have been a menace. We could not allow ASNE to be used by any powerful political figure that came along."[22]

Wiggins and three other editors, including Brucker of the Hartford *Courant,* William M. Tugman of the Eugene (Ore.) *Register-Guard* and Eugene S. Pulliam of the Indianapolis *News,* were not to be denied, however. In a slashing minority opinion that included a 15-page "Historical Summary of Some of the Conflicts between the Press and Legislative Branches of Government," the four members noted, "The people suffer some diminution of their right to know fully and comment freely upon their own government whenever a single newspaper, however worthy or unworthy, is subjected by one senator, however worthy or unworthy, to inconvenience, expense, humiliation, ridicule, abuse, condemnation and reproach under the auspices of government power."[23]

The day this report appeared, Chalmers M. Roberts said the Washington *Post* editorialized that McCarthy's "attempt at intimidation" of the press in the Wechsler case should be recognized for what it was.[24] Three days later McCarthy declared it incumbent upon the ASNE members who had signed the Wiggins statement to "investigate the extent" to which Wiggins had prostituted and endangered freedom of the press by "false, vicious and intemperate attacks upon anyone who dares to expose the undercover communists."[25] In keeping with the intent of the majority of the committee members, the ASNE board "didn't exactly distinguish itself."[26] It declined to become more involved in the McCarthy controversy and other political issues.

Wechsler alludes to such timidity in a related issue in his *Reflections of an Angry Middle-Aged Editor.* Referring to the inaction of publishers and elected officials concerning J. Edgar Hoover's efforts to apply advertising pressure in an attempt to stop a series of articles that criticized the FBI, Wechsler claimed,

Let a Congressman from Podunk try to intimidate a publisher from Squedunk and the boards of the American Society of Newspaper Editors and the American Newspaper Publishers Association will rise up in emergency protest. Let a newspaper be suppressed in Batavia, and the alarms are loud. But let Mr. Hoover engage in the crudest sort of pressure, as he did in this instance, and suddenly the nation's editorial pages find themselves absorbed with censorship of the press in Turkey.[27]

INFLUENCE AND EMPHASIS ON THE HOME FRONT

While concerned about the hot and cold wars abroad, ASNE focused on domestic problems. Particular emphasis was placed on the fight against attempts by public officials to restrict the gathering of thoroughly legitimate news.[28] Dwight Young, the editor-publisher of the Dayton *Journal-Herald,* helped establish the ASNE theme for the 1950s when he said: "It is true, and I think we all realize it, that in recent years we have gone in rather heavily for what I shall have to designate, for lack of a more expressive term, 'internationalism,' in its broadest sense."[29]

Things were done with a global perspective and with "our eyes wide open," he added, and with overwhelming support of the growing ASNE membership. As a board member, Young had voted to stimulate a better concept of freedom of expression in other parts of the world: "I certainly do not feel that our society's earnest endeavors in that field should be abandoned or curtailed. Rather, they should be expanded as any practical opportunity to do so presents itself. Those objectives were sound when they were initiated and they are as important today as they ever were."[30]

But Young said that there were other matters to which the society should give more attention: "Specifically, I mean the improvement of journalism in the United States." He announced that ASNE had retained Harold Cross to submit a comprehensive outline of his studies that brought together "the American union relating to the rights of newspapers and the various legal restrictions on their activities."[31]

FREEDOM OF INFORMATION EFFORTS

Cross, who had retired from Columbia University's graduate school of journalism, worked closely with James S. Pope, head of the Freedom of Information (FOI) Committee, and other committee members, until Cross' death in 1959. In 1953 their efforts produced a book, *The People's Right to Know.* This book, in turn, and Cross' testimony before legislative groups contributed to passage of the Freedom of Information Act in 1966.

Assessing the accomplishments of the FOI committee, Wiggins said in 1960 that Cross' book had won access to information rights for editors across the land. Specifically, he pointed out that the society had encouraged Congress to amend the Administrative Procedures Act, to open up payroll records, to open previously closed committee hearings and to improve state records laws so as to provide vastly improved access to information. Ultimately, he predicted, the efforts could form a foundation for federal statutes of this nature.[32]

Symbolic of the book's importance, the first copy was presented to President Eisenhower when he spoke at the opening luncheon of the 1953 convention. His first major speech since his State of the Union address was carried around the world by newspapers, radio and television. This speech was given during the presidency of Wright Bryan, who worked for newspapers in South Carolina and Atlanta before World War II. As a war correspondent before being captured by the Germans, he had covered Eisenhower. Bryan is best known for giving one of the shortest president's addresses on record and for holding the head of newly elected President Eisenhower, who was sick before his ASNE speech. At this time ASNE membership had increased to 560.

The growing influence of the ASNE freedom of information campaign can be seen in Mark Ethridge's remarks on the "Dynamics of Journalism." Ethridge, publisher of the Louisville papers, talked about information and its relationship to truth:

Basic to any understanding of the truth is knowing the truth. As a nation we do not know it. I am not talking about freedom of the press; I am talking about its handmaiden, freedom of information, without which freedom of the press is a mockery anyway. . . . Even so recently as 1950 when Basil Walters, Russell Wiggins and James Pope began to pull the bell rope of warning that there was a growing suppression of information, I had a supercilious attitude of amused tolerance. I did not realize that the bell was tolling for me, too. It tolls for all of us.

Additional evidence of ASNE's excellent leadership in the 1950s is found in a survey conducted by the University of Arizona after it had established the John Peter Zenger award (for outstanding promotion of freedom of the press). According to Raymond Moscowitz, a nominating committee of prominent newspaper executives selected two candidates, and then 30 outstanding newspaper editors chose one to receive the award. In 1955 twenty-nine editors responded. They chose Walters, executive editor of the Knight newspapers. Pope was named the next year. Two years later Wiggins received the honor. Thus, the Zenger award went quickly to the three men who were most prominent in ASNE's freedom of information efforts in the late 1940s and early 1950s.[33] By 1960, six of the seven recipients of the award were ASNE members, and Walters, Wiggins, Pope and Herbert Brucker had each served as ASNE president. E. Palmer Hoyt of the Denver *Post* was the first recipient in 1954. Virgil M. Newton, managing editor of the Tampa (Fla.) *Tribune*, was the 1960 winner. The only non-ASNE member who received the award before 1960 was John E. Moss, chairman of the House Governmental Information Committee, who worked with Cross in developing the Freedom of Information Act passed in 1966. By 1989, 8 of the 35 Zenger award winners had served as ASNE president.[34]

Wiggins later noted that the lack of a full-time ASNE staff would have been even more evident if the Moss committee had not carried the majority of the burden. "Presently it [the Moss committee] is helping the press more than the press is helping [itself] and we should not expect to lean on it forever for endeavors that we ought to be initiating ourselves."[35]

The choices for the Zenger awards during the early 1950s were especially fitting, writes Moscowitz, biographer of Walters. A diminutive, Indiana-born reporter and editor, Walters was one of 14 editors who served as president of both ASNE and the APME.[36] In his presentation of the Zenger award, Douglas Martin, the head of the University of Arizona journalism department, said Walters had won on the basis of his policy that "the people must know," a phrase that became identified with ASNE during the Eisenhower years. Walters, however, was quick to point out that neither he nor ASNE was responsible for the concept, which was slowly becoming a part of the American way of thinking.

The first great symbol of the campaign for freedom of information was John Peter Zenger, whose trial for seditious libel in colonial America, Walters suggested, rallied American colonists and helped spark the Revolutionary War. "We are now in a new type of war that calls for different tactics. We must not permit ourselves to be paralyzed into inactivity by the stultifying fear that the overall problem is so vast that we as individuals cannot make a contribution to its solutions."[37]

Walters stated that an important contribution to revival of newspaper interest in the people's right to know and to participate in important decisions was made by a weekly newspaper editor in Moose Lake, Minnesota, close to where Walters had once worked. Moscowitz wrote: "The county clerk wanted to write out for him the news from the records of his office the clerk thought good for the citizens and to omit that which he judged was none of the public's business. The dramatic fight that resulted drew national attention and was the 'Plymouth Rock' out of which has grown our whole modern day freedom of information crusade."[38]

Alice Pitts went back even further in the modern freedom of information battle. She referred to the claim by Kent Cooper of the Associated Press that an international news cartel had contributed to World War I by monopolizing the distribution of international news and by coloring the news in nationalistic hues to suit clients in each of the countries served.[39] Casper Yost helped to sound the warning as early as 1923 when he recommended that the ASNE "defend the rights of the profession when it is attacked or threatened by legislative or administrative powers."[40]

Ironically, despite his leadership in the FOI committee, Walters informed ASNE members that questions answered by Secretary of the Treasury George Humphrey in a convention appearance would be off the record. This practice was cited with surprise by Charles Withers of the Rochester (Minn.) *Post-Bulletin* in 1972: "Imagine that! Would ASNE today permit a public official (perhaps other than the President of the United States) to go off-the-record during the question period? I don't know, but I do not recall any such procedure in the 12 consecutive conventions I have attended."[41]

Along with Walters, Cross and Wiggins, Pope was perhaps the most influential ASNE member involved in the freedom of information efforts in the 1950s. As a city editor and managing editor for the Atlanta *Journal*, he had fought government secrecy. "The good editor—and perhaps any good and useful leader—has to wake up angry every morning," he said in a 1949 lecture at the University of Georgia. "He does not wait for the moment to crusade on a spectacular scale. He does not wait for an epidemic. He spots and cauterizes civic germs, regardless of the enemies it gets him, before an infection takes root."[42]

Pope's son, James, recalls that during World War II his father worked in the Office of Censorship for six months, handling press problems in Washington and helping to develop guidelines for voluntary censorship. "He fully understood the needs of national security, but he also felt strongly that many officials abused this excuse in order to conceal information that was merely embarrassing."[43]

During the three years he headed the committee on freedom of information, the Washington *Post* reported, Pope expanded his reputation as a tenacious and eloquent fighter for press freedom: "His battles, learned and reasoned, pitted him against seemingly everybody from the president of the United States and assorted members of both houses of Congress, to county clerks and sheriffs."[44]

Without a full-time ASNE staff, Pope's office at the *Courier-Journal and Times* became a clearinghouse for all who fought for information. The *Post* added: "He adopted the practice of personally writing to each public official against whom complaints were made, outlining his understanding of the facts and explaining just why he found the official's actions unjust. His letter, on an ASNE letterhead, often removed obstacles that had resisted the best efforts of editors of small local publications."[45]

Another strong proponent of freedom of information was Kenneth MacDonald, editor of the Des Moines *Register and Tribune*. Under his leadership, the *Register and Tribune* had won more Pulitzer Prizes than any other newspaper except the New York *Times*. Providing a laissez-faire working philosophy for investigative reporters such as Clark Mollenhoff, MacDonald gave them the time and freedom to pursue unusual subjects.[46] But the reporters also needed access to public records. MacDonald's primary objective was to reduce government secrecy. During World War II, he said, bureaucrats' desire to operate without public scrutiny was reinforced by the need for military security. This climate continued long after hostilities ceased; some government agencies actually issued written directives that no information was to be made public unless it reflected favorably on the agency.[47] MacDonald referred to ASNE efforts to fight this trend in a statement of objectives that appeared in the June 1955 *Bulletin*:

"There are many problems which need our attention. There is a puzzling and disturbing preoccupation with secrecy in the top levels of our governments which seems to persist despite valiant efforts of the freedom of information committees."[48]

MacDonald particularly praised the leadership of Walters, Pope and Wiggins. The latter two served at least three terms each as head of the Freedom of Information committee. "They both worked vigorously and aggressively at that assignment and devoted an incredible amount of time to conferring with public officials, writing letters and inspiring fellow society members to action in their respective communities."[49] The *Proceedings* of the 1950s contain lengthy reports of their activities. The report written by Wiggins, who was chair during MacDonald's tenure, filled 30 pages. "At that time we questioned whether we were accomplishing much, but I believe it is clear now that there is much greater access to information today because of ASNE's efforts, particularly the leadership of Walters, Pope, Wiggins and Cross, during that period," MacDonald said.[50]

DISPUTES ABOUT JOURNALISM SCHOOLS

Walters was concerned about another issue in addition to the right to know. *Editor & Publisher* in 1947 reported his concern that a program aimed at accrediting journalism schools might be a step toward licensing American journalists: "Walters charged the accrediting program, recently inaugurated by the American Council on Education for Journalism, with containing potentialities for becoming a bureaucratic monopoly . . . effectively putting the stamp of approval on the man or woman."[51]

As a result, Walters was ridiculed by acid-tongued Jenkin Lloyd Jones. Never one to avoid a verbal confrontation, Jones asked in the *ASNE Bulletin*, "What did Stuffy have to drink at the convention? Who dealt him up the Blue Moon of gin, vinegar, bitters, happy dust and a maraschino cherry? For unless I'm drinking the wrong stuff myself, I see no connection between Stuffy's horrendous forecast of a straitjacketed writing profession and the simple effort by the ASNE to improve the standards of journalism teaching."[52]

All the ASNE was trying to do, Jones said, was to put "a stamp of approval" on journalism schools, which, in the opinion of experienced newspaper executives, were doing their best to prepare students for newspaper work: "That is a positive service to students, newspapers and the press-reading public. It prohibits no one from hiring anyone. It damns no individuals. It merely seeks to raise a standard. And God knows, the standard should be raised."[53]

Kenneth E. Olson, dean of Northwestern University's Medill School of Journalism, and others, including Dwight Marvin, former ASNE president and current president of the American Council on Education for Journalism, also responded. With a tinge of nastiness directed at the growing number of group owners of newspapers, Marvin asked, "Isn't Mr. Walters seein' things at night? It is incredible that he, a working newspaperman, can be scared by such a synthetic ghost. . . . [Accreditation] is not half so dangerous as multiple newspaper ownership—the growing number of networks of chain organizations—in which Mr. Walters has been a willing participant. If newspapers cannot remain free from bureaucratic monopoly in spite of chains and accreditations, the whole business is a puling infant."[54]

Editor of the small-town Troy (N.Y.) *Record*, Marvin was among an increasing number of ASNE editors who challenged the growth of newspaper chains across the nation. As early as 1938, he had written to Carl Ackerman, recollecting when the little city of Troy had seven regular newspapers. By 1938 Troy had only the *Record* newspapers (one morning and one evening under single ownership) and a small Sunday paper. "What then becomes of freedom of the press?" Marvin asked:

It represents in this city my right—or, if he wishes to exercise it, the publisher's—to say my say. If I wish to be decent enough I can let people write me letters on the other side; but I don't have to do this. Nobody can speak his mind in Troy except on the platform or on my say-so. Why? Because I don't want him to? No, not at all! This is just what we are facing today in the trend toward concentration. If a man wants to say anything of which the newspaper doesn't approve he must hire a printer, print his broadside, distribute it at his own expense, and be considered queer.[55]

In a 1957 interview with Alice Pitts, Marvin commented on the major changes he had seen in journalism in his 50 years of newspapering. Foremost were the disappearance of the party organ and the increase in fairness and balance of news. Newspapers had become more fair, trustworthy and interesting, he believed. As for editors in the 1950s, Marvin said they had given in to what he described as "the corporate idea":

The old days produced the Greeleys, the Danas, the Wattersons, the Whites and the Hearsts. This personal leadership seems to have died, at least dropped precipitately, with the death of Grove Patterson. True, we have Spike Canham, Roy Roberts and half a dozen others of unusual capacity; but none of them overshadow their newspaper organs as did the giants of the past. I think the loss of the personal editor may have tended to make newspapers follow rather than lead.[56]

CASEY JONES—FIRST OF THE EXECUTIVE EDITORS

The trend toward fewer cities having competing newspapers also continued, with the percentages of competitive cities dropping from 8.4 to 6 percent between 1945 and 1954. By 1960 the percentage was only half what it was in 1940.[57] Mergers and takeovers also led to a new designation among ASNE presidents, that of executive editor. Whereas presidents in the past had primarily been titled editor, editorial page editor or managing editor, in 1951 Alexander "Casey" Jones of the Syracuse *Herald-Journal* became the first of 12 "executive editors" to preside over the society from the 1950s to the 1990s. He was also the second of five editors from either the *Star* or the *Post* to have the honor. B. M. McKelway was the first in 1950. He was followed by Jones, who in 1950 left Washington for Syracuse after nearly 15 years as *Post* managing editor. Described by *Fortune* as "cyclonic, convivial and incurably romantic" about his profession, Jones had come to Washington from the Milwaukee *Journal* in 1935 with a sense of hard news and how to portray it. Because of the turmoil surrounding news operations in the paper, a London *Times* correspondent had warned him, "Don't you know, old boy, that Pennsylvania Avenue is paved with the bones of former managing editors of the *Post?*"[58]

It was Jones who called once again for an ASNE secretariat in Washington. He wanted an executive secretary to ease the workload of officers and committee heads, who, Jones estimated, were devoting as much as half of their time to the work of the society: "I venture to say that the ASNE is today the only major society representing a great profession (I realize that technically we are not a profession) that does not maintain such a secretariat. That we have been able to function has been due to the loyal efforts of Alice and Freddy Pitts, who certainly should be an important part of a real secretariat, and to the unreasonable demands on the time of our committee chairmen."[59]

The second of three Joneses to be ASNE president was a feisty globe-trotter from Tulsa, Jenkin Lloyd Jones. (The third, in 1968, was Vincent S. Jones of the Gannett Newspapers.) The son of an old-school publisher, "Jenk" Jones had sprung into the limelight with a convention address on "Afghanistanism," or writing editorials about subjects that are safely far away. He also had headed a committee which investigated charges that 51 journalists (none of them ASNE members) were on the payroll of the state of Illinois.

Jones said his chief accomplishment took place even before his incumbency, when as program chairman he succeeded in getting members to acknowledge in 1956 that "the airplane was practical." This caused the annual meeting to be moved from Washington to San Francisco. As program chairman, Jones arranged for Canadian Prime Minister Lester Pearson to speak on what griped Canadians about Americans, but before the convention Pearson was defeated in a no-confidence vote. Jones recalled that Pearson "graciously offered to pass but I replied that with no official position, he could be even more honest. He came and blistered the ears of editors who imagined that Canada was merely a depository for moose and muskies and that all Canadians were puppy-friendly."[60]

Jones also found himself in another controversy because some members felt they did not have an opportunity to serve in the organization. In an article entitled "The Quiet Little Guy in the Back Row," Charlie Gallagher, managing editor of the Lynn (Mass.) *Item*, complained that although he had been in the society for eight years, he had not been asked to do anything. He queried, "Where does the novice find the brass ring which lands him on the escalator leading to committee work, a spot on the program directorship or even a second vice-presidency?" Gallagher recommended that ASNE follow the model of Rotary clubs and appoint new members to a committee immediately, and keep decision making out of the smoke-filled rooms.[61]

"Well, to hell with that," Jones responded to the Rotary recommendation. He stated: "The ASNE needs only a few committees, but those committees must work. The best committee is the smallest one that can present a wide enough exchange of views and ideas. It has been and it should be an honor to be on an ASNE committee, and loading them down with freshman members wouldn't help."[62]

As membership crept toward 550 in the mid-1950s, Jones agreed that there was a possibility of permanently overlooking able, but shy and retiring, members. "There is a growing danger that prominent and tested members may be called upon too often." The route to recognition, however, was not as Gallagher suggested—that is, buying drinks for the director—although that would be appreciated, Jones joked. Like Gallagher, Jones concluded that the society needed new blood, individuals who could say interesting things to members, say them well, and say them vigorously.

Although committee work may not have been easy to acquire in the 1950s, evidence shows a healthy turnover among policymakers, at least on the board of directors. "Then-and-now" pictures published in the *Bulletin* show that the board changed completely in the seven years between 1943 and 1950, except for past presidents serving ex officio terms.[63] Dwight Young said he saw no need for changes in the process of electing directors, because the average term on the board was only three and one-half years.[64]

THE FIGHT AGAINST SEGREGATION

During the 1950s, society members also worked to lessen the traditions of prejudice which continued to fester after the 1954 U.S. Supreme Court *Brown* v. *Board of Education* ruling that separate but equal educational facilities were unconstitutional. Some leadership came from ASNE members from southern states, most particularly Virginius Dabney and C. A. "Pete" McKnight. McKnight left the relatively safe and comfortable position as editor of the Charlotte *News* to direct the Southern Education Reporting Service (SERS), which was organized for the sole purpose of reporting events in the 17 states which practiced segregation at the time of the decision. He told members at the 1955 convention that he had taken a leave of absence from the Knight paper because he was intrigued by the wider journalistic horizons the Reporting Service opened up—the opportunity to cover an important and controversial story in-depth and beyond the capacity of the daily newspaper. McKnight said that such a service was important because of the poor coverage of racial matters in general and the progress made in desegregation:

In sum, desegregation more often than not has been accomplished in the past year, quietly and without incident, and more often than not Southern political leaders have not accurately reflected the views of many responsible Southerners. Yet the total picture which has emerged from the press coverage of the story in the past year, in my opinion, is precisely the opposite—that is, desegregation is usually accompanied by turmoil and near violence, and all segregationists are violent and inflammatory race baiters.[65]

In addition to Dabney as chairman, other ASNE members serving on the SERS board included Thomas Waring, Charleston *News and Courier*; Coleman Harwell, Nashville *Tennessean*; Frank A. Knight, Charleston (W. Va.) *Gazette*; Frank Ahlgren, Memphis *Commercial Appeal*; and Charles Moss, Nashville *Banner*. McKnight explained that the service had a corps of 20 experienced reporters or editorial writers who submitted material from the 17 states; its reports appeared in every state in publications which had a circulation of 30,000 or more and in many foreign countries. He said:

It is clear to me that we can, at best, reach only a relatively small audience, and that if this great dilemma of our democracy is to be resolved by the people of this country, our newspapers are going to have to do a better job than they have done so far in giving the people all the facts. More adequate coverage of this story, it seems to me, is a great challenge to us as newspaper editors. How well we serve our readers may very well shape not only the kind of South, but the kind of world we live in in the next century.[66]

Before heading the SERS board, Dabney had become a prominent figure fighting segregation as editor of the Richmond *Times-Dispatch*. His rhetoric was also aimed at the North's prejudice against the South. In a series of editorials and books, Dabney argued to end sectionalism and particularly to end misconceptions of the South. In a hard-hitting speech at a Phi Beta Kappa meeting at the University of Rochester, he declared that there can be no room for sectionalism if this country is to shape its ultimate development upon the anvil of destiny.[67]

Dabney also withheld confidential information about President Eisenhower's cautious approach toward integration, as shared with him during the 1958 ASNE meeting. In a letter to Miles H. Wolff in 1972, Dabney revealed a conversation he had with Eisenhower. Dabney stated that the president "chatted up a storm throughout the meal" but that there were "no digestive upsets, trembling hands or anything of that sort" such as had occurred when Eisenhower spoke to the ASNE in 1953. "I don't think he drank any of the wine at the luncheon, but he ate normally," Dabney wrote. Eisenhower also delivered the speech well, and Dabney liked what the president had said. "He said some confidential things during our conversation which I have never used in print," Dabney said. In his reply to Dabney, Miles Wolff said he was interested in "Ike's revelation that he had done everything he could to prevent the Supreme Court decision on schools in 1954."[68]

In his letter to Wolff, Dabney said he didn't know how such information could be used in 1972. He recalled that *Newsweek* magazine somehow heard of the conversation a week or two later, "but I wouldn't discuss it with them. Of course, Ike is long since dead, but I don't feel right about releasing this, even today. Do you agree?"[69]

In a September 6 response to Dabney, Wolff replied: "I think you were correct in keeping this information confidential, although it would have been a sensational piece of news."[70]

Norman Isaacs, ASNE president from 1969–1970, later expressed concern that more editors did not speak out on such important issues when they had access to information from prominent leaders such as President Eisenhower. "I do confess to being disappointed in both Virginius and Miles," Isaacs writes; "we would have practically little history to base the national record on if everyone in journalism felt it improper to disclose what a President had said about such major judicial decisions (or other equally important matters affecting governance). The longer I ponder on this exchange between the two very decent editors the more I keep wondering how much faith journalists really have in democracy."[71]

In his 1958 presidential message, George Healy, Jr., editor of the New Orleans *Times-Picayune*, joked that Reconstruction had really ended the day a member from the Deep South became president of the American Society of Newspaper Editors: "True, such fringe benefits as the election to the ASNE presidency of Walter Harrison and Jenk Jones from the Indian Territory, of Tom Wallace and Jim Pope from up Louisville way, of Wright Bryan when he was editor of the Atlanta *Journal* and of Virginius Dabney of the Virginia Dabneys have been hailed by some members as proof that the reign of the Yankees was over."[72]

A former president of both the Associated Press Managing Editors Association and Sigma Delta Chi, Healy was best known for his success in inviting Cuban leader Fidel Castro to address the 1959 convention, despite the fact that Castro had not been recognized by the United States government. In his biography, *A Lifetime on Deadline*, Healy says that several members of Congress didn't approve of his actions—nor did State Department spokesmen. Senator Wayne Morse of Oregon denounced him as a "meddler." One congressman claimed that Healy violated the Logan Act, which prohibits private citizens from interfering in foreign affairs. President Eisenhower's press secretary jokingly accused Healy of being the only ASNE president who ever ran the president of the United States out of Washington: Eisenhower was in Augusta playing golf when Prime Minister Castro came to Washington.[73] It wasn't much, but it demonstrated the growing influence of ASNE.

For others, including outgoing President Russell Wiggins, however, the Eisenhower years of the 1950s were not good ones for the society. In his 1960 address, Wiggins noted the strides made in freedom of information but also concluded that some aspects of the society were "downright discouraging":

We have found no one to carry out the great legal work of Harold Cross, and we are not likely to find anyone very soon. We have had the volunteer help of legal counsel of member newspapers, on demand, but this does not fill the real gap. We will never be able to push this contest as energetically as we should until we find another lawyer ready to make this cause his religion. The volunteer help of interested members must be our main reliance, but if it is our sole reliance we are going to fail to undertake many a legal fight we ought to make, and we are not going to even know of some that go by default.[74]

In a surprisingly frank discussion, Wiggins noted that most editors had gained their skills and abilities—their experience—from a prior age. "We are in the midst of changes more profound than those that have occurred over several generations; and I am afraid we have not adjusted our own perceptions to this new age readily enough," he warned. "The professional soldier, we are told, always gets ready to fight the last war, instead of the next one; are we mainly preparing ourselves to meet yesterday's communication challenges rather than tomorrow's? I am afraid so."[75]

As individuals, Wiggins said, ASNE members had little time for the long look ahead or for the reflective and thoughtful appraisal of what their society was doing or what it should be doing: "I must in candor say, on this occasion, that I think that the American Society of Newspaper Editors is not yet geared to the requirements of the next generation of our profession, as the society is now constituted. I think we are part of a profession that is, in many ways, the most important in the country; and I am afraid we do not approach our professional problems as though we thought this was true."[76]

NOTES

1. David Schoenbrun, "Would you trade today for life in the '50s?" *Parade Magazine*, December 6, 1987, 12.

2. French author Jacques Ellul's *The Technological Society* (New York: Vintage Books, 1964) analyzes the technical civilization and its standardizing effect on humankind.

3. Former journalist John Kenneth Galbraith's concern in *The Affluent Society* (New York: Mentor Books, 1958) is with the thralldom of a myth—the myth that production, by its overpowering importance and its ineluctable difficulty, is the central problem of our lives. His book, which added a new phrase to the U.S. language, is listed by Robert Downs as one of the *25 Books That Changed America*.

4. In *The Organization Man* (New York: Doubleday Anchor Book, 1956), William H. Whyte, Jr., argues that modern Americans find the jobs that provide security and a high standard of living and give up the hopes and ambitions that dominated earlier generations.

5. C. Wright Mills does not list the media among *The Power Elite* (New York: Oxford University Press, 1959), which includes celebrities and the Big Rich, the military, politicians and corporation executives. The Columbia University sociologist did see the mass media as a major cause of transformation of America into a mass society.

6. ASNE *Proceedings*, 1960, 28.

7. See John G. Fuller, *The Day We Bombed Utah: America's Most Lethal Secret*, New York: New American Library, 1984.

8. Jay M. Shafritz, *The Dorsey Dictionary of American Government and Politics*, Chicago: Dorsey Press, 1988, 110.

9. For a detailed account of the visit, see "A Long Wait for General MacArthur," Alice Fox Pitts, *Read All About It! 50 Years of ASNE*, Reston, Va.: ASNE, 1974, 278–280. See also "What Really Happened: MacArthur and the Editors," *ASNE Bulletin*, May 1951, 4.

10. Among the members were one past president, Nat Howard, and three ASNE presidents-to-be: Jenkin Lloyd Jones, Virginius Dabney and J. R. Wiggins. The other members were Edward Lindsey and Walter Lippmann. Referred to as a public philosopher, Lippmann earlier spoke to ASNE in 1925 on "Public Opinion."

11. ASNE minutes, October 14–15, 1950, 20A.

12. Ibid., 21A.

13. Quoted in Pitts, 189.

14. ASNE *Proceedings*, 1951, 177.

15. Jack Anderson and James Boyd, *Confessions of a Muckraker*, New York: Ballantine Books, 1979, 242. A personal friend of McCarthy before a "falling out," Anderson reports that by the end of June 1950, more than 40 daily columns and a like percentage of weekly broadcasts had been devoted in whole or in part to discrediting McCarthy's charges and disparaging his pre-crusade record in Washington and Wisconsin.

16. ASNE *Proceedings*, 1950, 98. Also quoted by Pitts, 284.

17. Ibid., 295.

18. Ibid.

19. See ASNE minutes, October 10, 1953, 78A. See also "Comment on the Wechsler Hearings" by the Special Committee on the American Society of Newspaper Editors, August 13, 1953.

20. In addition to Wiggins, members of the special committee which investigated the Wechsler charges were Paul Block, Jr., Herbert Brucker, Raymond L. Crowley, William H. Fitzpatrick, George W. Healey, Jr., L. D. Hotchkiss, Joseph W. Lee, James S. Pope, Eugene S. Pulliam, Jr. and William M. Tugman.

21. "Comment on the Wechsler Hearings," August 13, 1953, included as part of ASNE minutes, October 10, 1953, 1.

22. Russell Wiggins, telephone interview, December 5, 1990.

23. Ibid.

24. Chalmers M. Roberts, *The Washington* Post: *The First 100 Years*, Boston: Houghton Mifflin, 1977, 308.

25. Ibid.

26. Terminology used by ASNE president Loren Ghiglione in letter to Grambs Aronson regarding the account in *The Press and the Cold War*, July 30, 1990.

27. James Wechsler, *Reflections of an Angry Middle-Aged Editor*, New York: Random House, 1960, 139.

28. ASNE *Proceedings*, 1951, 13.

29. Dwight Young, "Objectives of the Year," *ASNE Bulletin*, June 1, 1950, 1.

30. Ibid.

31. ASNE *Proceedings*, 1951, 13. See also ASNE minutes, October 14–15, 1950, 21a.

32. ASNE *Proceedings*, 1960, 26.

33. Raymond Moscowitz, *"Stuffy": The Life of Newspaper Pioneer Basil "Stuffy" Walters*, Ames: Iowa State University Press, 1982, 124.

34. Other ASNE presidents who won Zenger awards were John S. Knight, 1967; J. Edward Murray, 1969; Erwin D. Canham, 1970; and Thomas Winship, 1985.

35. ASNE *Proceedings*, 1960, 22.

36. Other ASNE presidents beside Walters who served as president of the APME were Roy Roberts (1937), Walter M. Harrison (1938), N. R. Howard (1939), George M. Healy, Jr. (1946), Lee Hills (1950), Norman Isaacs (1953), Vincent S. Jones (1955), Michael J. Ogden (1959), J. Edward Murray (1961), John C. Quinn (1973), Richard D. Smyser (1974), Robert P. Clark (1975) and Ed Cony (1980).

37. Moscowitz, 124.

38. Ibid., 125.

39. Pitts, 169.

40. Ibid.

41. Ibid., 72.

42. New York *Times* Biographical Service, December 1985, 1523. See also "Former C J & T, Editor James S. Pope, Sr. Dies," December 15, 1985, E7.

43. James S. Pope, Jr., telephone interview, January 2, 1991; letter to the author, August 2, 1990, 1.

44. Washington *Post*, December 15, 1985, B6.

45. Ibid., B6.

46. George Mills, *Things Just Don't Happen*, Ames: Iowa State University Press, 1977, 163.

47. Kenneth MacDonald, letter to the author, July 30, 1990.

48. *ASNE Bulletin*, June 1, 1955, 1.

49. Ibid.

50. Ibid.

51. *Editor & Publisher*, July 5, 1947. Quoted in Moscowitz, 116.

52. Jenkin Lloyd Jones, "Jenkin Lloyd Jones Answers Walters on Accreditation," *ASNE Bulletin*, date unknown.

53. Ibid.

54. *Editor & Publisher*, July 12, 1947. Quoted by Moscowitz, 117.

55. Letter to Dean Carl W. Ackerman, Graduate School of Journalism, Columbia University, August 3, 1938. Quoted by Herbert Brucker in *Freedom of Information*, New York: Macmillan Co., 1951, 68.

56. Dwight Marvin (for 50 years a *Trojan* editor), interview with Alice Fox Pitts, *ASNE Bulletin*, October 1, 1957, 12.

57. In contrast to 1923, the year ASNE started, when 500 cities had two or more competing dailies (including 100 that had three or more), by 1991 there were only 44 cities where competition existed and 27 where competition was kept alive only through joint operating agreements.

58. Quoted by Roberts, 216.

59. ASNE *Proceedings*, 1952, 11.

60. Jenkin Lloyd Jones, letter to the author, July 16, 1990.

61. *ASNE Bulletin*, August 1956.

62. *ASNE Bulletin*, date unknown, 4.

63. "Few Directors Remain on Board after 7 Years," *ASNE Bulletin*, November 1, 1950, 3.

64. "Limitation of Board Service? Past President Sees No Need for Change in Electing Directors Citing Average of Only 3 1/2 Years Served by Present Members," *ASNE Bulletin*, March 1, 1952, 11.

65. ASNE *Proceedings*, 1955, 86.

66. Ibid., 88.

67. "No Room for Sectionalism," *ASNE Bulletin*, date unknown.

68. Miles H. Wolff, letter to Virginius Dabney, September 6, 1972.

69. Virginius Dabney, letter to Miles Wolff, July 14, 1972. In a letter to the author dated June 5, 1994, Mr. Dabney refused permission to allow reprinting of the contents of the conversation with President Eisenhower because it was made in "complete confidence."

70. Miles H. Wolff, letter to Virginius Dabney, September 6, 1972. Letter in possession of author.

71. Norman Isaacs, letter to the author, March 12, 1992, 3.

72. George W. Healy, Jr., "Presidential Message," *ASNE Bulletin*, date unknown, 3.

73. George W. Healy, Jr., *A Lifetime on Deadline: Self-Portrait of a Southern Journalist*, Gretna, La.: Pelican Publishing Co., 1976, 196.

74. ASNE *Proceedings*, 1960, 27.

75. Ibid., 28.

76. Ibid., 29.

Chapter 6

The 1960s: " . . . our prestigious but somewhat moribund society . . . "

Just about a year ago when I was concluding a hectic year as president of the American Society of Newspaper Editors, my successor (Norman Isaacs), a hard-nosed, hair-shirt wearer, asked me to head up a special committee to attempt reform of our prestigious but somewhat moribund society, which is composed of 700 of the nation's top newspapers.
—Vincent S. Jones, Gannett Newspapers, ASNE president, 1968–1969,
paper for the Humdrum Club, March 2, 1970

Shortly before he was elected president in April 1969, Norman E. Isaacs responded dramatically to ASNE's most tumultuous decade since it had been founded nearly 50 years before. The first non-American-born[1] journalist to head the society, the Louisville *Courier-Journal* editor was also one of the most vocal gadflies of American journalism and ASNE. Although he had been editor of the *Bulletin* and chairman of the committee on technology, Isaacs had not achieved what he needed to achieve to nudge ASNE into the main currents of a troubled nation.

Racial turmoil, civil rights issues, a youth rebellion, an unpopular war in Vietnam and ongoing efforts by government to restrict the free flow of information created serious challenges for the editors. Over the years Isaacs' colleagues in both the APME[2] and ASNE had rejected ideas for stronger ethics committees, outside media councils and serious reform in general. But Isaacs said he was too supercharged to be quiet.

"I think my own greatest asset—and maybe my own worst failing—is that I have a sense of mission," Isaacs once confided to colleague and former ASNE president Michael J. Ogden of the Providence *Journal and Bulletin*. "I'm an evangelist. I'm always preaching the way journalism ought to be. I try to instill things in the young guys. Whether I like a kid doesn't matter. I don't care if he's sassy or whatever, so long as he can produce. When I was on the firing line, I operated that way. I think I did things—for instance, that I changed the [Indianapolis] *Times* from a boisterous five-penny dreadful into a damn good civic-minded, responsible operation. A lot of us ought to make things happen. Instead, we stand around in bars talking about things we never accomplish."[3] When kindred spirit Vincent S. Jones handed over the ASNE gavel to him as incoming president in 1969, Isaacs said, "When I raise hell with the calling it is because I love it and want desperately for it to be better than it is."[4]

Before assuming the presidency, Isaacs told directors at the Shoreham Hotel that he and Jones had discussed "the persistent pressure on journalism." They considered recommending that the society seek out a major foundation to fund a broad, rigorous, unbiased study to assess the state of journalism. "The more we examined it, however," Isaacs said, "the more we were agreed that desirable as this might be, there was one necessary first step—a good look at the ASNE's own role."

Picking at old scabs, Isaacs once again referred to the ASNE founders' "knuckling under" to Fred Bonfils. He contrasted Bonfils with perennial patron saint William Allen White:

Perhaps it is much too late to make ASNE into a really select group instead of dispensing automatic prestige on the basis of circulation and a cashable check. There probably are several editors around this nation cut on the mold of William Allen White, but whose credentials are not measured on the merits of their papers, but rather on the basis of ABC's ledger clerks' testimony. There may be other serious flaws of our approach through the arbitrary structure of which we are merely the currently elected guardians.[5]

With Jones' approval, Isaacs submitted to the board a proposal for "a special committee of only five men to appraise the society and to present to the board at the earliest possible time consistent with serious deliberation, their recommendations as to the possible steps we might take to raise the society's sights and effectiveness, both for the membership and for the profession in general."[6] As committee members, Isaacs nominated Jones as chairman, John S. Knight, the society's oldest active ex-president; Otis Chandler of the Los Angeles *Times*, "the youngest of the dynamic new editor-publishers"; James Reston, "the newest of our members who is also one of the top figures in journalism"[7] and Isaacs' boss at the *Courier-Journal*, Barry Bingham, "who has the esteem of editors all over the world."[8]

A longtime member of ASNE, Bingham was an Isaacs favorite because he had supported Isaacs' move from eight- to six-column journalism and because he supported interpretive journalism in his Louisville papers. In the previous decade, Louisville editor James S. Pope had attacked interpretive journalism as "subjective and a means to translate, elucidate, construe in the light of individual belief or interest." To Pope (and many others in ASNE), interpretation was "the bright dream of saintly seers going beyond the scope of objective journalism."

On the other hand, Bingham argued that interpretive reporting became more necessary each week. Because of Bingham's insistence, the *Courier-Journal* became a major leader in interpretive journalism.[9] Bingham and the other committee members seemed naturals for what Isaacs envisioned to help reform the society.

Isaacs' recommendations were added to those of others in a bubbling of ideas for rejuvenation and reform which seemed to surface in ASNE every decade or so. In particular, Isaacs challenged the "glacial" progress of his profession in a decade of rapid change characterized by serious urban problems and accompanied by criticism of the media by the public, study commissions and the media themselves. Jones made a similar observation about the slow-moving society when he noted that Isaacs, "a hard-nosed, hair-shirt wearer," asked him to head up a special committee "to attempt the reform of our prestigious but somewhat moribund society, which is composed of 700 of the nation's top newspapers."[10] In a speech entitled "Does America Need a Press Council?" Jones publicly wondered what would come of all this: "Those of us in the ASNE leadership who have pushed this idea of an Ethics Committee have done so with the certain knowledge that its establishment might easily tear the society apart. This risk we have been willing to take because we believe that a smaller more vigorous society could be of more use to our profession and to the public that we are trying to serve."[11]

The concerns of Jones, Isaacs and outside observers as the 1960s drew to a convulsive conclusion differed little from the concerns articulated by Wiggins in 1960 when he said he did not think ASNE was geared to the requirements of the next generation of the profession.[12] In another broadside, Herbert Brucker claimed that the society vigorously repudiated "the concept of a referee, or policeman sitting in judgment upon and seeking to enforce, if only through some appeal to public opinion, conformance to a standard of performance which the referee may see as desirable in the public interest."[13] Brucker concluded that there was little chance of improvement because the society itself was a "continuing committee of the whole on self-examination and self-improvement. In other words, right back to home base: don't do anything."[14]

In contrast to the four firebrand presidents of the era—Wiggins, Brucker, Jones and Isaacs—the other presidents provided steady if not critical leadership. They focused their energy, office and talents on other areas essential to govern the society. They agreed with Wiggins' oft-used description of ASNE as "an organization which, if any more loosely organized, would fall apart, and if any more closely organized would be a menace." Turner Catledge of the New York *Times* told the 1961 convention: "We have tried to steer a middle course, and my administration closes in a state of purity, at least as far as any work is concerned."[15]

It was Catledge and a group of "elder statesmen," principally former presidents of the society, who Isaacs said had also killed the idea of a trial run for an

American Press Council patterned after the one that had proved itself in the British Isles. In particular, Isaacs blamed Catledge as the most vigorous antagonist of the idea that had increased in popularity after the directors held their 1969 fall meeting in London to assess the work of the British press council first-hand:

A man of immense Southern charm, one of the great raconteurs of his time, he was widely popular among fellow editors. Hence in both the personal sense and his newspaper connections, he wielded extensive influence. One of his arguments was greatly persuasive with many members. Journalism, he maintained, was not a profession like law and medicine and no editor had the right to pass judgment on what other papers did; editors had to be responsible to themselves for what was published and how, and the editors' society was threatening to impugn the integrity of editors by imposing a committee to pass judgment on whatever decisions they made in good faith. He let us all know that he intended to rise on the floor and to move for a hand-counted open vote.[16]

The same middle-road approach governed the administrations of Felix R. McKnight, Lee Hills, Miles H. Wolff, Vermont C. Royster, Robert C. Notson and Michael J. Ogden during the turbulent sixties as the society deflected attacks on its credibility and that of journalism as a whole. Journalism found itself challenged by a growing number of commissions, as well as the general public, into the 1970s. In 1964 the American press was chastised for its poor coverage of the assassination of President John F. Kennedy and for excessive detail concerning suspect Lee Harvey Oswald. Such charges were disputed by the Dallas *Times-Herald*'s McKnight. In a moving article in the *Bulletin*, McKnight described "a Texas editor's agony after the Kennedy assassination" and, despite the Warren Commission's charges, defended the press and his hometown against critics:

The indictment of an American city by a few drags American journalism to gutter stature. On a towering opposite, most of the American press held a terrible catastrophe in perspective—notably the *Wall Street Journal*, Nashville *Banner*, the Chicago press, and countless others. The offenders—some newspapers, magazines and the networks who suffered poisonous darts from context and rekindled fires of hatred from the death of a man who loathed them—need agonizing self-examination.[17]

"If I sound like an anguished man, I am," McKnight wrote. "In these past days my faith has been blunted by a few who misused their trust. I pray this experience never happens to you in your city. It is the saddest story in this world to cover." The charges made by the commission were also disputed by an ASNE press-bar committee, which was headed by Alfred Friendly of the Washington *Post*. The committee challenged the bar's unproven thesis that press coverage is a threat to a fair trial.

Four years later, the Report of the National Advisory Commission on Civil Disorders (Kerner Commission) called attention to the American press' inadequate coverage of the civil rights movement, claiming that the lack of coverage contributed in part to the creation of two Americas, one black and one white: "Events of these past few years—the Watts riots, other disorders, and the growing momentum of the civil rights movement—conditioned the responses of readers and viewers and heightened their reactions. What the public saw and read last summer thus produced emotional reactions and left vivid impressions not wholly attributable to the material itself."[18]

C. A. (Pete) McKnight, then the editor of the Charlotte *Observer*, made a similar observation while moderating a 1968 panel discussion on "Conflict in the Cities." Recalling his 1955 ASNE speech after the Supreme Court decision on desegregation, McKnight noted that the story had been much more important than editors had realized and that the race issue was more a national story than a southern one. He pointed out that between 1940 and 1950 the black population of the South had increased only 8 percent, while in other areas it had increased 50 percent.

"Over the years our public officials and our newspapers have paid a good deal of attention to the physical aspects of urbanization and not enough attention to the human beings caught up in and crushed down by the cold and unfeeling forces of urbanization," McKnight said in 1968. "So today we have conflict and violence in our cities, some of it understandable, some of it irrational; some of it racial, some of it class; some of it treatable, some of it yet defying diagnosis, much less treatment."[19]

Other critics and scholars charged that with the exception of a few outstanding newspapers, ASNE and the American media had abdicated responsibility for news coverage at home and abroad. In the past, criticism had focused on such issues as journalism schools which produced what the New York *Post* called "clerks of fact," or on monopoly ownership by publishers who cared little about professionalism and everything about profits, or on the fact that newspaper unions had become conservative under the auspices of nonwriting commercial employees with a seniority system and advertisers' influence on content. Now, however, the criticism was aimed at news coverage. The *Village Voice*'s Jack Newfield's criticism of 1960s journalism was "simply that it is blind to an important part of reality, that it just doesn't print all of the truth. It has a built-in value system that influences every editorial, every decision on hiring, what syndicated columnist to buy, what stories to cover, what copy to spike, what reporters to promote."[20]

In an article in the *Dutton Review*, Newfield said that Vice President Spiro Agnew's charges of an effete conspiracy were correct, but for the wrong reasons. "A few individuals do control the mass media in America. Only most of them are Republicans and conservatives." But Newfield also attacked the knee-jerk liberals and panicked network moguls who had responded to Agnew's jeremiad against the media by screaming "government censorship." "The disturbing reality is that the press censors itself, through superficiality, through bias, through incompetence, and through a desire to be the responsible fourth branch of government," Newfield said.

Newfield's charge that the media were controlled primarily by Republicans and conservatives was only partially accurate from the ASNE point of view. Its editors were widely scattered over the political and ideological spectrum from 1922 to 1991. A study of the 65 ASNE presidents, however, indicates that they were evenly distributed over a seven-point spectrum ranging from conservative Republican to liberal Democrat. Instead of following a single, stereotyped approach to politics and social issues, the editors both led and followed the American public, which was becoming more conservative during this period.[21] As puckishly noted by editor Jack Knight, the editors were "prolicons" progressive in outlook, liberal toward humanity and fiscally conservative (see Appendix D).

ASNE RESPONSE TO MEDIA CRITICISM

The growing criticism of journalism in general, and of ASNE in particular, during the 1960s should not detract from efforts to effect positive change. Such reforms, though limited, exceed those of ASNE's previous half-century. Efforts were made to combat growing attempts at legislative, executive and court control of the media and to respond to the public's criticisms regarding racism and the Vietnam War. These efforts to reform were aided by a growing number of reviews, books and articles written by both academics and professionals.

Along with others, Herbert Brucker filled the vacuum created by the loss of Carl Ackerman and other internal critics of ASNE. Brucker was a Columbia University graduate who helped lead the ASNE fight for freedom of information along with Wiggins, Creed Black, Brady Black, J. Edward Murray and others. Described by Dwight E. Sargent as "one of the driving spirits of American journalism," Brucker was well respected in academic circles, as well as in his profession, as the author of four books that helped provide philosophic backing for youth in the 1960s. Loren Ghiglione, ASNE president in 1989, remembers meeting Brucker when he (Ghiglione) was editor of the weekly at Haverford College, "a Quaker institution that treated journalism with about the same contempt that it displayed toward U.S. army recruiters."[22] Ghiglione believed "Herb was one of journalism's leaders, not just because of his presidency of the ASNE, but because he knew what was truly important."

In the previous decade Brucker decried Senator Joseph McCarthy's attacks on the press. He protested the Eisenhower administration's ban on reporters traveling to China. He backed sunshine laws to open government meetings to the press and the public and served as the first chairman of the Connecticut FOI commission. He endorsed press councils at a time when most editors regarded them as meddlesome institutions peopled by Benedict Arnolds.[23]

Four of Brucker's books symbolize the changes American journalism was experiencing. As noted by J. Herbert Altschull, "We need not fear to divide the years into decades, all with general descriptions—the conservative '50s, the revolutionary '60s, the complacent '70s, the transitional '80s. As central figures in their society during these decades, journalists in general have been equally conservative, revolutionary, complacent and transitional."[24] Brucker's first book, *The Changing American Newspaper* (1937), stressed that the mission of the newspaper had changed little since the first newspaper, *Publick Occurrences*, appeared in 1690. *Freedom of Information* (1949), Brucker's second book, explored the mores of the American newspaper and raised embarrassingly pertinent questions. *Journalist, Eyewitness to History* (1962) was essentially a guide for college students who were considering journalism as a career. His fourth book, *Communication Is Power: Unchanging Values in Unchanging Journalism* (1973), further analyzed the media's problems in the 1960s and openly discussed the ambivalence of journalists and ASNE in regard to issues such as the Hutchins Commission's recommendations.[25] "It is characteristic of the endless debate over this issue," he wrote, "that we boldly attacked the subject by expressing belief that the society, in the interest of the freest possible discussion of all public issues, should welcome critical studies of the press made in good faith by independent agencies," Brucker wrote. "But alas, the press is always thus marching up the hill to battle for the Lord, only to march down again."[26]

CHALLENGING PRESIDENT KENNEDY

One example of ASNE members' "marching up the hill" to confront a foe was when the Freedom of Information Committee challenged the Kennedy administration's attempts to manage news. Notwithstanding John F. Kennedy's image of being friendly with the press, and his appearances at ASNE meetings in 1960, 1961 and 1963, all was not as it appeared. ASNE minutes and other documents indicate that at least five times Kennedy and his aides attempted to control the press, from "management" to "outright lies," which were defended by Assistant Secretary of Defense for Public Affairs Arthur Sylvester.

As early as April 19, 1961, Eugene S. Pulliam, Jr., of the Indianapolis *News*, chairman of the committee on information, noted the discrepancy between Kennedy's rhetoric and actions, both before the 1960 election and after. Although Kennedy had written that he supported freedom of information,

Pulliam claimed that neither he nor his administration actually respected the principle. The defense and state departments in particular were keeping quiet, Pulliam charged in a report to board members.[27] Press Secretary Pierre Salinger had also purportedly upheld the principles of openness. "But as of this writing he has never answered a series of nine questions governing specific instances involving withholding of news," Pulliam said. Despite a letter sent two months before the meeting, Pulliam stated that Salinger had not responded. "To date, he hasn't, and there have been increasing complaints from the Washington press corps, most of them justified."[28]

If the media's response to the Bay of Pigs invasion of Cuba in 1961 is any example, however, Kennedy's animosity toward the press was not justified. At least three different accounts of the event indicate that requests from the Kennedy administration, as well as from James Reston, caused the New York *Times* to tone down its use of the word *imminent* before running Tad Szulc's exclusive story before the CIA-sponsored invasion ended in disaster. Although many newspapers had voluntarily censored copy, President Kennedy, in a speech before the ANPA in Dallas on April 27, asked newspapers to impose self-censorship. "Every newspaper now asks itself with respect to every story, 'Is it news?' All I suggest is that you add the question, 'Is it in the interest of the national security?'"

This speech so disturbed a number of society members that they went to the White House with ASNE president Turner Catledge to ask what Kennedy meant. When the president recalled a January 10 *Times* story about the invasion, Catledge noted that the essential details of the invasion had been reported by many papers. "But it was not news until it appeared in the *Times*," the president smiled. But at the same time, Kennedy called Catledge aside to tell him, "Maybe if you had printed more about the operation you would have saved us from a colossal mistake."[29] In his biographical remembrances, Catledge also criticized James Reston, who had yielded to Kennedy's requests to tone down the story: "He came to this country from Scotland when he was young, and perhaps his affection for it is even greater than if he had been native-born. I remember well his fascination with America and American folklore when we made a political scouting trip across the country in 1944."[30] "In the case of the Bay of Pigs story," Catledge said, "Scotty allowed his news judgment to be influenced by his patriotism. My own interest was less elevated—I wanted to print the story as fully as possible."[31]

Felix McKnight also recalled what he described as a highly successful discussion with Kennedy in the Oval Office—a three-hour, gloves-off give-and-take over a suggested government-imposed peacetime censorship. Kennedy's aides—Salinger and special assistants Theodore C. Sorensen and Arthur Schlesinger—were urging the president to implement such a policy after the Bay of Pigs fiasco. They contended that premature press accounts had ruined the invasion. McKnight said that the president had called him and requested that the presidents of ASNE, ANPA, AP, and UPI and representatives of the New York *Times* and Scripps Howard meet in his office. The press officials met in Washington, agreed on a statement of principles, and went to the White House the following morning. McKnight recalls that President Kennedy sat in a rocking chair, surrounded by the journalists and the "Three S's."

The President had a stack of folders in front of him containing alleged violations of national security that appeared in the American press. He only fingered the Bay of Pigs file and made a rather moderate charge that the invasion had gone awry because of premature stories. Turner Catledge, then managing editor of the New York *Times*, made an adequate rebuttal after lengthy discussions. Leaks from the White House were established and the President was annoyed. Frequently, his three aides sent over handwritten memos for his information that he turned face down and never used. We spoke frankly on both sides for a couple of hours—neither side pulling punches—and finally the President concluded the meeting with his own thoughts.[32]

Generally, Kennedy said, he abhorred censorship. He said that there would be no peacetime censorship, that he would unofficially recognize the same group of editors as a sort of "standing committee," and that if the need for further discussion arose, he would reconvene the same principals. "We never met again and the issue died," McKnight said.

Kennedy also instructed Salinger to sit down with McKnight, prepare a statement in his name and go outside to face a news conference: "Which we did. We did not get tough shafting the White House reporters and the publicized censorship threat just went away."[33]

Kennedy's inconsistency in dealing with the editors had a sequel in 1967, when the president's brother addressed ASNE's annual convention. In his remarks, Robert Kennedy said that the president had admitted that if the Bay of Pigs incident had been discussed more thoroughly in the media the fiasco might never have occurred.[34]

Such ongoing efforts to keep the flow of information open can further be seen in the leadership of ASNE and a handful of other journalists following the Cuban missile crisis. Despite recent attempts at revisionist history arguing that the media was negligent for not challenging the Kennedy account that the Russian missiles were a Russian offensive rather than defensive maneuver, ASNE and other public accounts show the following:

1. ASNE, through its Freedom of Information Committee chaired by John H. Colburn of the Wichita *Eagle and Beacon* and Creed Black of the Wilmington *News-Journal*, officially challenged the Kennedy administration's ongoing attempts at news management in general and in particular in regard to the missile crisis.

2. Of editors attending the Sigma Delta Chi convention, 52 disapproved of the Kennedy administration's handling of the Cuban problem, 44 were in favor.

3. Further public interest in the Cuban missile crisis issue was stimulated in other articles by Ben Bagdikian in the *Saturday Evening Post*, Hanson Baldwin in *Atlantic Magazine*, and Arthur Krock in *Fortune*.

4. As a result of the questions raised by the Kennedy administration's distortion of the crisis, and other news management, a Congressional inquiry was held on the issue. Among those testifying before the subcommittee on foreign operations and government information were Herbert Brucker, ASNE vice president, and Creed Black, member of the ASNE Freedom of Information Committee.

Although American journalists and institutions continued to rally around the flag as they had done in World War II, not all of them were taken in by the Kennedy administration. Skepticism from ASNE and others, including the National Association of Broadcasters and the American Newspaper Publisher's Association, coupled with the leadership of California Congressman John E. Moss, helped pave the way for the passage of the Freedom of Information Act (FOIA) and challenges concerning the Vietnam War in the same decade.

ASNE RELATIONS WITH PRESIDENT JOHNSON

Similar adversarial relations prevailed between the ASNE and President Johnson, who was drawn into the Vietnam quagmire which had been accelerated by Kennedy. In April 1963, Creed Black, chairman of the Freedom of Information Committee, reported on State Department policies about information from South Vietnam and on Senator Russell Long's bill to open government records to the press. Black advised the committee to retain a staff person with legal background to follow trends in the freedom of information fight and to assess legal aspects, as Harold Cross had done.[35]

In 1971, at the height of the controversy over the Pentagon Papers, Black testified before the House Subcommittee on Foreign Operations and Government Operations that the ASNE had been protesting government secrecy and manipulation over the Vietnam War during the period covered by the Pentagon Papers. Citing a 1967 report, Black recalled that Johnson's administration was the main factor in the credibility equation: "President Johnson continues to hurt his image and his credibility by consistently trying to make the news sound better than it is. The tendency, although evident with respect to many kinds of news, is most damaging in connection with Vietnam. The war has escalated to the accompaniment of an almost unbroken succession of pronouncements that it was going in the opposite direction, or at least that something else was happening."[36]

"A real paradox remains," Black wrote. "It is that an open society is trying to run a war against a closed society without imposing censorship, and this, instead of building confidence in the democratic process, has the opposite effect of widening the credibility gap." Black said that his committee had asked one top editor, who had representation in both Vietnam and Washington, about the adequacy of war reporting. The unnamed editor replied: "I do not think management of the Vietnam news is excessive. Indeed, I think a good case can be made for the institution of the sort of military censorship which would have applied had this been a properly declared war."[37]

Such views were rare, however, and not reflected in subsequent FOI committee reports on the increasing gap between the people, the press and their government. One example: "The credibility gap yawns wider in the Johnson administration than it did in preceding regimes, largely because the administration follows a policy of obscurantism for its own sake. All administrations manipulate the news to greater or lesser extent; all have been known to conceal, exaggerate, belittle, distort and even lie about important information when it served their interests to do so."[38]

"Coping with this is the task of every Washington reporter, and the ability to cope with it is what separates the men from the boys," FOI chairman Brady Black of the Cincinnati *Enquirer* wrote. "But under LBJ the coping is immeasurably more difficult because official deceit is practiced both when there is a reason for it and when there is not."[39]

ASNE MEMBERS CHALLENGE VIETNAM CONFLICT

ASNE members varied in their responses to the United States role in Vietnam. For example, the Washington *Post*'s Russell Wiggins, whom Johnson later rewarded with an ambassadorship to the United Nations, questioned without being overcritical. Like many other ASNE editors of the 1960s, Wiggins was "not a mindless hawk." According to Chalmers Roberts, Wiggins was repelled by the all-out-war proponents: "Essentially, like many of his generation within the administration, Wiggins was influenced by the memory of the democracies' failure to check the aggression that led to World War II. This was a central theme of *Post* editorials on Vietnam and no amount of argument that Vietnam bore no resemblance to Europe could shake Wiggins from his principle."[40]

Other editors were more critical. John S. Knight, who had been a censor in World War II, stated his position when he accepted the prestigious John Peter Zenger award. The '60s were precarious times, Knight noted. Americans were being deceived by their own government about the nation's entanglement in Southeast Asia. "The President forgets his responsibility to the people. It is one thing to hide facts which Hanoi, Peking or the Viet Cong don't know, and another thing entirely to misinform the public for no real security purpose."[41] According to biographer Charles Whited, Vietnam was a crucible, and Knight beheld the nation tumbling headlong into it. "So Knight, an Ohio Republican, social peer of pillars of conservatism, defended the ragged hordes of dissent, the hordes who smoked pot, listened to outrageous rock music, and wore the flag sewn on their tattered jeans."[42]

Another ASNE leader who challenged U.S. involvement in the Vietnam War was Georgia-born Eugene Patterson. A World War II veteran and former wire service reporter, Patterson had won a Pulitzer Prize for commentary on the racial crisis. Not until he joined the Washington *Post* did Patterson reverse his position on Vietnam. According to columnist Nicholas Von Hoffman, Patterson changed his mind when the Vietnam veterans bivouacked on Independence Mall: "This time they came to march to the Capitol and return the medals by throwing them on the marble steps. Gene, the news man, the editor, the father, the citizen and the old soldier had to go down and talk to those young soldiers spending the night in pup tents and sleeping bags."[43]

Patterson told the protesters, Von Hoffman said, how the older men in the news business, men he respected and had worked with, convinced him that Henry Wallace's third party movement was the impractical, ever-receding movement for peace. Patterson said he thought the young veterans who were illegally parked on the mall were making the same fight for peace he wished he'd gone on making as a young man. Von Hoffman concluded that he never thought "ASNE would make such a fine man its president. Not that I approve," he added. "Patterson has been misleading the public for years by giving the newspaper business a better reputation than it deserves."[44]

Vermont Royster, ASNE president in 1965, also questioned the Vietnam War. In his position as the chief editorial writer of the *Wall Street Journal* and as author of *The American Press and the Revolutionary Tradition*,[45] *Journey through the Soviet Union*[46] and *My Own, My Country's Time: A Journalist's Journey*,[47] he portrayed the loyalties and conflicts of many ASNE members during the 1960s—particularly in regard to the war. In his autobiography, Royster recalls a 1963 conversation he had with Henry Morgenthau while in Saigon: "What are we doing in this country, anyway?" he asked. "Having travelled over as much of the country as was thought militarily secure, I had no satisfactory answer. I never found one, but I regret it was a long time before I would let the *Journal* pose the same question publicly. I was too long intimidated by the idea of 'responsibility' to support American policy."[48]

Although the *Wall Street Journal* challenged Kennedy's Vietnam policy from the start, its critical editorials moved slowly toward support of the war.[49]

On May 25–26, 1967, explaining Vietnam in its political context, the paper reluctantly acquiesced to the Johnson administration's policy, using logic that influenced other newspaper agendas: "In both national policy and political tactics we think the Administration's least unfavorable course is more or less the current one, unless there is a sudden shift in the context of the war. . . . The full scale U.S. commitment is only two years old, after all. . . . Though it may be sad to say, the best course may be to hang on and hope."[50]

Following the Tet offensive, which had threatened even the American embassy in Saigon in 1968, the *Journal* published several editorials demanding that the United States pull out of the war-torn nation: "The people must prepare for the bitter taste of a defeat beyond America's power to prevent." Written jointly by Royster and Joseph E. Evans, the editorials were picked up by press and wire services and widely distributed and reprinted.[51]

In addition to the Vietnam War, Royster said that the racial problems that divided the country made it difficult for him to support Johnson against Barry Goldwater in the 1964 presidential campaign. As usual, Royster said, his editorials endorsed neither candidate. Unlike prior elections, when most newspapers and ASNE editors had endorsed Republican candidates, most endorsements in 1964 were for Johnson, the Democratic candidate. Writing in 1983, Royster said that he still could not say whether Barry Goldwater would have been a successful president.

It's clear, though, he could hardly have done worse. The next four years of Lyndon Johnson would turn into a shambles for the country, at home and abroad. As he enlarged the war in Vietnam, sending more Americans to fight for Asian boys, getting us deeper into a land war in Asia, all his campaign promises about "peace for all Americans as long as I am President" came to have a hollow ring. On that score the country might as well have elected Goldwater.[52]

Notwithstanding his distaste for Johnson's inconsistencies and hypocrisy in handling international affairs, Royster used the president's operating procedures as a model for some of his dealings within the ASNE. Spotting an inconsistency and injustice in the nominating and voting system, Royster enumerated the problems, prescribed new wording for parts of the constitution and made it simple to remedy a serious defect in the organization. One member said, "If it didn't risk insulting Vermont, I would say that in knowledge and mechanics of the operations of ASNE's government, he is our LBJ."[53]

RETURNING TO AN INTERNATIONAL OUTLOOK

Royster pulled off a major coup in convincing ASNE members to hold their annual meeting in Montreal, Quebec, Canada. Although ASNE had left

Washington, D.C., for previous conferences in Atlantic City, New York City, San Francisco and New Orleans, the 1966 meeting was the first outside United States borders. During this period the society also formally resumed its foreign involvement, which had shifted to a back burner in the 1950s. This change was highlighted by trips to the Soviet Union in 1962 and 1969. These were followed in 1972 by what was later described as the society's most significant trip abroad, a journey to the People's Republic of China.

As executive editor of the Dallas *Times-Herald*, McKnight led 12 ASNE members on a 23-day visit through the Soviet Union in 1962, during which a news-gathering tour turned into a long-standing debate on free enterprise versus communism. McKnight recalls that the following year a delegation of Soviet journalists came to the United States, and ASNE reciprocated by hosting them around the country. "The whole project opened some doors that had been tightly closed—particularly for those Western journalists who had been tightly held within the parameters of the Moscow area."[54]

McKnight was followed in the ASNE presidency by Lee Hills, an executive for the Knight Newspapers. Former president of the Associated Press Managing Editors (APME), the Inter-American Press Association and Sigma Delta Chi, Hills had gained national attention for his efforts to bring about the transition from the personal newspaper chains of the pre– and post–World War II periods to modern media companies. Along with other ASNE leaders, Hills helped to shape the old-fashioned newspapers of the past into those that defined newpaper ownership in the 1960s and beyond: chain ownership, local monopolies, joint-operating agreements, cross-media ownership of newspaper and television stations in the same city, and media conglomerates.

North Dakota–born, but raised in Utah, Hills was one of the most important of the post–World War II editors who brought about fundamental and often radical changes in newspapers, accommodating daily journalism to the increased tempo of modern living. He emphasized writing that was terse, colloquial, and designed to explain complex issues in terms that could be grasped quickly by readers with heavy demands on their time. He redesigned newspapers to give them greater eye appeal through the increased use of bold headlines, white space and pictures. Hills strongly believed that newspapers could better serve the public by utilizing surveys and other available information on that public. He also advocated better interpretive and investigative reporting, believing that newspapers often fail to get at the facts underlying a news development because of their "obsession with objectivity."[55]

Despite being overshadowed by his boss, John S. Knight, Hills helped introduce or refine such management techniques as recruitment and personnel testing. Many of his ideas were continued through other Knight-Ridder leaders, such as C. A. (Pete) McKnight, Don Shoemaker, James K. Batten, Bill Baker, Rolfe Neill, Eugene Roberts and David Lawrence, Jr., also members of ASNE.

FULL-TIME SECRETARIAT

Much of the society's success in traveling abroad and challenging government censorship resulted from the creation of a full-time secretariat. Since the society's inception, ASNE officers had used makeshift facilities and filing systems. In the 1960s ASNE's first full-time offices were created. Hills noted that when he became president in 1962, ASNE was in an important transition period, with new headquarters, new financial problems and a new secretariat. In one of many tributes to the outgoing Pitts couple, Herbert Brucker noted the influence of an efficient staff:

ASNE presidents come and go. They make about as much imprint on affairs in their care as the French ministers in the revolving door cabinets of pre-de Gaulle days. But the Pittses have gone on forever. Alice Pitts, as executive secretary, functions behind the scenes. But she is the one who has told and still does tell ASNE presidents what to do and how to do it. And Freddy presides over *The Bulletin*. This is the cohesive force of ASNE, the bond that holds us all together between conventions whether we come to Washington or not.[56]

The new executive secretary of the society, replacing the Pittses, was Angelo (Gene) Giancarlo, former secretary to Turner Catledge of the New York *Times*. A native of Allentown, Pennsylvania, Giancarlo had been involved with society affairs since 1954, when he assisted Catledge in his job as ASNE program chairman. Giancarlo had also served as an aide to Felix McKnight at the New Orleans convention. Giancarlo's appointment, which began January 1, 1963, at a $10,000 annual salary, coincided with ASNE's shifting headquarters from Wilmington, Delaware, to the ANPA offices in New York City.[57]

The administration of Herbert Brucker was followed in 1964 by that of Miles Hoffman Wolff, executive editor of the Greensboro (N.C.) *Daily News*. The son of the president of Gaston College, Wolff taught high school briefly before entering newspaper work in North Carolina. After a stint as the Baltimore AP bureau chief, he joined the Baltimore Sun papers. In his unpublished autobiography, Wolff describes how he was fired from his post as managing editor of the Baltimore *Evening Sun* after Neil Swanson claimed he was "not capable of handling a metropolitan paper."[58] Wolff spent many years with both APME and ASNE, serving as chairman of the *ASNE Bulletin*. He became ASNE president during urban riots and the Vietnam War controversy, both of which were major items on ASNE convention programs.

HIRING LEGAL HELP

In addition to creating a full-time secretariat, ASNE retained two prominent attorneys to promote freedom of the press and to litigate cases involving that issue. The minutes state: "When the board has voted to intervene in a case, discussion brought out the feeling that intervention in certain cases is a proper function of the society, that the number of such cases may increase, and that each case would have to be examined in view of budgetary considerations."[59]

The first attorney retained after the death of Harold Cross was William P. Rogers, former attorney general under President Dwight Eisenhower. Rogers remained for nearly three years. During this period his annual fees were $1,500. Then the board suggested that he be replaced by Richard Cardwell of the Indiana Press Association, who it hoped would perform "more energetically" on behalf of the society.[60] Rogers returned to the ASNE meetings in 1969 as secretary of state for newly elected President Richard M. Nixon. "No appointment by President Nixon could have been more popular with American editors than that of William P. Rogers as Secretary of State," Norman Isaacs said in his introduction. "As everyone here knows, the secretary served for some years as ASNE's counsel with high skill, a sure knowledge of newspaper problems and with that unusual blend of strength and charm that has made him so effective and appealing as friend, as lawyer and as public official."[61] Rogers joked that when he worked for ASNE he filed the client under a category entitled "High Prestige, Low Pay." His secretary thought ASNE stood for "Always Some New Excuse."[62] Richard M. Schmidt, Jr., followed Cardwell on December 1, 1968. He had served as head of the United States Information Agency until his appointment.[63] A Democrat by registration but an appointee of many Republican officials, Schmidt helped ASNE file friend-of-the-court briefs in numerous cases of the 1960s to protect journalists' sources and provide greater access to public records.

CHALLENGING COURT INTERFERENCE WITH INFORMATION

ASNE presidents and board members had another serious problem during the 1960s: proposals to restrict coverage of court proceedings.[64] Much of this concern was caused by the outcome of the *Sheppard* v. *Maxwell* case, which was brought about by the Cleveland media's sensational reporting and by the American Bar Association (ABA) Reardon Committee's subsequent recommendations to control activities of both the bar and the media. These recommendations proposed to restrict release of prejudicial information by officers of the court and by others involved in proceedings—lawyers, defendants, witnesses, court personnel, and law enforcement officers. The committee recommended the issuing of contempt citations to anyone who disseminated information that affected the outcome of a trial or who violated a court order not to reveal information disclosed in the courtroom.

Even before the publication of the Reardon Committee's findings, the ASNE directors approved a motion praising the committee's highly informative report and instructing FOI and Press-Bar Chairman J. Edward Murray of the Detroit *Free Press* to continue discussions with the committee. However, the board was concerned that limitation of information at the arrest stage might pose challenges to the American system of an open arrest book.[65]

Alfred Friendly's carefully reasoned ASNE Press-Bar Committee report, which was issued at the 1965 convention, had little effect on Reardon's prestigious ABA committee. "In all our meetings with him," Murray reported, "Justice Reardon personally was urbane, gracious, charming and seemingly the personality of conciliatory approach. But he was also iron-willed." When the massive report became available, Reardon told ASNE it was only tentative, and subject to modification through criticism. But such was not the case. Murray told the 1967 convention:

I think all of us realize that freedom of information lost rather than gained during the year because the Supreme Court and the American Bar Association simply scared a lot of lawyers and policemen into suppression of legitimate news. The fallout was fierce from the Sheppard decision and the Reardon Report. Lawyers and judges . . . overreacted atrociously to both, carrying lesser law enforcement people in their wake . . . The mere possibility that the tentative Reardon proposals for news restrictions may eventually be formalized is causing almost daily attempts to muzzle the press so law enforcement can operate behind closed doors.[66]

Robert C. Notson of the Portland *Oregonian,* ASNE president in 1966, helped ASNE fight bar intrusion on the people's right to know. With much experience in covering the courts, Notson served five years on the Oregon Commission on the Judicial Branch. Many of the commission's recommendations for the Oregon courts were adopted. Notson helped to organize the ASNE Bar, Press and Broadcasters Committee, which created a set of guidelines adopted by some 25 states in varying forms. These guidelines were designed to ease growing hostility between the bar and the news media concerning the public's right to know and the right of a fair trial.[67]

Notson also helped formulate Oregon's voluntary bar-press "Statement of Principles," which became a national signpost toward responsible journalism in reference to police and court matters.[68] On both the local and national levels, Notson worked for press and bar understanding and for open meetings and open records. Congress adopted the open records law during Notson's ASNE administration, and despite some tart exchanges with staff, the bills gained the approval of President Johnson.[69]

A highlight of Notson's ASNE presidency was his address to the Georgia Press Association on Free Press and Fair Trial. This followed a rejoinder to the Reardon report. At that time it appeared that the bar and the courts were moving to suppress most pretrial information; Notson pointed out that this would obscure from public view 80 percent of the facts of criminal cases. The lack of scrutiny, he maintained, would damage the judicial system: "Justice thrives in the light; corruption in the dark."[70]

The result of overreaction to the Sheppard decision and the Reardon report, according to Notson, was to deny or restrict public knowledge of criminal procedures. "At year end ASNE stands under a threat of fait accompli," he warned members at the 1967 convention. "Lawyers control both the bar and the courts. And the bar and the courts can adopt canons and rules in this area which have force of law, all without any enactment by a legislative body."

ELIMINATING SYNDICATE PARTIES

Notson also strongly opposed the practice of syndicates' paying for parties for ASNE convention goers. "ASNE would be better off without this peripheral activity," he responded in a poll conducted by Loye Miller of the Knoxville *News-Sentinel*. "It does seem a little inconsistent that we should editorialize and be resolute against government employees free-loading and then ourselves seek such favors."[71]

The ASNE president who eventually ended the questionable practice of having syndicates subsidize post-convention parties, however, was Vincent S. Jones, executive editor of the Gannett newspapers. Jones lived and worked in New York before becoming Gannett executive editor in 1955. In that role he supervised a group of editors from Illinois to Connecticut to New Jersey to Florida.

Jones described the task of stopping the syndicate parties as "throwing the money changers out of the temple."[72] He observed, "A society such as ours, dedicated to the highest principles of journalistic ethics, should avoid the acceptance of commercial hospitality." The board agreed and gave him approval to handle the matter, so he sent a letter to each of the former hosts: "The ASNE very much appreciates the generosity and goodwill that your organization and others have displayed towards our members over the years. The number and size of these festivities have reached such proportions, however, and the ASNE has grown so large, that what once seemed liked a harmless social custom assumes today an appearance of possible impropriety. Neither you nor we can afford any such appearance."[73]

Not all members applauded the move. Some saw the action as hypocritical because there were more serious problems within and without the society. Referring to his own efforts at reform, as well as those proposed by Norman E. Isaacs, Jones stated: "My guess is that we will proceed slowly and cautiously, but that within the reasonable future some sort of review procedure will be established. I hope we get to do it."[74]

ASNE RELATIONS WITH RICHARD NIXON

In contrast to the adversarial relations with Presidents Kennedy and Johnson, relations between ASNE and President Nixon during 1968–1969 were more cordial. Before his election, Nixon appeared before ASNE in 1968 for the fifth time, this time on a panel entitled "The New Nixon." After his election, Nixon appointed four ASNE members to high-ranking positions in his administration: Walter Annenberg as ambassador to the Court of St. James; William P. Rogers, former ASNE legal counsel, as secretary of state; Creed Black as assistant secretary of health education and welfare for legislation; and Herb Klein as director of communications for the executive branch.

Comments about the new press relations spearheaded by Klein were almost rhapsodic in the FOI report the following year. FOI chair Howard Cleavinger of the Spokane *Daily Chronicle* quoted Samuel Archibald of the Washington FOI Office:

There are two reasons Klein—the first government official to have the title Director of Communications and to have the administrative muscle that goes with it—has been getting the praise of the press so far; first, he is an acknowledged expert in the communications business, having served as a reporter and editor for many years before becoming candidate Nixon's perennial campaign adviser; second, Nixon accepts advice. . . . Not since the role of presidential press secretary was created by Franklin Delano Roosevelt have any of the Federal Government's top publicity men had the administrative muscle that Herb Klein does.[75]

The honeymoon was not long-lived, however. Speaking of a memorandum that established procedures for compliance with congressional demands for information, Sam Ragan of the Raleigh *News & Observer* said that his FOI committee report contained cautious optimism which seemed justified. But the report added that those close to the scene had their fingers crossed. "It was well they did," Ragan said. "For as time went on, the visibility of Herb Klein became less and less and the White House itself became at times almost impenetrable."[76]

NOTES

1. Although Isaacs was born in Manchéster, England, in 1908, his parents moved to Montreal, Canada, two years later. In an autobiographical chapter in *Untended Gates: The Mismanaged Press* (New York: Columbia University Press, 1986), Isaacs says his ethical views were shaped in part by his father, whom he describes as a liberal who leaned toward state socialism, under which all natural resources would be publicly owned (37).

2. In addition to Isaacs, 13 other ASNE presidents have served as president of the APME. Roy A. Roberts, the second APME president, was one of the APME founders with Oliver Owen Kuhn in 1933. Others include N. R. Howard, Walter M. Harrison, Basil Walters, George W. Healy, Jr., Lee Hills, Vincent S. Jones, Michael J. Ogden, J. Edward Murray, John C. Quinn, Richard D. Smyser, Robert P. Clark and Ed Cony.

3. Quoted by Michael Ogden in *Gentlemen of the Press*, edited by Loren Ghiglione, Indianapolis: R. J. Berg & Co., 1984, 189–190.

4. Quoted in Alice Fox Pitts in *Gentleman of the Press*, 93.

5. ASNE minutes, April 14, 1969, 390–391.

6. Ibid.

7. Like Isaacs, Reston was foreign born—in Scotland. A protégé of Ohio publisher James Cox, who helped put him through the University of Illinois, Reston was one of the foremost columnists and an executive of the New York *Times* when Isaacs recommended him for the committee.

8. In addition to being chairman of the board of the two Louisville papers, the Binghams were also supporters for Democratic candidates and liberal causes. Bingham was an early supporter of press councils; his newspaper was the first in America to name an ombudsman in 1967.

9. William Rivers, "The New Confusion," 236, in *The Reporter as Artist: A Look at the New Journalism Controversy,* edited by Ronald Weber, New York: Hastings House, 1974.

10. Vincent S. Jones, "Does America Need a Press Council?" paper for the Humdrum Club, March 2, 1970.

11. Ibid.

12. ASNE *Proceedings*, 1960, 29.

13. Herbert Brucker, *Communication Is Power* (New York: Oxford University Press, 1973), 204–205.

14. Ibid.

15. ASNE *Proceedings*, 1961, 11.

16. Isaacs, 110–111.

17. Felix McKnight, *ASNE Bulletin*, January 1964. Quoted by Pitts, 332.

18. Kerner Commission, *Report of the National Advisory Commission on Civil Disorders*, New York: Bantam Books, 1968, 362–389, 365.

19. ASNE *Proceedings*, 1968, 30.

20. Jack Newfield, "Journalism: Old, New and Corporate," *Dutton Review*, No. 1, in *The Reporter as Artist.*

21. For a detailed discussion on this issue see "Prolicons: A Study of Political Leanings and Preferences of Presidents of the American Society of Newspaper Editors, 1922–1990," presented by the author at the West Coast Journalism Historians Conference, Berkeley, Calif., March 1, 1991.

22. Loren Ghiglione, "Herbert Brucker, 1899–1977," *ASNE Bulletin,* June 1977, 23.

23. Ibid.

24. J. Herbert Altschull, *From Milton to McLuhan: The Ideas behind American Journalism*, New York: Longman, 1990, 297–298.

25. Brucker, *Communication Is Power.*

26. Ibid.

27. ASNE minutes, April 19, 1961, 228.

28. Ibid.

29. Quoted by Harrison Salisbury in *Without Fear or Favor*, New York: Ballantyne Books, 1980, 158.

30. Turner Catledge, *My Life and the Times*, New York: Harper & Row, 1971, 262.

31. Ibid.

32. Felix R. McKnight, letter to the author, July 21, 1990. For additional information, see James E. Pollard, "The Kennedy Administration and the Press," *Journalism Quarterly*, Winter 1964, 3–14.

33. Felix McKnight, letter to the author, July 21, 1990, 4.

34. ASNE *Proceedings*, 1967, 235.

35. ASNE minutes, April 20, 1963, 276.

36. ASNE *Proceedings*, 1967, 260.

37. Ibid.

38. ASNE *Proceedings*, 1968, 256.

39. Ibid.

40. Chalmers Roberts, *The Washington* Post: *The First 100 Years*, Boston: Houghton Mifflin, 1977, 374.

41. Charles Whited, *Knight: A Publisher in the Tumultuous Century*, New York: E. P. Dutton, 1988, 257.

42. Ibid., 258.

43. Nicholas Von Hoffman, "The Night they tore old Gene down," *ASNE Bulletin*, date unknown, 23.

44. Ibid.

45. Washington, D.C.: American Institute for Public Policy Research, 1974.

46. New York: Dow Jones, 1962.

47. Chapel Hill, N.C.: Algonquin Books, 1983.

48. Royster, *My Own, My Country's Time*, 216.

49. Lloyd Wendt, *The Wall Street Journal*, Chicago: Rand McNally & Company, 1982, 394.

50. Ibid.

51. Ibid., 396.

52. Royster, *My Own, My Country's Time*, 222.

53. Quoted by William H. Fitzpatrick in *Gentlemen of the Press*, 364.

54. Felix R. McKnight, letter to the author, July 21, 1990.

55. Alf Pratte, *American Newspaper Publishers, 1950–1990*, edited by Perry J. Ashley, Detroit: Gale Research, 1993, 129–134.

56. Herbert Brucker, "Our Next Forty Years," *ASNE Bulletin*, February 1964, 7.

57. ASNE minutes, October 12, 1962, 257–258.

58. Quoted by Harold A. Williams, *The Baltimore* Sun, *1837–1987*, Baltimore: Johns Hopkins University Press, 1987, 255, 264. See also Michael J. Ogden, "The Full, Busy World of Miles Wolff," *ASNE Bulletin*, April 1964, 8–10.

59. ASNE minutes, April 14, 1965, 293.

60. ASNE minutes, October 29, 1967, 358; see also minutes for April 14, 1965, 293; May 16, 1966, 311, and April 15, 1968, 363.

61. ASNE *Proceedings*, 1969, 47.

62. Ibid. 48.

63. William Hornby and Ann Schmidt, "Who the Hell Is Dick Schmidt?" *ASNE Bulletin*, date unknown, 3–6.

64. ASNE minutes, April 20, 1963, 282.

65. ASNE minutes, September 12, 1966, 327.

66. Quoted in Pitts, *Read All About It! 50 Years of ASNE*, Reston, Va.: ASNE, 1974, 241–242.

67. Robert C. Notson, letter to the author, July 18, 1980, 2.

68. Ghiglione, ed., *Gentlemen of the Press*, 299.

69. Notson, July 18, 1990, 3.

70. Ibid.

71. Quoted in Pitts, 306.

72. Letter from Vincent Jones to author, July 24, 1990.

73. Quoted in Pitts, 307.

74. Ibid., 8.

75. ASNE *Proceedings*, 1969, 247.

76. Quoted in Pitts, 217.

Chapter 7

Looking upon Themselves as Potential Publishers

We encouraged editors "to begin looking upon themselves as potential publishers," so as to provide such enlightened proprietors as Jack Knight, Nelson Poynter and Otis Chandler with rounded candidates for the top job instead of ceding it to bean counters. Editors were disabused of fears they were arithmetical illiterates, and primed to rule.
　　　　　　　　　　—Eugene Patterson, from a letter to the author, July 20, 1990

William Hornby summarized well the issues that dominated ASNE in the 1970s. In his 1980 president's report describing the journalistic challenges of the previous decade, the Denver *Post* editor recalled "persistent problems," including the state of journalism ethics, the superficiality of reporting and the influence on the press by special interest groups. The other nine presidents of the 1970s each faced the lack of minority representation, the need to maintain a free press, the decline of accuracy, the erosion of literacy, the denial of public access and shrinking readership. "These and many other topics," Hornby emphasized, "concerned us during the 70s."[1]

In a similar summary in 1978, an editor from the South, Eugene Patterson, observed that ASNE editors were in a period of "search and change" and were moving toward a new dimension of journalism:

We remember the generally obedient press born of depression and world war, which tended through the 1950s to respect the authority of established power to define this nation's purposes and interest. We well remember the convulsive switch to adversary journalism in the late 1960s and early 1970s, when domestic discord and a mistaken war turned the society as well as the press from a general obedience to an adversary sense of fallibility of the powerful institutions we live under.[2]

Patterson told ASNE members that the adversary press of the 1960s had contributed to a sturdier press and a stronger society. "But I sense a current self-examination in the press, addressing the question of whether throwing rocks at authority is enough, whether better reporting of issues should be added to our investigative approach," he added.

The St. Petersburg (Fla.) *Times* editor challenged ASNE and journalists to move toward "explanatory journalism": that is, journalism which reports issues in whole, not in part, enumerates pros and cons and informs readers with a comprehensible simplicity. "Just as the major part of our adversary role is to watch those who exercise power, we carry a major obligation to be guides to the people so that they can more clearly comprehend the issues which the wielders of power may be managing and mismanaging, and especially those vital issues they may be avoiding." Besides its responsibility to monitor official handling of their own agenda, the press had to identify primary sources independent of political authority.

Patterson also reported the society's progress in emphasizing ethics, recruiting minorities, adopting new technology and promoting readership and research. In particular, he called attention to the Readership and Research Committee, headed by Michael J. O'Neill of the New York *Daily News*, which had markedly altered editors' opinions of companion elements in the news business. "This new posture moves us somewhat away from the defensive crouch we have maintained for a good many reasons and a good many years when we were invited out of the henhouse by what we took for the fox," Patterson said, referring to ASNE's new cooperation with the ANPA and the Newspaper Advertising Bureau (NAB). Leo Bogart later described this move as "an unprecedented cooperative attempt by the American newspaper industry to halt the downward trend in newspaper readership and circulation."[3]

The new ASNE approach caused editors to assert editorial values as part of the Readership Council, an organization which before had been only a well-funded creature of ANPA and NAB. Introducing editorial guidance into the council's direction, ASNE channeled thousands of project dollars into readership research and the start-up of the publication *Editor's Exchange*. And ASNE and ANPA stopped "shying."[4] In a comment that symbolized the transition of the old-time editors into the new era of high finance, Patterson also encouraged editors "to begin looking upon themselves as potential publishers," so as to provide enlightened proprietors such as Jack Knight, Nelson Poynter and Otis Chandler with rounded candidates for the top job instead of ceding it to the bean counters. Editors were disabused of fears they were arithmetical illiterates and primed to rule.[5]

ASNE president John Hughes of the *Christian Science Monitor* made similar comments in his 1979 report. He observed that many newspaper editors of the past had viewed circulation and advertising and business departments of their newspapers as "heathens." That is changing, Hughes said, "perhaps partly because some editors have become born again and recognize the benefits of sensible and ethical cooperation with noneditorial departments, and perhaps partly because increasingly editors are joining the ranks of the erstwhile heathen themselves and are themselves assuming responsibilities as publishers."[6]

The new ecumenical alliance among the groups came about after a number of scorching speeches, memos and recommendations given by western states presidents, including Howard H. (Tim) Hays of the Riverside (Calif.) *Press-Enterprise* and George Chaplin of the Honolulu *Advertiser*. In his presidential report, Hays referred to the "deplorable" financial state of ASNE, a problem which contrasted with the picture painted by his predecessors. After a year or two of deficit financing, the society had a balanced budget. "But I have qualms about how it had to be balanced," he stated. Hays, who had a law degree from Harvard, was particularly troubled by two outlays he regarded as unfair and shortsighted: those for legal counsel and those for the services of the executive secretary.

In a stinging rebuke, Hays charged that "niggardliness" toward the executive secretary's office had caused different problems. Without referring to the low salary paid to Alice and Freddy Pitts over the years, Hays said he was concerned about the increasing burden on the three-member staff. "If the society expands its activities, as I am convinced it will, the problem will become even more critical."

Hays also charged that the very modest retainer paid to attorney Richard Schmidt was not proportionate to the heavy and increasing demands placed on him. "The society should intervene in more of the court cases which raise significant First Amendment issues. But when our FOI chairman and our counsel consider such interventions, they are often restrained by financial limitations."[7] The board increased the salary of the executive secretary from $40,000 to $45,000 in 1980 and raised Schmidt's retainer from $13,000 to $15,000.[8]

Hays' skill in strengthening the role of committees also contributed to the improved organization of the society. He recruited a record number of committee members, introduced the concept of a midyear meeting for most committees and of two-year service for committee heads, changed the role of the nominating committee, arranged for more *Bulletin* coverage of committee activities and appointed a Committee on News Research. Before the committee's establishment, the profession had doubted its value; many felt the best responses were produced by editors who used only their intuition for guidance.[9]

COMMITTEE SYSTEM BROADENED

Before Hays' tenure, committees selected nominees for election to the ASNE board of directors by a series of elimination ballots conducted by mail. What was happening, in essence, was a measuring of name recognition and popularity among committee candidates. As noted in Charles Gallagher's 1956 concern over a lack of broad-based representation, too often outstanding younger members who

were beginning to make significant contributions were passed over in the nomination process; older, better-known members, past the prime of opportunity and
willingness to contribute, were chosen instead. Hays determined that ASNE
could expect better results if a nominating committee gathered information on
possible nominees, then met to compare them. He thought the time for a popularity contest was not during the nomination process but in the election. With the
approval of the board, he appointed a smaller committee to select nominees.[10]

A strong new committee member who helped transform the ASNE during
the 1970s was George Chaplin. He headed the committee guiding the society to
a record membership. He provided quiet leadership, nudging the editors to think
beyond their own "kuleanas," or areas of jurisdiction in the newsroom, to
greater visions. Having transformed Honolulu's ultraconservative *Advertiser*
into a moderately liberal competitor for the Honolulu *Star-Bulletin*, Chaplin had
the experience and personality of a reformer.

He moved to Hawaii shortly before its statehood, having served as editor of
papers in Camden, New Jersey; San Diego and New Orleans. In the words of
Bill Ewing, managing editor of the competing *Star-Bulletin*: "Statehood, Henry
J. Kaiser, jet airplanes and George Chaplin hit Hawaii at about the same time.
I'm not quite sure where to list them in order of importance." In the early 1960s,
using the same personalized letter-writing skills he later employed to increase
ASNE membership, he was able to raise funds for a Pearl Harbor Memorial.
Interested in planning, he coauthored *Hawaii 2000: Continuing Experiment in
Anticipatory Democracy*. Chaplin was an early supporter and longtime member
of the Honolulu Media Council.

According to Hays, who watched Chaplin help boost ASNE membership
above 800, it may well be that Chaplin knew more members than anyone else.
"And this is a measure of his remarkable capacity for friendship. For he is
neither a back-slapper nor a vote-counter. He doesn't step forward with his hand
out. On the contrary, he is a bit reticent. He builds new friendships with warm
response and nurtures them with empathy. This is probably one of the reasons
why he has gotten where he is in the society, but only one among many."[11]

Chaplin's and others' vision of an expanded leadership role for the organization
in the 1970s was translated into action by a special finance committee headed
by Michael O'Neill of the New York *Daily News*. In addition to ideals such as
freedom of the press, O'Neill said, ASNE needed to focus on immediate and
brutally practical problems such as "whether we're going to let market experts
edit newspapers or whether we're going to do the job ourselves." He stated,
"Right now, most editors are playing second fiddle to their business offices.
Somebody with a calculator is telling them what space they'll have. Ad directors are trying to call the tune on everything from real estate pages to special
food sections. Market analysts are busy saying what readers want to read. And it
will get worse before it gets better."[12]

The bottom line, according to O'Neill, was that editors needed a powerful organization, imaginatively led, well staffed and well financed, capable of balancing the business orientation of the groups now dominating industry policy and, above all, equipped to provide strong editorial leadership at the national level. The poorly financed ASNE, he said, was not such an organization: "The ASNE, of course, is the industry's welfare case. It has only 664 active members, representing only 504 daily newspapers! These active editors, plus 148 retirees and three distinguished service members, paid a mere $92,325 in dues in 1975. And we have a grand total of only three full-time employees."[13]

O'Neill charged that the ASNE program was even more limited than the ASNE staff and financing. Except for occasionally speaking out on press rights, the society had historically done little more than hold annual conventions. "It has been very self-contemplating, taking a narrow view of its role in the industry and leaving a vacuum, which has allowed other disciplines to develop an unbalancing degree of influence on the councils of publishers."

In a general discussion of the draft of an "Editorial Leadership Program" devised by O'Neill and his committee, Eugene Patterson said the gut issue was the overall balance of forces among elements of the newspaper industry, not only in the readership project but also in the future shape of the industry. "Editors must stand up and protect their interests—in Charles Bailey's term, 'hang in there'—because if the ASNE effort fails, it threatens long-run editor control of editorial content."[14]

Another forceful advocate for editorial judgment was Denver *Post* editor William Hornby, who, while strongly supporting research, argued that editors should never forget the raison d'être for newspapers. In particular, he was distressed over surveys that indicated readers were turned off by serious news and government affairs:

The newspaper is an institution that sets out to do more than just maximize its market.... The press has never been and never should be in business to give the people just what they want . . . its purpose is first and foremost to provide news. . . . If the hard, spot news of what's happening becomes more and more capsulized in easy doses, between columns of matter on how to take a bath, newspapers will move away from the central human need they particularly exist to satisfy. . . . Their product must produce a profit to exist, but the product doesn't exist for a profit.[15]

In his 1978 presidential statement, Patterson reported that as "activists in an ecumenical alliance," ASNE participants had encountered respect, not hostility, for editorial integrity from publishers and advertisers. And while there were skirmishes along the way, he said, ASNE received support to establish certain guiding principles to be formally offered in the industry's cooperative Readership Project. ASNE's new position was far more productive than the alternate isolation of defensiveness and resistance, which would have had ASNE believe it could only rattle its chains.[16]

NEW POST FOR PETE MCKNIGHT

President Patterson announced the appointment of Pete McKnight as ASNE project director in mid-1977. The directors created the permanent staff position to manage the society's expanding efforts to attract readers and restore credibility. McKnight continued to hold the title of associate publisher of the Charlotte *Observer* along with the ASNE position. He had also been president of the North Carolina Press Association.

McKnight had been a major factor in what Jack Claiborne described as "The Knight-McKnight Revolution" in Charlotte from 1955 to 1965, a revolution which helped to energize southern papers during the '70s. A North Carolina native, McKnight invigorated news gathering, photography and typography on the *Observer*. He also introduced liberal views on race and poverty to the group-owned publication. His efforts helped change the newspaper from one of the worst in the South into what *Time* magazine described as one of the best.[17]

McKnight could not have changed the paper without the support of owner-publisher John S. Knight, who set the *Observer*'s tone after buying it on December 29, 1954. Lee Hills, the Knight group's executive editor, also assisted in the transformation by recruiting McKnight for the paper. The two continued the long tradition of Knight executives who would serve as presidents of ASNE. Seven served in the first 70 years. No other newspaper group provided so many presidents for ASNE.

One of three talented sons of a wholesale grocer, Colbert Augustus McKnight had intended to become a Spanish teacher but instead became a reporter. A tall, frail, nervous intellectual, McKnight wrote prizewinning editorials before moving up the executive ladder, where he became recognized for recruiting outstanding talent. That talent brought the *Observer* its first Pulitzer Prize in the mid-1960s. Each spring and fall, McKnight and his managing editor, Tom Fesperson, took recruiting trips to major journalism schools. According to Claiborne, McKnight developed a knack for spotting people of exceptional promise. He had a simple test: If I were a news source, would I like being interviewed by this person? When he felt the hair rise on the back of his neck in an interview, McKnight knew he was facing an extraordinary applicant.[18]

McKnight served as staff and liaison for the Readership and Research Committee and for the two major task forces under that committee: writing improvement, and editorial content and technology. He also functioned as the staff liaison with ANPA and NAB and for the ASNE president, managing the president's activities on the steering committee of the Newspaper Readership

Council. In addition, he organized and managed the ASNE writing awards established in 1978 and provided administrative backup for standing committees on ethics, minorities, freedom of information, education for journalism and international communication.

Patterson, Hays and Tom Winship of the Boston *Globe* helped establish the writing awards as a means of encouraging excellence in American newspaper writing. Of the 625 first-year entries, Cynthia Gorney of the Washington *Post*, Carol McCabe of the Providence *Journal-Bulletin* and Ellen Goodman of the Boston *Globe* were among the finalists who received awards at the 1979 convention banquet.[19]

Under the direction of McKnight and executive director Giancarlo, ASNE conducted independent studies and participated with other organizations in determining why newspapers were no longer a part of many American homes. Studies examined readability and credibility. Ruth Clark conducted a number of studies on the changing needs of readers; they proved to be best-sellers in the industry. Surprisingly, many non-newspaper customers ordered copies, including the Cleveland Browns of the National Football League.[20]

In spite of the popularity of the "Changing Needs of Changing Readers," which became the most widely circulated document yet produced on newspaper research, Clark's methodology and the conclusions endorsed by ASNE were questioned. In a detailed case history of the Newspaper Research Project, Leo Bogart says that by proclaiming the message that the public wanted fun rather than facts about the world's grim realities, ASNE legitimized the movement to turn newspapers into daily magazines with the pelletized, palatable characteristics of TV news. In this respect the ASNE results contrasted with the conclusions of a large-scale survey the Newspaper Advertising Bureau had conducted with financial support of the newsprint companies.[21]

In a well-documented critique, Bogart argued that although a number of Clark's findings accorded well with the conclusions drawn earlier from large-scale surveys, some of the most publicized ASNE results were directly at variance with the NAB results. In contrast to Clark's reaffirmation of the editor's traditional notion that local news was what people were most interested in, Bogart said the analysis actually showed that while readers wanted news of all kinds:

[T]hey were more interested in news of the nation and the world than in the news of their own localities. These conclusions fit with the trend toward education and a more cosmopolitan outlook reinforced by exposure to network television news. It also jibed with the shifts in population and the heightened daily mobility that made it increasingly hard to define the territorial boundaries of individual local concerns and sense of identity within a sprawling metropolitan region.[22]

In a letter to the author, O' Neill strongly disagreed with the characterization of Clark's work. He said she had been selected to assure skeptics that the editors had their own research person (not the ad bureau's), someone with a good track record. "On both counts, Ruth Clark filled the bill: she already had won a lot of fans because of work she had done at the major newspapers (including mine)," O'Neill said.[23]

O'Neill added that the editors helped assure that editors got a full voice in the development of newspaper industry policy and sold the general membership on Clark's approach to the overall project: "We were breaking the old crockery about separation of church and state because all this did was surrender initiatives to advertising circulation, etc. We did not want to FIGHT them—merely to be taken into the industry council so editorial could influence things that affected all parts of the business."[24]

O'Neill found the methods of Clark and Daniel Yankelovich more useful for searching out subtle attitudinal tendencies that gross numbers did not catch. The social indicators system was both innovative and heavily used by Yankelovich's commercial clients. The government has also used a similar methodology.[25]

J. Edward Murray disagreed, arguing that both Bogart and Clark operated on the false premise that their research methods could determine what readers wanted. "I don't believe that," he emphasized. His experience on four newspapers told him that readers didn't really have a clue to what kind of overall newspaper they wanted until they saw what their choices were in newspapers conveniently available to them. Only then did their choice yield an answer to what the readers wanted:

So, findings based on even the most scientifically sound research on what the readers say they want is flawed. And that's one reason why we now have so many newspapers, with shallow formulas of celebrity trivia and local-local, human interest tidbits, losing share of market to electronic competitors. In other words, I believe in the central role of the editor who selects the news menu on the basis of what she or he thinks the readers need to know to be informed citizens, intelligent parents, and concerned residents of a community.[26]

FOSTERING DIVERSITY

ASNE's efforts to come to grips with new readers they had failed to attract and old readers they had lost touch with also coincided with programs to make the newsrooms more diverse by adding women and blacks. After years of neglect and only "casual involvement" in providing leadership, the editors were nudged by the Kerner Commission Report (1968), which indicted the press. This was followed by what Norman Isaacs was to describe as a "new sense of urgency" and the naming of committees to deal with the problems that had accumulated since 1922.

Evidence of the glacial progress in promoting diversity can be seen in the fact that it was not until ASNE's 50th anniversary that McKnight appointed a special committee headed by Isaacs and Sylvan Meyer of the Miami *News* to conduct a joint study on minority employment and minority enrollment in schools of journalism. A series of committees appointed by all presidents followed.

The minorities committee, headed by Neal Shine of the Detroit *Free Press* and Reg Murphy of the San Francisco *Examiner*, encouraged newspapers to recruit and hire minority employees in the 1970s. After completing a national survey on hiring minorities and reporting minority issues, the society made it a goal to attain a percentage of minority employees equal to that of the national population by the year 2000. It encouraged "not waiting to be prodded, but acting because it was right." A 1974 ASNE report found that minorities constituted no more than 1 percent of professional newsroom staffs. By 1992, the percentage had only increased to just over 9 percent.

One of the most visible ASNE members of any minority committee was John H. Sengstacke, editor and publisher of the Chicago *Daily Defender* and head of the Sengstacke Newspapers Group. The nephew of Robert S. Abbott, who in 1905 had founded what became the cornerstone of the largest black newspaper group, Sengstacke was elected to the ASNE board in 1970—the first black board member. Shortly after his nomination, the society launched its campaign to recruit more black journalists.[27]

WOMEN IN ASNE

Of equal concern to ASNE during the 1970s was the question of women's rights in the United States, in newsrooms around the country, and in ASNE, which included only eight women among 800 members.[28] The increased sensitivity toward female editors is seen in the minutes and at the annual meetings: a few more women began to appear on panels and in prominent positions. Judith W. Brown of the New Britain (Conn.) *Herald* was chiefly responsible for bringing women to ASNE's agenda. Her efforts were rewarded in 1972, when President Ed Murray appointed Brown and Clayton Kirkpatrick of the Chicago *Tribune* to head a committee to discover why there weren't more women in ASNE.[29] In a survey sent to members, Kirkpatrick studied a cross section of newspapers to determine whether women and men were treated equally, to ascertain the main prejudices against women and to explore avenues for raising the industry's consciousness of women and their potential contributions.[30]

Preliminary responses, reported to the board at its November meeting, indicated that 59 women were eligible for membership in the society but that only 7 of them were from papers with circulation in the over-20,000 category. Acting on the survey's results, Brown suggested that the society "by indirection find directions out," that the findings of the committee be published in the *Bulletin*, and that reactions and results be evaluated before any specific policy was considered.[31] In 1974 the board approved an initiative permitting a newspaper to enroll an additional member in ASNE if at least one of the paper's members were a woman who fulfilled all the other regular membership criteria.[32]

CREDIBILITY AND ETHICS

Lingering ethics questions resurfaced in the 1970s under the persistent goading of Norman Isaacs, Herbert Brucker and others. In 1975, a special committee headed by Robert P. Clark of the Louisville papers had the unenviable task of revising the 1923 code into a more palatable statement of principles. As noted by former President Erwin Canham in an address on ethics enforcement, "I am not sure how the vote would come out on the issue of whether or not John Peter Zenger should be disciplined for his independent actions as an editor. Sometimes the vote of one's peers under certain circumstances is no more a guarantee of independence than would be the intervention of some external authority."[33]

In the 1975 discussion, Mark Ethridge, Jr., said that even the title, "Code of Ethics" or "Canons of Journalism," troubled the committee who was revising the holy doctrine: "There is no way, short of forming a closed shop editor's union, whereby more than 800 editors, or 1,700 daily newspapers, can be ordered to conform to a mold like lawyers and penalized for breaking that mold. We sought, instead, to agree upon a statement of principles, which is what we finally called it."[34]

In addition to revising the code, ASNE members had a lively debate on whether to support media councils—community or national groups designed to prompt the press toward a better job. Clark, in 1975, presented an 81-page report which included one of the most extensive bibliographies ever compiled on the subject. Despite these efforts, however, Clark said it was still too early to make a full evaluation of the National News Council. "That may sound chicken, but I don't believe it is," Clark said. "It has been in operation less than two years."

Aggressive efforts by Isaacs and others to enhance ASNE credibility also received impetus from Vice President Spiro Agnew, who attacked the media in a number of speeches, beginning in 1969. "I assume full responsibility for plunging the society into the center of the dispute started by Vice President Agnew's attacks on television and newspapers," Isaacs said in his 1970 president's report in San Francisco. "Some few members resented my speaking up. I happen to be proud that I did. I consider the vice president's continuing attacks on the news media a calculated campaign to erode further our credibility with the American public."[35]

In keeping with ASNE's tradition of fairness, however, Agnew was invited to speak at the society's 50th anniversary in 1972. Rather than continue the polarization, Warren Phillips quoted Scotty Reston of the New York *Times*, noting that Agnew was a man who said what he thought. Agnew, in return, chose not to speak about the media before the editors, saying he had more serious matters to discuss concerning President Nixon's position on Vietnam.[36]

Presidents Pete McKnight and Edward Murray each noted elected officials' attacks on media credibility in their annual reports or through ASNE counsel Richard Schmidt. The attorney said the White House's relationship with the press had evolved from the "news management" of the Kennedy administration to the "credibility gap" of President Johnson to the Nixon administration's "communication gap." Some relief came in the wake of attacks by the Nixon administration, which Murray said had poisoned many wells:

More subpoenas to get reporters to reveal confidential sources. More reporters in jail. More closed courtrooms and closed public meetings throughout the land. Increasing use of the Fairness Doctrine, or versions of it, in an effort to impose self-censorship on television programs. Fewer presidential press conferences, which permit tough questioning. More government from behind the wall of silence created by executive privilege. And, currently, a new big effort to increase government secrecy through a revision of the federal criminal code which would amount to an official secrets act.[37]

Murray also referred to "the festering national wound of Vietnam." The Nixon administration not only "shamelessly" managed the news in presidential prime time on the networks, but constantly implied that the press was unpatriotically overreporting the horrors of the war. All of this changed, however, shortly before the 1973 convention, Murray said. The press' adversary role, vis-à-vis the executive branch, at least, was sharply readjusted toward a more reasonable balance. Watergate looked like President Nixon's Waterloo in his long fight with the free press: "For the press, certainly, Watergate is a watershed, demonstrating for our generation the indispensability to the nation and to the democratic government of unfettered investigative reporting."[38]

As the Watergate scandal edged toward impeachment in the spring of 1973, the White House further damaged its own credibility by stonewalling the nation's news media on all details of the scandal. Murray met several times with Nixon's press representatives in an effort to keep news channels open for all the media. On one occasion, he headed a small group of editors who went to the White House expecting to see the president, in the hope of getting him to modify his self-defeating cover-up policy. But, at the last moment, all they got was an abortive late-afternoon cocktail hour with spokesman Ron Zeigler.[39]

In brief remarks at the close of his presidency, Murray summarized Nixon's "misbegotten campaign" against the press on many fronts, concluding with a well-deserved tribute to the Washington *Post* and other newspapers for the Watergate revelations that finally led to the president's resignation.[40]

JOURNALISM EDUCATION

ASNE president Tim Hays noted that the much publicized Watergate case and its heroic investigative reporters had contributed to a burgeoning enrollment in journalism schools. He expressed concern that too many young people, many of them unqualified by any valid standard, were being allowed, sometimes even encouraged, to believe that opportunities were waiting for them in daily journalism: "I hope to see that day when journalism schools are more strict about whom they admit and whom they graduate. I would like to see more graduate, professional schools with admission requirements comparable to those of law and medicine."[41]

Hays made some observations on the American media environment during the 1970s. "First, I fear that our readership has not yet felt the full erosive force of two significant phenomena: the distraction of television and the deterioration of instruction in reading and writing in our schools. Second, I think the problem of public distrust should be recognized as more serious and fundamental even than our problems with the courts and the legislatures." For newspapers to compete with other media, Hays suggested that editors make better use of their competitive advantages:

Whatever the variety that television can occasionally offer, the fact is that we alone—even with the present economic restrictions—still have the space for information which may appeal to only a fraction of our readership. We have an unrealized potential for focusing on specialized audiences: the young, of course, the poor, working women, racial minorities, the retired. If we cannot yet offer them special editions, we should be looking to the day when we can.[42]

Hays said the print media could recoup readability by inviting scrutiny, stimulating discussion with ombudsmen, and emphasizing codes of ethics, press councils, and candid corrections. "Such things may be bothersome, or even embarrassing, but surely we of all people should encourage an informed public dialogue on our role, and just as surely, this is in our interest."

A related topic addressed by several ASNE presidents in the 1970s was the excitement over investigative reporting. "We seem to go in cycles of interest," Hays said. "Once it was foreign correspondence; then it was race relations and urban affairs reporting; then it was consumer affairs reporting. It is not that there is too much investigative reporting. Quite the contrary. Indeed, every reporter should be encouraged to think of himself as—and more important, to be—an investigative reporter, whatever the beat or assignment."[43] John Hughes also expressed his enthusiasm for investigative reporting during the 1979 convention. "Without it, we wouldn't have uncovered the excesses of Vietnam or the corruption and mismanagement symbolized by Watergate."

During his 1977–1978 administration, Eugene Patterson demonstrated to ASNE the need for a new dimension in U.S. reporting that would accompany investigative reporting without detracting from it. He described this "explanatory reporting" as the art of explaining the complexities of almost incomprehensible modern issues through clear writing and an educated grasp.[44] Subsequently, the Pulitzer Prize board added a new category in its competition, that of explanatory reporting.[45] Patterson also inserted other items on the ASNE agenda in the 1970s, including occupation of the leading edge of First Amendment and freedom of information initiatives and, extending across the nation, Socratic dialogues on ethical conflicts between the media and the law. Thirty-five such sessions were scheduled during the year.

Murray also tried to extend ASNE influence beyond its membership with a 1973 speech at the University of Georgia. Using the title "New Trends in News Reporting," he summarized what he thought newspapers should be doing to survive the juggernaut of television, which two-thirds of Americans said was their main news source. These included solution-oriented reporting, systems thinking, team reporting, reporting which emphasizes the changing mores, consumer reporting and ecology reporting. Although the speech received modest favorable reaction from a few editors and journalism department deans, Murray says he doubts it had any substantial influence. "In fact, all but a score of the best newspapers have remained pretty much immune to either these or other new methods of reporting."[46]

ASNE GOES TO CHINA

With the help of Warren Phillips of the *Wall Street Journal,* several other editors, and Executive Secretary Giancarlo, Murray organized a 4,000-mile trip inside China for ASNE editors in 1972, including what proved to be a three-hour interview with Premier Chou En-lai. To some China watchers, the trip was described as the "longest and most comprehensive visit by American newspapermen since the Chinese revolution in 1949." Michael Ogden, the only member who went to both Russia and China, said it was ASNE's most significant trip abroad.

Aside from what we learned about the Chinese, it's fairly certain they got an insight into Americans. Unlike the trips to Soviet Russia, where the ASNE delegations found themselves fighting a running battle with their hosts on the merits of capitalism versus communism, here the subject almost never came up. In fact, for some days, the editors thought they sensed a complete lack of curiosity about the United States. The dam broke as both sides got to know each other.[47]

During the Chou En-lai interview, described in his unpublished autobiography, Murray said the Chinese leader accused him of being "naive" because he didn't think the Kennedy assassination was the result of a high-level conspiracy. "That's because you have a conspiratorial mind," Murray countered.[48] The ASNE editors knew from visits to villages, communes, factories and schools that the ongoing cultural revolution was a bloody undertaking, Murray said, although they had only anecdotal evidence of individual deaths to prove it. But Chou En-lai repeatedly insisted with a straight face that there had only been minor skirmishes and no fatalities.[49]

On October 6, 1972, the ASNE board of directors attempted to produce a historical document as a by-product of the visit. The hope was that Chinese journalists would join the Americans in signing what ASNE chose to call "The Peking Declaration."[50] Pitts concludes: "Possibly because Chinese editors are not weaned on 'the right to know' or the American belief 'in the freest flow of information,' our Oriental colleagues expressed no interest in a joint signing of the declaration. Nothing daunted, ASNE issued the pronouncement itself. The Peking Declaration received some mild publicity in the United States, but scarcely enough to rank its history with say, the Monroe Doctrine or the Magna Carta."[51]

As did other touring editors, Murray says he produced a good series for the Knight newspapers from the trip. The *Free Press* displayed the series in a booklet entitled "4,000 Miles across China," and the series was nominated for a Pulitzer Prize. The China trip was a main theme for Murray's speeches as ASNE president, including a major address at Davidson College. Because state control of media was central to his China speech, Murray was able to work into it an account of the very beginning of what became an important world issue: demand for a new world information and communications order. Debate on this issue continued in many third world countries well into the 1980s and was kept alive until the end of the cold war by the United Nations Educational, Scientific and Cultural Organization (UNESCO).[52] Murray said the idea was made irrelevant by several developments, including the growth of the global economy, which requires free media; the ongoing global communications revolution based on computers and satellites, which overwhelmed efforts at internal media control by any one nation; and the loosening of media controls in the USSR and some of the Soviet bloc nations.[53]

O'NEILL URGES BROADER INTERNATIONAL VISION

Michael O'Neill also became involved in this UNESCO discussion, as did other members of ASNE's board seeking to help Americans develop a better sense of the world. In an examination of the failings of American journalism, O'Neill described the "profound ethnocentricity" that projects the whole world onto American screens, looking at incoming images through the prisms of American culture and translating issues into American stereotypes, so that we do not see other societies as they see themselves and do not see ourselves as others see us: "From Vietnam to the dispatch of Marines to Lebanon, our history is littered with tragic miscalculations based on an ethnocentric view of the outside world. A tiny example of our own field was the overreaction of many newspaper editors to the so-called new world information order championed by UNESCO. Their outrage was defined entirely by their own constricted view; there wasn't the slightest hint that some Third World complaints were justified."[54]

When O'Neill was president (1981–1982), he tried to infuse ASNE with an understanding of journalists and others in developing countries. He promoted the idea, and followed through with it to some extent, of working constructively to help Third World journalists, rather than merely denouncing UNESCO. Some of the flavor of this approach can be seen in a 1982 speech he gave at the Women in Communications convention.

What we need, rather, is a more subtle strategy—one that is not so arrogant as understanding, not so combative as persuasive, not so aggressive as patient, not so dogmatic as tolerant of cultural and intellectual difference. I'm not talking about compromise, either of principle or ideal—only about understanding the mighty forces at loose in the world and making intelligent use of this understanding to develop practical ways to help our cause.[55]

Another program aimed at bringing about better understanding between nations was implemented by John Hughes, the second foreign-born ASNE president (1978–1979). He was especially aware of the society's steps to encourage journalistic interns, particularly those from the Third World, to observe firsthand the "failings and strengths" of American journalism through a number of programs in the 1970s:

I felt that if they could be exposed to all the vitality, the independence, the argument, the opposing viewpoints that go into the making of American newspapers it would make them sturdier defendants of the kind of journalistic principles we treasure. Years later, when they were in positions of leadership in their own countries, their having been steeped in these American traditions would serve them well, perhaps when dictatorial regimes tried to suppress them. My idea was translated into exchanges sponsored by ASNE and others, and today there is quite a lively passage to the United States by foreign journalists.[56]

Born in South Wales and reared in South Africa, Hughes was the second ASNE editor from the *Christian Science Monitor* and the third ASNE president (with Arthur C. Deck and Hays) to win a Pulitzer Prize in the 1970s. Boston editor Tom Winship said that because of his "Welshness," Hughes had the capacity to look at the whole Anglo world with fresh eyes. "And his passion for dogs has given him a convenient index for classifying the rest of humanity."[57]

During Hughes' presidency ASNE expanded its knowledge of China by sending its third delegation there in the fall of 1978 and by playing host a second time to a return delegation of the Chinese editors earlier the same year.[58]

As Hays pointed out at the 1975 convention, the society's midyear committee meetings around the country produced some unexpected results, one of them of international significance. The International Relations Committee, headed by Dick Leonard of the Milwaukee *Journal*, invited representatives of all significant international journalistic organizations to a meeting in Wisconsin, where the World Press Freedom Committee was born. That organization continues to play an important role in protection of press freedom around the world.[59]

Phillips was the second of three presidents from the *Wall Street Journal* to lead ASNE. A native of New York, he went to Germany after World War II after being denied entrance into Columbia University. Starting as a copyboy after his return to the United States, he rose rapidly with Dow Jones. In ASNE he served effectively on several committees. He also was president of the American Council for Education in Journalism (ACEJ).

During his ASNE presidency, Phillips advocated product improvement as an answer to statistics which showed that newspaper circulation was down 2 percent in 1974, to the lowest level since 1965. Although the number of American households had grown almost 24 percent in 10 years, and the population had increased by almost 10 percent, the circulation of American newspapers had increased only half of one (0.5) percent.[60] Phillips believed that a remedy lay in the suggestion of Ed Miller, head of the new Newspaper Evaluation Committee and Allentown (Pa.) *Morning Call* editor. Miller's idea was to develop ways in which local editors could systematically and more accurately improve their operations relative to other newspapers with comparable circulation and resources. The effort would embrace quantitative, objective data (newshole [the amount of space left for news after advertising], staff size) and such subjective yardsticks as initiative and creativity.[61]

Phillips and Sylvan Meyer of the Gainesville (Ga.) *Daily Times*, who had both served as the journalism education committee chair, warned members that the federal government was becoming more involved in the journalism accreditation system in the 1970s. Their particular concern was that the Department of Health, Education and Welfare, in trying to make accreditation agencies conform to guidelines, would eventually affect journalism substance areas such as curricula and faculty qualifications, and thus raise the question of First Amendment infringement.[62]

Education committees spent much of their time in the 1970s (1) creating programs to increase cooperation between journalists and professionals and (2) working with regional journalism councils, which ASNE established in 1972. Education committee topics included enrollment problems and opportunities for journalism graduates. Committee members and guests discussed midcareer learning opportunities and reactions to journalism education.[63] ASNE continued its liaison with the Newspaper Fund, managing the editor-in-residence programs under which its members visited colleges and universities. ASNE and the Dow Jones Newspaper Fund served as a clearinghouse for the project. The purposes were obvious: to give students and faculty contact with editors in the mainstream of journalism, to provide answers to career questions and to allow students to explore journalistic issues with practicing newspeople.[64]

When Phillips was president of ACEJ, a major effort was made to encourage journalism schools to reflect in their teachings the needs and qualities advocated by the nation's editors. The objective was to reduce the rising influence on school curricula of the more "academic," esoteric and theoretical "mass communications" proselytizers. "I hope we made a difference in advancing these issues, even though they are all still very much alive today," Phillips observed in a letter in 1990.[65]

SUPPORT FOR FEDERAL SHIELD LAW

ASNE continued to fight for freedom of information under the aggressive leadership of attorney Schmidt. A former disc jockey and sports announcer before earning his law degree from Stanford, Schmidt had served as counsel for the U.S. Information Agency before being named ASNE counsel in December of 1968. He became the link between journalism and the bar as chair (1969–1973) of the American Bar Association's standing committee on communications and as a leading member of the ABA Task Force on the Courts.

Schmidt's most time-consuming issue in the 1970s involved support for federal shield legislation—support which fluctuated throughout the decade. Prompted in part by the *Branzburg* v. *Hayes* ruling and by the decision of some states to pass their own legislation, ASNE joined the action on April 14, 1971. It passed a resolution that "the society endorse the principle of a federal shield law and assume the leadership in mobilizing support for it."[66]

Two years later, however, William Hornby briefed the board on several adverse court rulings and on the bleak outlook in Congress for an absolute shield bill. With passage of the bill unlikely, the FOI committee and Schmidt supported H.R. 5928, the so-called Kastenmeier–Cohen bill, as a compromise. During a lengthy discussion on the matter, Robert P. Clark noted that the journalism profession was looking to ASNE for leadership. In light of the Supreme Court statements, other judges' decisions and the tenor of the country, Clark argued that ASNE should continue to grapple with the question.[67]

Debate about how actively ASNE should support a shield law culminated in 1975, when Robert Chandler of the Bend (Ore.) *Bulletin* questioned whether the board should get involved in the shield law question at all, after the FOI committee voted six to six on the question.[68] The committee remained split down the middle in a similar vote the next year.[69] Vacillation over the issue may have prompted President Arthur Deck of the Salt Lake City *Tribune* (1973–1974) to provide this optimistic outlook without budging one centimeter.

I am as adamant as anyone that we should have unqualified shield laws, both at national and state levels. But I am not persuaded that anything effective will emerge on the national level, and efforts to set up an effective one already have been shot down in the Utah legislature as in other states, so I look upon this as a continuing effort that isn't going to be solved in the relatively near future.[70]

As the courts became more involved in cases such as the invasion by police of the Stanford *Daily* and in the halting of publication of the *Progressive* magazine, however, sentiment changed. In 1979, Charles Bailey of the Minneapolis *Tribune* announced that the FOI committee had voted 11 to 1 to support a federal shield law. Hornby detected a distinct change in most members' attitudes "because of the beating the [journalism] business had taken over the past year." Bailey urged the board to take a position immediately on a federal shield law. He outlined the traditional arguments to the directors: the series of adverse Supreme Court decisions; the fact that 26 states had already adopted shield laws; the fact that the First Amendment, as it was being defined, was a far cry from Justice Black's definition of it and the need for a federal law to organize the chaos wrought by the variations in state laws. The final vote was 21 to 3 in favor. John Quinn, Claude Sitton and Edward Miller voted no.[71]

Schmidt also managed the society's efforts to pass SB 1 in 1976, and to remove and prevent further privacy restrictions and efforts to stifle the press in the courts. Addressing the issue of SB 1, Schmidt warned that because of leaks in the CIA, particularly the naming of CIA agents, and because of the death of agent Richard Welch, more members of Congress were inclined to support the national security sections of SB 1. This would have made the leaking of classified information and the nonreturn of such information a crime.[72]

Schmidt warned the directors that the FBI was out to "get" the press in the battle over open records under the FOI Act. He reported that FBI director William Webster had stated that the FOI Act got informants killed, a charge Schmidt denied.[73] In 1976 ASNE joined three other news organizations to denounce new federal laws and regulations designed to protect individual rights to privacy, calling them a dangerous step toward wholesale conversion of public records to private records. The Reporters Committee for Freedom of the Press, the ANPA and the National Newspaper Association joined ASNE in the denunciation.[74] FOI committee head Clayton Kirkpatrick of the Chicago *Tribune* praised ASNE's success in finding allies to influence privacy legislation and amend the FOI Act. "The alternative to hanging together is to hang separately," he noted in a 1975 board meeting at the Bermuda Castle Harbour Hotel.[75]

George Chaplin said that freedom of the press was under heavier assault in the bicentennial year than at any time since the period of the Alien and Sedition Acts. Speaking as the 46th society president (1976–1977), Chaplin cited polls which showed that the public mistrusted the press. "And it seems increasingly evident that, if we are to stem losses in readership and generate more public confidence, newspapers must be made more relevant to a society tossed and tumbled by accelerated change."

At the 1977 convention in Hawaii, Chaplin stated that ASNE had experienced few changes, except an increase in membership. At the convention 20 years earlier, he recalled, the program featured "How Goes Freedom of Information?" There had been changes in degree and emphasis, but editors in 1977 were still concerned with those same problems, among others—including the need to better educate the public that freedom of the press belongs to it, and that editors are surrogates.[76]

Hornby nevertheless noted areas of ASNE's solid progress in his summary of the decade. The work of the ASNE, he said, had led to newspapers that were more ethically aware, more thoughtful and significant in content, fairer to minorities and more accessible to the public than they were before 1970. Newspapers were better equipped technologically, had better trained staffs and were better organized to protect themselves in courts and legislatures. In general, he added, editors launched an efficient campaign, along with other segments of the industry, to improve readership.[77]

Hornby, however, noted goals that were not reached in the 10-year span. "If anything, the accuracy of our newspapers is declining, a very serious matter. If we editors would just make accuracy our fetish for the 1980s, we'd probably do the most for our cause." He cited superficial reporting of a complex world as an overlooked problem. Ending optimistically, Hornby asked that members of the society be recognized for the unique individuals they were—unique not in any superhuman characteristics but in the sense that they in their diversity represented an exceptional human institution. "This daily newspaper on the North American continent is really an extraordinary private institution."

NOTES

1. ASNE *Proceedings*, 1980, 81.

2. Ibid.

3. Leo Bogart, *Preserving the Press: How Daily Newspapers Mobilized to Keep Their Readers*, New York: Columbia University Press, 1991.

4. Eugene Patterson, letter to the author, July 20, 1990.

5. Ibid.

6. ASNE *Proceedings*, 1979, 79.

7. ASNE *Proceedings*, 1975, 43.

8. ASNE minutes, September 27, 1979, 803.

9. Howard H. (Tim) Hays, Jr., letter to the author, August 7, 1990.

10. Ibid.

11. Howard H. (Tim) Hays, Jr., "What Took So Long?" *ASNE Bulletin*, April 1976, 12.

12. Michael J. O'Neill, memo to special finance committee, "Expanded Leadership Role for the ASNE," October 19, 1976, 1.

13. Ibid., 6.

14. ASNE minutes, May 5, 1977, 742.

15. William H. Hornby, "Beware the Market Thinkers," *Quill*, January 1976, 14–17. Quoted by Leo Bogart, 113.

16. ASNE *Proceedings*, 1978, 86.

17. *Time* magazine, September 27, 1976. Quoted by Jack Claiborne, *The Charlotte Observer: Its Time and Place, 1869–1986*, Chapel Hill: University of North Carolina Press, 304, 308.

18. Despite using sophisticated personnel practices bequeathed by Hills, Claiborne (246) says McKnight recalled two top reporters who slipped through his fingers. One was Tom Wicker, a Hamlet native working for the Winston-Salem *Journal*. McKnight interviewed him for an editorial writing job but decided that Wicker was too liberal for the *Observer*. McKnight also dismissed Patrick J. Buchanan, who showed up at Columbia University with a copy of *The Conscience of a Conservative* under his arm. McKnight decided Buchanan was too conservative and advised him to look elsewhere. Buchanan went on to work for Casper Yost's old newspaper in St. Louis and later served in the Nixon and Reagan administrations as director of communications. Wicker went on to the New York *Times* as a columnist and later as an executive (Claiborne, 263).

19. ASNE *Proceedings*, 1980, 302–303.

20. ASNE minutes, September 27, 1979, 804.

21. Bogart, 138–139.

22. Ibid., 141–142.

23. Michael J. O'Neill, letter to the author, July 17, 1992.

24. Ibid.

25. Ibid.

26. J. Edward Murray, letter to the author, June 29, 1992.

27. ASNE minutes, April 12, 1971, 503.

28. ASNE minutes, April 15, 1974, 632.

29. ASNE minutes, April 22, 1972, 571.

30. Ibid.

31. ASNE minutes, November 20, 1972, 592.

32. ASNE minutes, April 15, 1974, 638.

33. ASNE *Proceedings*, 1971, 22.

34. ASNE *Proceedings*, 1975, 271.

35. ASNE *Proceedings*, 1970, 201.

36. ASNE *Proceedings*, 1972, 193–199.

37. ASNE *Proceedings*, 1973, 23.

38. Ibid.

39. J. Edward Murray, *Eye for an I*, unpublished autobiography, in possession of author from Mr. Murray, July 3, 1990, 331.

40. Ibid.

41. ASNE *Proceedings*, 1975, 45.

42. Ibid., 46.

43. Ibid., 45.

44. Eugene Patterson, July 20, 1990, letter to author.

45. Ibid.

46. Murray, 351.

47. Alice Fox Pitts, *Read All About It! 50 Years of ASNE*, Reston, Va.: ASNE, 1974, 164.

48. Murray, 339.

49. Ibid.

50. The full text of the document is published in the *ASNE Bulletin*, November–December, 1972, 18.

51. Pitts, 166.

52. J. Edward Murray, letter to the author, June 29, 1992.

53. Ibid., 346.

54. Michael J. O'Neill, letter to the author, August 4, 1990, 2.

55. Speech at Women in Communications convention, Denver, October 1982. Quoted in August 4, 1990, letter.

56. John Hughes, letter to the author, August 20, 1990.

57. Warren Phillips, quoted in Ghiglione, ed., *Gentlemen of the Press*, Indianapolis: R. R. Berg & Co., 1984, 180.

58. ASNE *Proceedings*, 1979, 79.

59. Ibid.

60. ASNE *Proceedings*, 1976, 20.

61. "Warren Phillips on the Year Ahead," *ASNE Bulletin*, May–June 1975, 20–21.

62. ASNE *Proceedings*, 1975, 274–275.

63. Ibid.

64. Warren H. Phillips, letter to the author, July 12, 1990.

65. Ibid.

66. ASNE minutes, April 14, 1971, 520.

67. ASNE minutes, October 27, 1973, 623.

68. ASNE minutes, April 18, 1975, 671.

69. ASNE minutes, April 15, 1976, 694.

70. Quoted by Norman Isaacs in *Gentlemen of the Press*, 65.

71. ASNE minutes, May 2, 1979, 823.

72. *Editor & Publisher*, February 28, 1976, 29.

73. ASNE minutes, April 6, 1980, 823.

74. "4 News Organizations Warn against Misuse of Privacy Act," *California Publisher*, February 1976, 1.

75. ASNE minutes, October 23, 1975, 680.

76. "What Will George Chaplin Mean to ASNE?" *ASNE Bulletin*, April 1976, 11.

77. Ibid.

Chapter 8

Editor-Businessman: The Changing Character of ASNE in the 1980s

Indeed, as I look at the editor's universe, change seems to be the one constant that confronts us. The role of the editor is changing for some members of this society even as we meet. In addition to serving as a community conscience, psychiatrist, monitor, priest, prophet, constant critic and occasional booster, there is that new role of editor-businessman.

—John Seigenthaler, April 12, 1989

And they surely did not like bean-counters, those people from the advertising, production and circulation sides who worried about mundane things like revenues. These were the keepers of the church, in the old ASNE, and they would not understand a lot of the people I am looking at today, including myself.

—Eugene Patterson, past ASNE president, April 14, 1989

One way to sense the changing character of ASNE, and to some extent of American journalism in the 1980s, is to refer to statistics cited by society President Richard Smyser of the Oak Ridge (Tenn.) *Oak Ridger*. In his presidential address in April 1985, Smyser noted the change in titles of the 1,000 members, resulting from policies that were adopted in the 1970s to encourage editors to become publishers and to permit former editors-turned-publishers to remain in ASNE. Referring to the problem of achieving a proper balance between the news and boardrooms when more and more editors were becoming publishers, Smyser said that the title "editor" was held by 42 percent of ASNE members in 1955, while only 31 percent retained that title in 1985.[1]

A 1986 survey conducted by Larry Allison of the Long Beach (Calif.) *Press-Telegram* showed that the society's 923 members represented only 448 daily newspapers, or less than 25 percent. Of 259 remaining editors who responded to the question of what would induce them to join the society, 10 percent said they would do so if dues were reduced. Another 66 percent said they would "seriously consider membership" under such terms.[2] In a 1989 report, L. John Haile of the Orlando *Sentinel* said the membership committee was "uncomfortable with the numerous exceptions the board was making to its membership policy."[3] Haile reported that the committee had made aggressive efforts to recruit editors of small newspapers, despite difficulty in getting the smaller newspapers involved in ASNE.

Another survey conducted by Ted Natt of the Longview (Wash.) *Daily News* in 1987 asked what members thought was the best thing about ASNE. Their replies were the *Bulletin*, minority workshops and early-bird workshops at the convention. Missing from ASNE they said, were a "nuts and bolts emphasis" and workshops between conventions. Those polled said the worst things about ASNE were too many conventions in Washington, D.C., an East Coast dominance and an "elitist" attitude.[4] In all, Smyser said that while he had seen "vast benefits coming from the news side because brilliant and caring editors had become brilliant and caring publishers," there were still serious questions: "What will be the effects if, increasingly, the position of editor is less an end in itself and more just another rung on the ladder to corporate management? Is the brilliant editor who moves up ever really able to completely turn over the editor's role he or she has ably filled to someone else so that they may be an editor, only an editor, because every newspaper needs at least one editor who is only an editor."[5]

Similar concerns were raised by former ASNE president Gene Patterson at a 1989 panel on "The Editor's Job: How Has It Changed?" Patterson recalled that when he first joined ASNE in 1957, "giants walked these halls." Members were "very testy fellows" who did not go to early morning workshops, which were said to be beneath an editor: "And they surely did not like bean-counters, those people from the advertising, production and circulation sides who worried about mundane things like revenues. These were the keepers of the church, in the old ASNE, and they would not understand a lot of the people I am looking at today, including myself."[6]

Patterson's remarks helped contrast the independent editors, described at the first ASNE meeting by Casper Yost as "gods within the machine," to more modern editors with a corporate mind—looking upon themselves as potential publishers and as editor-businessmen. He saw the so-called Bermuda Resolution, which was passed during Warren Phillips' administration to liberalize membership rules, as "the great watershed": "Instead of throwing out arbitrarily any editor who was not a directing editor, we decided some publishers, if they came up through the editor's office, could also be members of ASNE."[7]

Along with Smyser, Patterson questioned whether the liberalizing of membership policies had been a net gain: "Or have we lost some of that sharp edge of competition between God and man, between church and state? Have we softened the edge of First Amendment advocacy to the point of making it jibe with the bottom line? What have we lost in the process of gaining so much, beyond he old system of simply rattling our chains?"[8]

Other members raised concerns over the continuing exceptions to the membership policies. Designed to create a more diverse membership and financial foundation they actually resulted in an overabundance of retired members and publisher types. In 1981 Michael G. Gartner asked for a rule specifying that no publisher could join ASNE unless the operating editor were also a member. "I think it is terrific that publishers want to be members. We not only get their money, but we may also get their hearts as well. But I worry lest the publisher belong to ASNE instead of an editor."[9] Two years later the board recommended changing the bylaws to extend membership to those who hold "significant ultimate responsibility" for the news or editorial activities of daily newspaper companies, news services of daily newspapers or major national news organizations serving daily newspapers. According to President John Quinn (1982–1983), the changes would give the board "elbow room" to deal with newspaper questions at a time when newspaper titles were changing.[10] As interpreted in the discussion, any publisher would be welcome. Journalism school deans, on the other hand, were still excluded. Proponents believed that the changes would not mean a change in the character of the society.[11] The membership rejected the proposed change in a close vote.

Notwithstanding the rhetorical questions raised by Smyser, Patterson, Gartner and others about the change in titles of editors and the character of the society, new models and approaches to the editor's role were developing in the 1980s. Not only did ASNE broaden its membership to include publishers, small-town editors, and a variety of other supervisory types, but the membership joined in supporting an agenda which was established more and more by leaders who were elected from the major groups of the new corporate media world. These included newspaper chains and groups who were intimately involved with broadcasting media. Ithiel de Sola Pool described the situation as a convergence of modes.[12] This did not necessarily detract from the society's ongoing emphasis on traditional concerns: education in journalism, ethics, the First Amendment, freedom of information, international communications and the press, bar and public affairs. In addition to the innate, immediate problems of print, the editors now became more involved with issues revolving around technology, economics and social problems. ASNE became more concerned too with protection for broadcasters and even advertisers under the First Amendment. More than in any other era, newspaper editors had to be ready for change, including becoming more involved in business. An example is noted in the 1992 presidential address of David Lawrence Jr. To some, the address sounded more like a businessman's speech before the Chamber of Commerce than a traditional journalism speech.

Lawrence said that ASNE represented an industry and further described journalism as "our industry," "our business," "smart business" and "our franchise" while quoting from the Economic Policy Institute. "Some of us will need to lower our profit expectations, adjusting as other enterprises are doing," he warned. "I see nothing wrong with that."[13]

A further sense of the changes in journalism is apparent in comments by the first woman ASNE president, Katherine Fanning (1987–1988), when she recalled the personal and institutional changes the Anchorage *Daily News* underwent after withdrawing from a joint operating agreement with the Anchorage *Times* and entering a merger agreement with the McClatchy newspapers:

I was no longer a sole entrepreneur. Now I answered to a boss—and the first few months I didn't do it very gracefully. McClatchy sent in a management consultant with whom I immediately tangled. She saw my management style as oppressive. I was trying to be everywhere, involved in every decision. Back off, she said, and so did my bosses. Now that someone else's investment was at stake, I was even more intensely devoted to the paper's success. Reluctantly, I did back off and learned to delegate better. The whole newsroom staff no longer fit on our "one green couch" as reporter/columnist Suzan Nightingale had described it. Now I was an editor once-removed from the news staff, responsible for the content and editorial policy of the paper but also for an ever-growing business side.[14]

After years of close association with some of her managers, Fanning, like a whole new generation of editors, had to adjust relationships with her staff, readers and community. What was successful during the early years of struggling to establish her family-owned paper was no longer effective. With a newsroom staff that burgeoned from 12 to 60 (and eventually to 300 when she moved to the *Christian Science Monitor*), there were lessons to be learned "to delegate, to be willing to listen, to allow all levels of staff to advance ideas and take credit, to avoid involvement with every detail, to let others take the lead in meetings and listen to their views before giving mine—and I'm still learning."[15]

Similar observations about change were noted by John Seigenthaler in his 1989 presidential address: "Indeed, as I look at the editor's universe, change seems to be the one constant that confronts us. The role of the editor is changing for some members of this society even as we meet. In addition to serving as a community conscience, psychiatrist, monitor, priest, prophet, constant critic and occasional booster, there is that new role of editor-businessman."[16]

Along with those of three other group executives, Seigenthaler's career dramatizes the evolution from editor to businessman; it also demonstrates the growing affinity of ASNE leaders with the group (or corporate) mind in the 1980s. Two other group executives were also from Gannett: John Quinn, who had left the Providence *Journal-Bulletin* to join Gannett in 1963 and then helped launch *USA Today* in 1981, and Michael Gartner, who worked for Gannett papers in Des Moines and Louisville before joining NBC as vice president of news. The third, Robert P. Clark, joined Harte-Hanks newspapers after serving as editor of the *Florida Times-Union* and Jacksonville *Journal* and executive editor of the *Courier-Journal* and *Louisville Times*. The only ASNE presidents of the 1980s who were not from newspapers owned by large groups were Smyser; Mrs. Fanning, who had left the McClatchy group to join the *Christian Science Monitor* in 1983; and Loren Ghiglione of the Southbridge (Mass.) *News*.

As editor of the Nashville *Tennessean* and editorial director of *USA Today*, Seigenthaler was no stranger to changes in the media and in his local and national communities. As a reporter for his hometown *Tennessean* during the first stirrings of the civil rights movement in the late 1940s and 1950s, he, along with former *Tennessean* colleagues Creed Black, David Halberstam, Fred Graham, Bill Kovach and Jim Squires, saw many southerners adjust slowly to the idea of a society that includes blacks. Seigenthaler became caught up in the South's evolution. He left his job as one of the most tenacious investigative reporters in the South to serve as Robert F. Kennedy's assistant in the Department of Justice and to be the chief negotiator with the governor of Alabama during the 1961 Freedom Rides. At one time he was attacked by a mob of whites, and he suffered a fractured skull.[17]

Seigenthaler returned to the *Tennessean* at age 34, becoming the youngest editor of a major daily U.S. newspaper. His "instinct for the story"[18] served as a catalyst for change in newsroom operations, news gathering and editorial writing. He lost his early animosity for newpaper groups after the Gannett Company bought the previously home-owned *Tennessean* in 1979. Joking about the day he was "sold into chains," Seigenthaler became what one biography describes as "a strong, independent and valuable voice for Gannett." When offered the job as editorial director of *USA Today* in 1983, Seigenthaler eagerly accepted the opportunity. He kept his job in Nashville and commuted regularly to *USA* headquarters in the Washington area. This placed him closer to the new ASNE headquarters in the ANPA building in Virginia.

In Washington, Seigenthaler faced equally great leadership challenges on the ASNE board of directors and later as president (1988–1989) in a decade later described by Kevin Phillips as "a second Gilded Age of conservative politics." It was a period characterized by labor difficulties, tax reductions and a concentration of wealth under the "Teflon" administration of Republican Ronald Reagan.[19] Despite a growing population, newspaper circulation was not keeping up with the growth. Women and minorities were still absent from newsrooms. Journalism students shifted toward advertising, public relations and broadcasting. As head of the Education Committee, Seigenthaler warned in 1985 that newspapers no longer attracted the best students. Outstanding students were opting for other careers: "While newspaper editors seem to be satisfactorily filling their openings at present, the possibility exists that the supply may not be plentiful in several years. There are data suggesting that newspapers are losing talented people in mid-career and that newspaper salaries are not keeping pace with other fields."[20]

LOW NEWSROOM SALARIES

The following year, ASNE's first newsroom salary survey showed that many beginning reporters earned substantially less than starting schoolteachers. The report further confirmed that journalism educators were having difficulty attracting bright students. David Lawrence of the Knight-Ridder group recommended that the survey findings be distributed to publishers, who needed to understand the difficulties that low salaries presented to the newsroom. Seigenthaler described the salary results as "devastating." Larry Jinks, also of Knight-Ridder newspapers, said that the low salaries paid by small newspapers were a persuasive reason for bringing more of those newspapers into ASNE.[21] President Clark pointed out that salaries were "disgraceful." A beginning reporter on a small daily (under 10,000 circulation) started at $13,350 a year on the average. On a somewhat larger paper (20,000 to 30,000 circulation) the average starting salary was $16,000. Television news beginning salaries were comparable.

Speaking on "Greed Is Dangerous," Clark said that one reason for the low salaries was the groups' desires to keep profits up. The average profit is close to 20 percent—a handsome return for any business, he said. "In the past 10 years, newspapers have been among the brightest stars in the firmament of American business." Clark recalled that when he was executive editor of the *Courier-Journal and Times* from 1971 to 1979, the profit margin dropped to between 2 and 3 percent, a low figure that presented a problem: "There was fear that some members of the Bingham family, the owners, would want to sell their interests to get a better return elsewhere. So costs were cut, rates were raised and the return increased. Later family members got into a bitter squabble and the papers were sold to the Gannett Company."[22]

Clark pointed out the decline in quality of the Louisville newspapers after they were purchased by Gannett. A reporter and managing editor who led the Louisville papers to three Pulitzer Prizes during his tenure, Clark said the problems were caused in part by a cutback in human resources.[23] Vice president for news after the Harte-Hanks group was reduced to 10 dailies and several weeklies, Clark later became more vocal over the dangers of "bottom-line journalism."

DEBATE ON GROUP OWNERSHIP

Notwithstanding the apparent contradiction between the high profits of group-owned papers and the low salaries in the industry, most ASNE members accepted the inevitability of the business evolution. Appearing on a 1986 convention panel on "Mergers and Acquisition Frenzy in the News Business: Where Will It All End?" Seigenthaler recalled the conference in Honolulu 10 years before. He said that Gannett's purchase of his own newspaper had contributed to what he described as "a better paper, a more attractive paper, a more readable paper, with stronger Washington coverage, a larger staff and more reporters travelling outside the city to other assignments. There was also more investigative reporting and more resources. It was a more competitive paper in the market, and I acknowledged that."

Along with several other ASNE presidents, Ben Bagdikian, a journalist-turned-academic, questioned the growing trend of group and conglomerate newspapers at the 1986 meeting. As a self-proclaimed "skunk at the garden party," Bagdikian reminded the editors that it was splendid to have Rolfe Neill of the Knight-Ridder chain as moderator. Yet it would have been more interesting, he said, if ASNE had a representative from each of the chains, to put all of the names in a hat, stir them around and pick them at random. "And we might have picked out Thomson of North America or some other chain. The presence of John Seigenthaler, of course, reminds us that the distinguished paper of which he is the editor and publisher achieved its distinction under local ownership."[24]

Calling attention to the Knight-Ridder chain as one of the better newspaper groups in the nation was not entirely inappropriate. Known for its high degree of local autonomy[25] and for its reinvestment of money into its editorial departments in the 1980s, Knight-Ridder had also come to dominate the top leadership of ASNE. Only the Gannett Company with four, and the *Christian Science Monitor* and *Wall Street Journal*, with three presidents each, had made such institutional commitments to ASNE in the society's first 70 years. Seven of the 65 ASNE presidents from 1922 to 1992 were Knight executive editors or editors of newspapers controlled by the group.

Other Knight editors made important contributions to the society before and after the death of patriarch Knight in 1981. These included Everett Norlander, managing editor of the Chicago *Daily News*; Brodie Griffith, who trained ASNE presidents McKnight and Wolff and numerous other journalists in the South at the Charlotte *News* before the *News* was purchased by the Knight group in 1950; associate editor John D. Pennekamp and editorial page editor Don Shoemaker of the Miami *Herald*; Rolfe Neill of the Charlotte *Observer*; and Dorothy Jurney, who worked for the Philadelphia *Bulletin*, Detroit *Free Press* and Miami *Herald*. For many years she conducted surveys on women in the newsroom for ASNE. Along with Judith W. Brown of the New Britain (Conn.) *Herald*, Jurney provided major stimulus for the long-delayed and tortuous route of women into positions of ASNE leadership, culminating with the election of Fanning as president in 1987.

These editors and many more adopted the John Knight–Lee Hills philosophy that Knight editors should shy away from corporation boardrooms and, like Knight, be active in civic and professional groups.[26] At Knight's death in 1981, his $1 billion a year enterprise included 32 daily newspapers and partnership in several other papers and supply firms. The company had also become a model for other groups who were striving to gain acceptability and to rid themselves of the broadbrush attack on all newpaper chains. But even so-called "good" newspaper chain models, as noted by retired ASNE president Basil "Stuffy" Walters, had dangers: "In this continuous centralization of communications control, unless it is balanced off with strong grassroots newspapers which provide intelligent forums for debate and dissent. There's a danger of national brainwashing in mass communications. . . . We're going to need a lot of independent thinking 'rebels,' operating out through provinces to keep these giants in line."[27]

Bagdikian also challenged the popular thinking of the 1980s in ASNE by arguing that in the long run he did not think that chains benefited journalism or that they should dominate the thinking in that field. Unlike independent owners, Bagdikian said, most major chains sought expansion and acquisition on a national and even international scale. Consequently, he continued, their subsidiaries, including their news subsidiaries, were under pressure to produce maximum fast profits—not profits to survive and keep a paper economically healthy, but profits to feed the firm's national strategy. "And newspapers, especially monopoly newspapers, are usually easy to squeeze for surplus profits by cheapening content. And in most chains, this pressure is usually greater than in most independent papers." Specifically, Bagdikian pointed out that chain newspapers carry 23 percent less local and national news than independent papers, because local news is more expensive than syndicated matter.[28]

Bagdikian argued that larger organizations led to bureaucracies and to demands for uniformity and regularity: "The MBAs are moving into the newsroom."[29] Also, he discussed conflicts of interest that came with interlocking directorates and other pressures on editors. To illustrate the tension, he cited a 1980 survey which found that a third of the chain editors did not feel free to publish stories which damage the interest of their paper's parent firm. That survey was conducted, Bagdikian joked, "by the notorious troublemaking organization," the ASNE.[30]

Using the *Bulletin* and other publications, critics such as Norman Isaacs argued that although group giants such as Knight-Ridder and the Times-Mirror Corporation accorded publishers high degrees of autonomy, this was not the general pattern. Isaacs contended that, in general, the observable pattern was to release seasoned local executives and install younger, lower-salaried officers from smaller newspapers in the chain organizations, to adopt standard typographic patterns and to transmit computerized budgets from central headquarters. Isaacs quoted Malcolm Mallette, the American Press Institute's director of development, who noted that many publishers and editors were moved around like pawns. "It is hardly a system one can call dedicated to consistent and continuing service in the public interest."[31]

At least three other ASNE presidents, or presidents-to-be, challenged the growing movement toward groups of both large and small newspapers—groups which by 1987 controlled 80 percent of the nation's newspaper circulation. While the society's board of directors avoided taking positions on the issue, it was discussed openly and bluntly in the *Bulletin*, which served as the major forum of debate after the practice of introducing and debating resolutions was dropped. Tim Hays charged in 1987 that ASNE had been "ill served" by ignoring the warning of Hutchins Commission member Zechariah Chafee 40 years before about journalism's falling into fewer and fewer hands:

What little reaction to this trend there has been within the profession has focused on the question of whether newly acquired papers are improved or harmed in the short run. That's understandable. But the debate has been inconclusive. Time spent addressing long run consequences for the whole of American journalism would be more productive, for these are more discernible. And they point to trouble ahead for the press clause in the First Amendment.[32]

ASNE President Seymour Topping (1992–1993), director of editorial development for the New York Times Company, argued that purchase of a newspaper by a group does not always diminish quality and public service. Many papers improved after being acquired by a chain, Topping responded in a commentary in the *Bulletin*. Most retained editorial autonomy. Many groups instructed their publishers to be highly responsive to reader needs and community concerns. "However, unless there is a strong continuing commitment on the part of group management, the standard company practice of rotating publishers, who are rewarded in the first instance by the size of the profit margins, does not guarantee that community needs will be satisfied."[33]

Topping and Ghiglione expressed further concern about the growing number of U.S. newspapers which were being purchased by foreign owners—for example, the Canadian-owned Thomson newspapers and those of Conrad Black, a Toronto-based publisher. Black's views hardly agreed with the traditions of journalism in the United States, Topping charged.[34] In a special issue of the *Bulletin* on "When a Chain Adds a New Link," Barrie Zwicker examined the purchases by the Southam and Thomson groups, who controlled about half of Canada's circulation (10 Canadian chains control 80 percent of the country's daily circulation). "Is there a lesson in the Canadian experience for U.S. editors?" asked Ghiglione.[35]

Bagdikian challenged ASNE to conduct "its own study in a detached, scientific, non-defensive way to see if people like me are wrong." He said ASNE might use careful survey methods to view chain versus independent newspapers for such characteristics as quantities of local and national hard news, for the journalists hired per non-advertising page, or newsroom budgets as a percentage of profit margins. "I think it would show that on the whole, a good cross section of independent newspapers would come out better than a good cross section of chain papers. If that were done in an honest, careful survey, and I turned out to be wrong, I promise to personally sell *USA Today* for one hour at high noon at the corner of 14th and F."[36] During his tenure as president, Ghiglione took up Bagdikian's challenge by naming a committee to study group ownership. Previously, Ghiglione had conducted an in-depth study of 10 newspapers which had been purchased by chains: three newspapers improved, three remained the same, and four deteriorated.[37]

ASNE RELATIONS WITH BROADCASTERS

Not only did Seigenthaler modify his stand on group journalism, he also changed position to become more favorable toward broadcasters as equal partners under the First Amendment. So did the ASNE presidents from groups such as Knight-Ridder and Harte-Hanks newspapers. In the past the print media and broadcasters had competed for news and advertising dollars, but in the 1980s they became joined in corporate marriages through interlocking directorates, joint operating agreements and a multitude of other sophisticated financial and legal arrangements that made the former rivalries dated. Leaving past frictions behind, Seigenthaler now evoked what he interpreted as Thomas Jefferson's support of the electronic media: "When the freedom of any of us is threatened, the freedom of all of us is in jeopardy. I urge you to do all that you can do to protect and preserve freedom for all the media." Michael Gartner made a similar plea to support freedom for advertising and commercial speech in his 1987 presidential speech on behalf of broadcasters. He claimed that the U.S. press was not free because of infringements such as the Smith-Mundt Act, the Securities Act of 1933 and other laws which censored or impaired freedom of speech.[38]

Not all editors embraced the broadcast media as enthusiastically as Seigenthaler, Gartner and other group representatives. Minutes of board debates about continuing to support the Fairness Doctrine (as ASNE had since 1949) show early concerns to retain the doctrine. It was a twelve to six vote in May 1982.[39] Before the decade was over the vote to reject the Fairness Doctrine was unanimous.[40]

Three other ASNE presidents, however, raised questions about the electronic media in their annual reports. William Hornby warned that to some extent newspapers had let television news "lay off its value system to us—the obsession with personality, the competition to stress who's ahead, the episodic and capsulized treatment of important issues."[41]

In one of the lengthiest and most bitter[42] presidential addresses in ASNE history, Michael O'Neill charged that the very processes used to inform the public had been badly distorted by television and, to a lesser degree, by a whole range of other phenomena from investigative reporting to adversary journalism. "So not only have we failed to match new responsibility to new power, we have also yielded to trends that are hurting the cause of a well-informed citizenry." He contended that television helped to reverse U.S. national policy in Vietnam and ultimately to destroy the presidency of Lyndon Johnson. Moreover, O'Neill continued, "Television has played a decisive role in the revolution of rising expectations. It has strongly stimulated the consumption culture. It has dramatized the gap between the 'haves' and the 'have nots,' helping to create a runaway demand for more and more government services and for equality of result as well as of opportunity. . . . Television has also indelibly changed the democratic process by establishing a direct communications link between political leaders and their constituents. Now, as never before, those politicians are able to bypass the print media and the troublesome business of depending on reporters to represent them to the public."[43]

Creed Black also raised concerns about the merging of the two historically different media in the minds of the public. Speaking at the 1984 annual conference, Black bemoaned the print business' decreasing credibility, despite improved performance. A major problem, Black said, was that the public lumped the printed press and television together as "the media," making little distinction between the two. "The result is that we are blamed for the sins and shortcomings of what television—which remains basically an entertainment medium—calls news."

Black criticized television as "show biz and non-news, with little opportunity for dissent or criticism and lacking a standard mechanism for correcting errors." He offered ASNE members suggestions for confronting problems created for newspapers by television. Referring to an article by Stanley Cloud of the Los Angeles *Herald-Examiner*, Black urged editors to curb the use of the troublesome word *media*. The gradual replacement of "the press" by "the media," he said, had the effect of all but eliminating the distinctions between various purveyors of information. "By acquiescing in the use of 'the media,' we play directly into the hands of those who benefit from riding on the coattails of serious, responsible journalists."[44]

Concern over becoming too closely associated with broadcasters was also expressed by other members in the *Bulletin*. Arnold Friedman, editor of the Springfield (Mass.) *Union-News*, complained that editors were sending the wrong message when they reached into the "enemy camp" of broadcasters to procure speakers and panel moderators for ASNE conventions. In separate broadsides at 1990 luncheon speaker Dan Rather of CBS and at Carole Simpson of ABC, who moderated a panel on minority hiring in 1991, Friedman charged:

I don't remember the last time I read about a newspaper editor playing an important part in a TV executives' convention. Nor do I remember the last time I read through an ASNE convention program without a TV personality. I know we have to accept the fact that TV news does some things we can't (but not many). But maybe the program committee doesn't know that the TV folks are the enemy, at least in the competition for advertising dollars and readers' attention.[45]

Black also opposed efforts to revive the National News Council, which died in the 1980s. Because it was quite an active issue, Black says he did more than "watch" in his role as an ASNE president: "Instead, I strongly opposed the effort to pump new life into the corpse, often citing John S. Knight's statement that 'no self-respecting editor should surrender his judgment to a self-appointed group of busy-bodies.'"[46]

Norman Isaacs, ardent supporter of the news council concept, pointed to the discrepancy between Black's call for a standard mechanism to correct errors and the failure of editors to support institutions such as media councils which were intended to do just that. "Reading Black contend that TV was still in its adolescence reminded me of the prejudices we all carry, and how too often we abuse the privilege of using printing presses and air waves to vent private grievances," Isaacs wrote in a largely autobiographical book about the failure of editors to serve as skilled managers in journalism. "The distrust voiced to pollsters about journalistic fairness shows how astutely the citizens have divined how poorly those editorial gates are tended."[47]

O'Neill, who preceded Black as ASNE president, did not entirely agree with Isaacs' assessment on the death of the National News Council: "The trouble was that it was established as a kind of judicial tribunal. Aside from the fact that the council had no staff etc., to investigate grievances very well, it was quickly subverted into being kind of a quasi-extension of our legal system. Lawyers used our ethical guidelines and council statements as evidence in courts, so what was supposed to be voluntary became coercive."[48]

Vincent S. Jones joined Isaacs in the 70-year-old battle over ethics enforcement. In an essay on the state of the newspaper business, Jones observed that the rich were no longer getting richer in 1992—but no tears were being shed for the publishers whose profit margins had dropped from a gaudy 20 percent to a still robust 15 percent, or even a respectable 10 percent. In another shot at the "arrogance and irresponsibility" that were causing some readers to view the press as "a big ruthless, institution," Jones reminded ASNE members of the lack of an American media council, which was due to a lack of financing, and more importantly, of the failure to enlist broad support and cooperation from the industry's leadership: "Regrettably, ASNE does not attempt to enforce its lofty 'Statement of Principles,' which replaced its 1922 'Code of Ethics,' or 'Canons of Journalism,' which turned out to be toothless when challenged."[49]

The position of the society, in regard to the codes and voluntary guidelines, can be better seen in the challenge by Federated Publications, Inc., against Washington state Judge Byron L. Swedberg, who attempted to have reporters sign a voluntary agreement. Although the agreements were upheld by the Washington Supreme Court, ASNE fought such practices, along with several other attempts to restrict press freedom by the courts and by the Reagan administration. A survey by ASNE counsel Schmidt cited seven instances in which the ASNE Statement of Principles was introduced to support the argument that journalists were not reasonably prudent.[50]

ASNE STUDIES AND BOOKS

In addition to Ruth Clark's surveys on readership, or the lack of it, ASNE conducted studies on minorities, women and high school students. One report revealed the extent to which high school journalism had influenced professionals. The study by the Education for Journalism Committee showed that students with high school newspaper or yearbook experience achieved higher scores and grades than their counterparts.[51] In her second readership study in 1984, Clark noted that the United States had seen inflation, recession, unemployment, international crises and loss of prestige and competeiveness in world markets. Underlying many national polls was a deep-seated anxiety about the danger of nuclear war—not in the distant future, but in the lifetime of 1980s readers.[52]

In addition to ASNE publications, individual members and presidents published a variety of books in the 1980s, as they had since the 1920s. Following Casper Yost, Herbert Brucker and Vermont Royster as ASNE's most prolific president/authors was Loren Ghiglione. In addition to editing *Gentlemen of the Press* (1984), a series of profiles of ASNE editors that appeared in the *ASNE Bulletin* over the years, Ghiglione edited *Evaluating the Press: The New England Daily Newspaper Survey* (1974); *Improving Newswriting* (1982); *The Buying and Selling of America's Newspapers* (1984) and *The American Journalist: Paradox of the Press* (1990), which was written with a $325,000 grant Ghiglione received for an ASNE Library of Congress exhibit to celebrate the 300th birthday of the American newspaper.[53]

Other ASNE publications during the 1980s included *Playing It Straight*, a book on ethics written by John Hulteng, and *Improving Newswriting*, which was based on ASNE writing awards. This latter publication sold 7,500 copies and earned nearly $20,000 for the ASNE Foundation.[54] The spate of books being published by the society prompted President Creed Black to question whether ASNE should publish books unless markets could be determined for them. He asked, "Shouldn't we aim for projects that will return money to the foundation?"[55]

The ASNE Foundation, started in 1979, was the major tool through which organizations made tax-free gifts for projects dealing with minorities in journalism, readership, world press freedom and similar issues. By 1988, William Hornby announced that the Foundation had assets of $500,000.[56] In addition to providing funds for ASNE project reports, the *Editor's Exchange*, newspaper career booklets, cash prizes to winners in the writing contests and scholarships for minorities through a $100,000 endowment, the foundation also contributed $10,000 annually to bring foreign journalists to America. Hornby's successor, William Burleigh of the Scripps-Howard group, announced April 11, 1989, that ASNE Foundation funds exceeded $1 million for the first time.[57]

STAFF AND FINANCES

Lee Stinnett and a full-time staff of five others were the center of ASNE publications and research, which operated out of the ASNE headquarters in Reston, Virginia. In a 1992 report, shortly before the creation of the Newspaper Association of America from the blending of the 106-year old American Newspaper Publisher's Association (ANPA) with the Newspaper Advertising Bureau (NAB), president David Lawrence described ASNE as "among the most frugal organizations of my acquaintance." Lawrence also announced a restructuring committee headed by Seymour Topping that would streamline operations and cut costs after the two years of deficits by ASNE due to the American recession and a drop in ASNE membership to 917, the same number as in 1984.[58]

Among the proposals for change were that the vice president and treasurer would assist the president in overseeing committees; the secretary would head a board committee of four to review membership applications to the board of directors, who had ultimate responsibility for approving membership applications; ASNE would become an active participant in the the newly formed council of presidents, facilitating cooperation and communications among various news-editorial associations.[59]

A former reporter in New Orleans and Charlotte, Stinnett had joined ASNE as project director in 1981 and succeeded Gene Giancarlo as executive director in 1983.[60] Although his official charge was "to assist officers, directors and committee members in carrying out goals and policies of the society and to manage the headquarters," Stinnett was also an active researcher, writer and occasional contributor to the *Bulletin*, as well as being active in community organizations. In October 1988, Stinnett thanked officers and the staff for their support in a year in which he publicized the fact that he was gay. He told directors that he decided to publicize his involvement with various organizations, including the Whitman-Walker Clinic and the Arlington Gay and Lesbian Alliance.[61]

Just as Seigenthaler and Quinn represented ASNE editors who saw greater value in group ownership, Michael Gartner symbolized editors who were merging into related media areas. Gartner may be the best example of the new editor in the era of change. A former reporter and a one-third owner of his own newspaper, Gartner had a law degree that helped him through the intricacies of the increasing number of legal and financial problems facing ASNE's 1,000 members. He wrote a syndicated column on words and a viewpoint column for the *Wall Street Journal*. The First Amendment was attacked during the Reagan years. As ASNE president, Gartner pushed for an expanded view of the First Amendment in broadcasting and advertising. As chairman of the Freedom of Information Committee while at the Des Moines *Register & Tribune*, he had warned that the Freedom of Information Act was in "grievous danger" of being dismantled by the Reagan administration. He recommended that ASNE form a "SWAT team" to meet with President Reagan and possibly with ANPA representatives. Although some members expressed concern over having editors lobby, Gartner and former FOI Chairman Bailey said that because of their experience, they had no qualms about lobbying for the First Amendment.[62]

TROUBLE WITH THE REAGAN AND BUSH ADMINISTRATIONS

The Reagan administration's major attack on the people's right to know occurred on October 27, 1983, when the press was forbidden to accompany U.S. troops on their invasion of the island of Grenada. Military commanders also denied the press firsthand accounts. As a result of this news blackout, President Black and Edward R. Cony sent a telegram to Reagan that vehemently protested the restrictions. "It is deplorable for Americans to be depending on Radio Havana as a major source of news during the first few days of the invasion." The telegram, drafted by the FOI committee, said that ASNE understood fully the military need not to telegraph any invasion in advance, but that ASNE could not comprehend the refusal to allow U.S. reporters to accompany the troops. "From D-Day in 1944 through the Korean and Vietnam wars, U.S. reporters have been at the front with U.S. troops without endangering military security. What has changed?"[63]

More important was the follow-up initiative of Black and ANPA president William Marcil, who brought together 10 press organizations to take positions that would be effective in achieving a goal of early access to invasions and other military operations in the future. Producing a statement of principle on press access to military operations, the group declined membership on the Sidle Commission, which the Pentagon set up to establish guidelines for press access to combat zones.

Although there were subsequent controversies with the Pentagon over war coverage during the Gulf War in 1991, Black feels the ASNE and other press groups played an imporant role in fighting for access.

Prior to the Gulf War, Gartner had called further attention to First Amendment abuses by the Reagan administration and Congress. These included legislation forbidding dissemination of Voice of America material in the United States; the Domestic Mail Manual; the U.S. Code, which made it a crime to broadcast lottery information; and the Securities Act. Gartner, president of news for NBC, also challenged Supreme Court rulings on commercial speech and libel cases, including *Keeton* v. *Hustler, Calder* v. *Jones,* and *Bose Corp.* v. *Consumer's Union.*[64] In 1991, Gartner received national exposure for his articles which supported the right of the media to publish the names of rape victims. ASNE did not take a similar position.

The society's FOI committee and legal counsel became involved in dozens of issues, media alerts and *amici* briefs during the 1980s. For example, Peter Prichard of *USA Today* reported that ASNE had taken a leading role in trying to dissuade Congress from reenacting the Fairness Doctrine with a "press alert" which generated about 20 editorials on the issue. Other committee actions included the following:

The committee

1. opposed attempts in the U.S.–Canada trade agreement to define a journalist.

2. urged a Senate subcommittee to let in "sunshine" through the open meeting law.

3. opposed visa denials on the grounds of advocacy of unpopular ideas.

4. fought proposed restrictions on commercial satellite sensing systems.

5. supported ham operators' rights to gather news in emergencies.

6. protested attempts by Western Kentucky University to limit the rights of a student newspaper.[65]

To challenge what Press, Bar and Public Affairs chairman John Craig of the Pittsburgh *Post-Gazette* called "the monumental level of ignorance on the part of the judiciary," the ASNE published an updated second edition of *Free Press* v. *Fair Trial*. Published in the previous decade, it served an important role, paving the way for passage of the Freedom of Information Act. It was challenged by the executive and legislative branches in the 1980s.

ASNE also received national attention after the publication of its report revealing that a significant minority of newspaper editors believed that even a free press ought to have legal limits. The report, *Free Expression and the American Editor*, was a survey of the 900-member organization that found wide disagreement among editors on how much legal protection to afford different kinds of speech. While editors were generally more supportive than the public of media and speech rights, two related studies stated, a surprising number said the press should not be free to say just anything. For example, only about one-half of the ASNE members would give unconditional legal protection for newspapers' reporting that could influence trials, name juvenile suspects or rape victims, or disclose politicians' sex lives. "There are without a doubt editors who don't believe in free expression. It's astounding they're in the business," said Seigenthaler. As chair of the ASNE First Amendment Committee, he helped finance the $80,000 survey along with Gannett Foundation and Middle Tennessee University.[66]

INTERNATIONAL PROJECTS

According to Norman Pearlstine of the *Wall Street Journal*, a program sponsored by the International Communications Committee (ICC) was furthered by ASNE's ongoing effort to help foreign journalists understand how the U.S. press works. In addition to sponsoring foreign journalists in the United States, ASNE sent 12 members to the Soviet Union in November 1987. It was the third ASNE group to visit the USSR since 1984. In return, a delegation from the USSR visited New York, Washington, San Francisco and Los Angeles under ASNE auspices.[67] In 1984, A. M. Rosenthal of the New York *Times* objected to a visit by Soviet journalists on the grounds that they were journalists in name only: "They are propagandists for the Russian government. To engage in such an exchange makes a mockery of the free press."[68] President Creed Black suggested that such objections be discussed with the Russians during their visit. He said that editors, who understood the differences between American and Soviet journalists, could still benefit from the exchanges. He asked for a vote to reaffirm support for the exchange and received unanimous approval.[69]

Illiteracy, which affected about one in five adults in the United States, became a new problem for the ASNE to face in the 1980s, since it had an obvious impact on newspaper readership. In response to the problem, the society formed the Literacy Committee, which was to act as the chief instigator of numerous reading activities. In 1988, Jay Ambrose, then editor of the El Paso *Herald-Post,* cited a dozen programs in which ASNE was participating, along with such organizations as the ANPA Newspaper in Education Committee, the Education Writers Committee, the Foundation of the International Newspaper Advertising and Marketing Forces and the Southern Newspaper Publishers Association Foundation.[70]

ASNE WRITING AWARDS

To foster better writing, ASNE continued to recognize outstanding writers with $1,000 awards at its annual meetings. Shortly after the scandal at the

Washington *Post* when reporter Janet Cooke created a fictional composite character, however, ASNE found it had a problem of its own. David Laventhol of *Newsday*, head of the Writing Awards committee, provided written documentation that one of the award-winning articles by Tom Archdeacon of the Miami *News* contained a small amount of material which had appeared elsewhere. After an investigation by the *News*, editors were satisfied that the borrowed material was an isolated case.

ASNE insisted that public disclosure of the case was essential to the credibility of the awards and the profession. Although the incident appeared to be a journalistic misdemeanor, not a felony, a mistake rather than plagiarism, the board deplored such gross carelessness and sloppiness as part of the working procedure of such a talented writer. "We hope full public airing of what took place will discourage such casual practices in the future, both for the individual involved and for all those who might take shortcuts under deadline pressure."[71]

EXPANDING ROLE FOR MINORITIES AND WOMEN

Along with its new problems, the society continued to grapple with blights that had plagued journalism for decades. Among the most persistent problems were recruiting, hiring and advancing more minorities and women in newsrooms nationwide as well as within its own ranks. The topic dominated board meetings, annual meetings and presidential addresses. President Thomas Winship of the Boston *Globe* emphasized the need of the print media to confront minority underrepresentation, warning board members that they were sitting on a "time bomb."[72] Winship repeated his concerns in an impassioned president's address when he scolded members, "Our casual attitude toward minority employment is particularly embarrassing because our mission is semi-public and because it is protected by constitutional guarantees. Yet newspapers, with a nearly all-white face, attempt to portray accurately a mixed society."[73]

Richard Smyser and Robert P. Clark also addressed minority representation in their presidential addresses. The son of a minister, Clark said that along with poor credibility and the lip service paid to education in journalism, the small number of minorities in the newsroom was a major blind spot for editors. Although progress had been made, he added, ASNE still had a long way to go. He saw the issue as an economic as well as a moral issue: "Every time we gain a few percentage points in the minority representation in our newsrooms, the general population is surging ahead that much faster. By 1990 minorities will be 25 percent of this country's population. By the year 2000, 29 percent. And here we stand in our newsrooms at something over 6 percent."[74]

Smyser cited minority employment as the first of four major ASNE concerns ahead of strains between government and the press, the role of the editor, and the credibility problem. As a well-known symbol of small-town journalism, Smyser had served for many years on the minorities committee, where he and Seigenthaler were instrumental in creating the salaried position for Carl Morris, the society's first minority affairs director. Robert Maynard of the Oakland *Tribune* and William A. Hilliard, the executive editor of the Portland *Oregonian*, also provided valuable assistance on the issue of minority representation. In October 1990, the board elected Hilliard ASNE treasurer. As such, in 1994 he became the society's first black president.[75]

New members recruited in the 1980s reflected the small percentage of women in top editing positions.[76] Concern about underrepresentation of women in ASNE and newsrooms was closely related to the concerns over minority recruiting problems. The issue was brought forward again when Judith W. Brown called for the resurrection of a 1973 survey which showed the small number of women in newsrooms. Brown herself had broken a sex barrier in 1978 with her election to the board. She was followed by Tina Hills, wife of former ASNE president Lee Hills, of Puerto Rico. But by 1987 only three other women in addition to Katherine Fanning had made it to the predominantly male preserve. One recommendation made to the directors was to create a committee to examine the problem. Although Charles W. Bailey pointed out the tendency to create committees on everything and suggested that the creation of a committee for women would be a step backward, the directors continued to support efforts by Mrs. Brown and others to encourage more women to join ASNE. By the 1990s, women were being nominated to positions on the board after being in the society for only a short time. The 1991 board included five women, 25 percent of the board. The society took a major symbolic step forward when Mrs. Fanning became its first female president in 1987. As noted by Michael Gartner, who succeeded her, stories about Mrs. Fanning's becoming the first female president of the 65-year-old organization had begun when she first stepped on ASNE's leadership ladder in 1983. Mrs. Fanning gave credit to those women who had labored in the newsroom many years before her: "I am not kidding myself. I know that I would have had to go to the end of a much longer line before ascending the so-called ladder of the ASNE if it had not been for ASNE's clear desire to diversify newsrooms and bring in women and minorities."[77]

Like Robert Clark before her, in her presidential address Fanning called attention to the growing trend toward group ownership. She also acknowledged Ed Cony of the *Wall Street Journal*, who, after being elected president, resigned and received a standing ovation from convention attendees. Cony, a persistent advocate of press freedom and openness, insisted on revealing the full facts behind his resignation: he had been diagnosed as having Alzheimer's disease.[78] The first *Journal* reporter ever to win a Pulitzer Prize (for his analysis of a timber transaction which drew attention to the problems of business ethics in

1981), Cony was known for his attempt to reduce the proliferating number of ASNE committees. Committees had contributed to management problems, he said, and as president-elect he had proposed to reduce the number from 15.[79]

Through a greatly expanded *Bulletin*, speeches and news releases, Gartner, Fanning and numerous others helped to expand the image of ASNE, if not its influence, more than during any other decade in ASNE history. This new aggressiveness included joint efforts with the ANPA to stop AT&T's attempts to enter the information business following the deregulation of the telephone company in the early 1980s. Some expressed concern about the ANPA's willingness to have editors join in their lobbying efforts. Clayton Kirkpatrick noted that although ANPA needed to lead, it would welcome the support of ASNE, which should continue as is because "there is going to be a lot of guerrilla warfare and that is where editors shine."[80]

An editor who placed himself in this activist category was Ghiglione, who served as ASNE president from 1989 to 1990. Ghiglione created four new committees: Newspapers and the Disabled, Prison Journalism, Ownership, and History and Newspapers. In his 1990 presidential address, Ghiglione called for a more active ASNE in the 1990s. Among other things, he challenged editors to form a "Press Corps"—a newspapers' Peace Corps. "News people in the 1990s must retool their thinking and rededicate themselves to action and change in order for newspapers to keep pace with a changing America," he said. "The '90s require our action. Not every action need be earth-shattering, but the more we try to achieve, the more we will achieve. Passivity and neutrality, watchwords of journalism in the '80s, must be replaced in the '90s by a passionate, persistent commitment to action."[81]

Along with the board of directors, ASNE president Burl Osborne, editor and publisher of the Dallas *Morning News*, focused attention on the freedom of expression in the marketplace of ideas, on international relations brought about by the breakdown of the former communist empire and on diversity in the workplace.[82] During 1990–1991, he reported that minority employment was about three times greater than the previous year, or about nine-tenths (0.9) of one percent, the largest 1-year improvement in 13 years. That increase was encouraging for two reasons, Osborne told members at the Boston convention, which was held to celebrate the 200th anniversary of the Bill of Rights. First, it occurred during a period with a sagging economy, which caused some to fear that the minority percentage would decline. And second, it suggested that ASNE progress does not have to be linear—that it may be possible to accelerate.

A longtime Associated Press reporter and bureau chief, Osborne relied heavily on market research[83] to revitalize the *Morning News* and eventually eliminate the Dallas *Times-Herald* from competition. He also warned of the dangers of the political correctness movement's inhibiting free speech and thus constituting a threat to the First Amendment. On the darker side of the first year of the decade, Osborne expressed concern over attacks on the press by the military, and in particular, Osborne said that the military had carried out "a textbook job" on the battleground of public opinion and had clobbered the press in coverage of the Persian Gulf War. Responding to criticism that ASNE did not join in lawsuits to challenge the military censorship, Osborne pointed out: "We did not see the need to get involved in litigation, because we were involved in negotiations with the Department of Defense. The war ended so quickly that in essence the matter became moot. We are continuing to negotiate with the military to achieve a better basis for covering future conflicts."[84]

As predicted by Osborne, president David Lawrence continued efforts to strengthen the First Amendment values, while continuing the campaign for pluralism. Among the major ASNE accomplishments cited by Lawrence was that minorities in 1992 made up 9.4 percent of newsroom journalists, up from 8.7 the previous year.

In his outgoing speech, utilizing the language of the business community, Lawrence expressed a strong feeling of optimism for an industry and country that, though they were beset by economic, social, informational and professional problems, had for the most part successfully grappled with those problems during the ASNE's more than 70 years of existence. In an increasingly fragmented society, with increasingly fragmented media, Lawrence saw that what newspapers did best was necessary for the future of democracy. Though newspapers have never been better, he claimed, they must be still better. "ASNE will continue to be a leader in the pursuit of such excellence."

Lawrence's sucessor, Seymour Topping, director of editorial development for the New York Times Company, noted the profound changes in relationships between editors and publishers in one of his first notes to the membership in the summer of 1992. An underlying complaint of many publishers at their annual convention was that editors had allegedly isolated themselves in an elitist manner from the concerns of the marketing departments. Editors, on the other hand, perceived "encroachment by advertisers" as a growing threat to their editorial integrity as a major problem in the 1990s.

As one means of looking into the problem, the ASNE ethics committee gathered evidence to support warnings from business writers about the threat to editorial integrity. Topping also said he had submitted a proposal for broadened cooperation between the editors and publishers. The arrangment did not impinge on the independence of ASNE, Topping said. It was designed to bring about closer cooperation through uninhibited discussion. "It will fit into the emerging editor-publisher dialogue upon which the future of our newspapers may turn."[85]

Following Topping as the society's 64th president was William A. Hilliard, editor of the Portland *Oregonian*, and ASNE's first black president. A low-key administrator who had worked his way up from copy boy, Hilliard said he wished it were not noteworthy that a black man was coming into the leadership position of a national organization. But he said the country had not changed enough for that. He said he viewed his arrival as a signal to young people that there was a place for minorities in news organizations.

"The thing that bothers me more than anything else," Hilliard said, "is what I see as more and more racial divisions in the country today. And I think newspapers are the ideal education tool to correct it."[86]

The editor who succeeded Hilliard, Gregory Favre, executive editor of the Sacramento *Bee*, shared similar sentiments concerning minorities as well as a broad range of activities as he assumed leadership of the 893-member professional group in April, 1994.[87] "I hope the coming year will see ASNE help our industry take additional steps toward achievement of our diversity goals and continue our fierce protection of First Amendment issues," he said. "In addition we will examine the whole process of change in newspapers, including a major effort in the area of new media and values," Favre said in describing a process that had continued since the time of Casper Yost.

NOTES

1. ASNE *Proceedings*, 1985, 13.
2. ASNE minutes, April 7, 1986, 1053.
3. ASNE minutes, October 7–8, 1988, 1145.
4. ASNE minutes, October 9, 1987, 1115.
5. ASNE *Proceedings*, 1985, 13.
6. ASNE *Proceedings*, 1989, 212.
7. Ibid.
8. Ibid.
9. ASNE minutes, April 20, 1981, 855.
10. An example of the increased leeway given to editors can be seen in a 1989 discussion concerning the approval of senior editors at *USA Today*, recorded in the April 11, 1989, ASNE minutes, 1169. After a question by Ted Natt, it was reported that there were 20 news executives from *USA Today* in Washington who were ASNE members. Additional discussion on the changes in membership can be seen in ASNE minutes, October 11, 1984, 1009.
11. ASNE minutes, May 8, 1983, 930–932.
12. See Ithiel de Sola Pool, *Technologies of Freedom*, Cambridge: Harvard University Press, 1983.
13. David Lawrence, Jr., "The Future for Newspapers," Presidential Address, April 8, 1992, 5.
14. Mrs. Fanning is quoted by Judith G. Clabes, ed., in *New Guardians of the Press: Selected Profiles of America's Women Newspaper Editors*, Indianapolis: R. J. Berg & Co., 1983, 71.
15. Ibid.

16. ASNE *Proceedings*, 1989, 7.

17. Gannett corporate biography of Seigenthaler in author's possession. See also Pam Janis, "Seigenthaler retires after 42 years," *Gannetteer*, February 1992, 8–9; Frank Sutherland, "Reporter, Editor, Publisher, Role Model: Which John Seigenthaler Are We Writing About?" *ASNE Bulletin*, February 1990, 15–21; Peter Prichard, *The Making of McPaper: The Inside Story of* USA Today, Kansas City: Andrews, McMeel & Parker, 1987, 156.

18. Author and journalist David Halberstam, who worked with him in the 1950s, says Seigenthaler was the first reporter he ever knew who had the ability to contribute to his career as a brilliantly tuned reporter (*ASNE Bulletin*, February 1989, 16).

19. See Kevin Phillips, *The Politics of the Rich and the Poor: Wealth and the American Electorate in the Reagan Aftermath*, New York: Random House, 1990.

20. ASNE minutes, April 9, 1985, 1022.

21. ASNE minutes, April 8, 1986, 1058.

22. Robert P. Clark, "Bottom-Line Journalism," *Editor & Publisher*, May 26, 1990.

23. Robert P. Clark, telephone interview with the author, July 25, 1990.

24. ASNE *Proceedings*, 1986, 225.

25. Norman Isaacs, *Untended Gates: The Mismanaged Press*, New York: Columbia University Press, 90.

26. Don Shoemaker, "Lee Hills, Executive Editor, Knight Newspapers," in Loren Ghiglione, ed., *Gentlemen of the Press*, Indianapolis: R. J. Berg & Co., 1984, 160.

27. Raymond Moscowitz, *Stuffy: The Life of Newspaper Pioneer Basil "Stuffy" Walters*, Ames: Iowa State University Press, 1982, 183.

28. ASNE *Proceedings*, 1986, 226.

29. One example of this is seen in the fact that two of the ASNE presidents in the 1990s—Burl Osborne and David Lawrence Jr.—are graduates of the Advanced Management Program at Harvard.

30. ASNE *Proceedings*, 1986, 227.

31. Isaacs, 90.

32. Howard H. Hays, Jr., "In a world of chain newspapers, do we need a bill of rights for editors?" *ASNE Bulletin*, July–August 1987, 30.

33. Seymour Topping, "The single-minded pursuit of profits will trip up newspapers in the end," *ASNE Bulletin*, September–October 1988, 14–16.

34. Ibid.

35. Loren Ghiglione, "When a Chain Adds a New Link," *ASNE Bulletin*, February 1981, 15.

36. ASNE *Proceedings*, 1986, 228.

37. Loren Ghiglione, *The Buying and Selling of America's Newspapers*, Indianapolis: R. J. Berg & Co., 1984.

38. ASNE *Proceedings*, 1987, 6–14.

39. ASNE minutes, May 3, 1982.

40. Ibid., 892; May 7, 1982, 911; October 7–8, 1988, 1142; April 11, 1986, 1163.

41. ASNE *Proceedings*, 1980, 82.

42. Term used by Al Romm of Ottaway newspapers to describe O'Neill's comments on "The Power of the Press: A Problem for the Republic—a Challenge to Editors,"

ASNE *Proceedings*, 1982, 19. The speech was later included in *Representative American Speeches, 1982–83*, edited by Owen Peterson, 97–111.

43. ASNE *Proceedings*, 1982, 13.

44. ASNE *Proceedings*, 1984, 12.

45. Arnold Friedman, "TV headliners: Why Do We Continue to Invite 'The Enemy' into Our Camp?" *ASNE Bulletin*, May–June 1991, 40.

46. Creed C. Black, letter to the author, July 29, 1992, 2.

47. Isaacs, 13. See also Norman Isaacs, "Circuit Preacher on Journalism's Sins," *ASNE Bulletin*, March 1984, 23–26; Watson Sims, "Monitoring the Monitor of the Press," *ASNE Bulletin*, July–August 1980, 14.

48. Michael J. O'Neill, letter to the author, August 4, 1990. Further discussion of how codes of ethics can be used against newspapers can be seen in ASNE minutes, October 11, 1984, 1007.

49. Vincent S. Jones, "Under fire from all sides, newspapers are still expected to perform aggressively," *ASNE Bulletin*, April 1992, 32–35.

50. ASNE minutes, April 7, 1987, 1099.

51. *High School Journalism Confronts Critical Deadline*, a Report by the Journalism Education Association Committee on the Role of Journalism in Secondary Education, Blue Springs, Missouri, 1987.

52. ASNE *Proceedings*, 1984, "Relating to Readers in the 1980s," 107–117.

53. ASNE minutes, April 12, 1988, 1132.

54. ASNE minutes, May 7, 1984, 986.

55. ASNE minutes, October 21, 1982, 915.

56. William H. Hornby, "Foundation assets reach $500,000; Bill Hornby steps down as president," *ASNE Bulletin*, April 1988, 9.

57. ASNE minutes, April 11, 1989, 1164.

58. David Lawrence, Jr., "Strong and vital ASNE remains critical; tough times affect Society, too; restructuring is under way," *ASNE Bulletin*, January–February 1992, 2.

59. "ASNE members taking on more duties: restructuring aims to improve communication, planning," *ASNE Bulletin*, January–February 1992, 32.

60. In the November 13, 1980, minutes, President Thomas Winship refers to Stinnett as "made to order for us." Vice president Michael O'Neill said that of all the candidates, Stinnett is "the stick-out." "He has newspaper background, plus experience with ANPA in functions that we are interested in. He is bright, enthusiastic and well-recommended." See also Michael Gartner, "Introducing the Staff," *ASNE Bulletin*, July–August 1986, 2; John Seigenthaler, "Here is some hard data on ASNE's anonymous—but efficient staff," *ASNE Bulletin*, November 1988, 2.

61. ASNE minutes, October 7–8, 1988, 1161.

62. ASNE minutes, October 1, 1981, 873.

63. ASNE minutes, October 30, 1983, 950.

64. Ibid.

65. ASNE minutes, April 11, 1989, 1163. Another example of the ASNE's increasing involvement in legal issues can be seen in the October 7–8, 1988, minutes, 1142.

66. George Garneau, "Some editors say press should not be free," *Editor & Publisher*, May 4, 1991, 17.

67. Norman Pearlstine, "Exchanges, Trips, Protests, Pools—ASNE International Efforts Growing," *ASNE Bulletin*, April 1988, 15.

68. ASNE minutes, May 7, 1984, 990.

69. Ibid.

70. Jay Ambrose, "Opening an Encyclopedia of Reading Activities," *ASNE Bulletin*, April 1988, 20–21.

71. ASNE minutes, October 21, 1982, 922.

72. ASNE minutes, April 25, 1981, 866.

73. ASNE *Proceedings*, 1981, 335.

74. ASNE *Proceedings*, 1985, 63.

75. "Hilliard will be next ASNE treasurer," *ASNE Bulletin*, November 1990, 29. For a complete account of blacks in ASNE, see Alf Pratte, "Ending this history of neglect of a truly integrated press: ASNE rhetoric and reality in fostering racial diversity, 1922–1991," paper presented to Western Journalism Historians Association, Berkeley, Calif., February 1992.

76. ASNE minutes, April 11, 1989, 1169.

77. ASNE *Proceedings*, 1987, 228. For a full account of women in ASNE, see Pratte, "'A Torturous Route Growing Up': The Rise of Women in the American Society of Newspaper Editors," *Journal of Women's History*, Vol. 6, No. 1 (Spring 1994).

78. ASNE *Proceedings*, 1988, 3.

79. ASNE minutes, October 9, 1987, 1109–1110.

80. ASNE minutes, November 13, 1980, 839.

81. Loren Ghiglione, "The 1990s: A Time for Frontline Fighters and a New Kind of Peace Corps," *Newspaper Research Journal*, Summer 1990, 6.

82. Burl Osborne, interview with the author, Dallas, Texas, July 15, 1992.

83. Peter Elkind, "High Stakes in Dallas: Is the *Times-Herald* Still in the Game?" *Washington Journalism Review*, June 1986, 27.

84. *ASNE Bulletin*, May–June 1991, 39.

85. Seymour Topping, "Where does news fit in the marketing world? 'Team' play should not mean an end to editorial independence," *ASNE Bulletin*, July–August 1992, 2.

86. William Glaberson, *The New York* Times, March 4, 1993, A6.

87. *ASNE Bulletin*, June–July 1994, 19.

Chapter 9

A More Far-Reaching Effect

It follows then that the acts of this Society should have an influence on journalism as a whole, and upon the public attitude toward journalism, proportionate to the powers of the press which it represents. What we do here, therefore, may have a more far-reaching effect than that which touches our personal, or even collective interests as a group.

—Casper Yost, ASNE *Proceedings*, 1924

One of the more difficult responsibilities of historians is to assess the influence of the subject they write about. It is relatively easy to gather relevant information, then weigh and even interpret the data in light of other sources. The hundreds of variables that exist, however, make determination of causal relationships or actual influence (the ability to form or control) difficult, if not impossible. Only slightly easier is the effort to assess leadership—that is, the ability of individuals or institutions to crystallize, organize or set agendas for other individuals or organizations. Former ASNE president Lee Hills (1962–1963) observed this difficulty:

ASNE is and must be loosely organized. It doesn't speak for "the press." No one can do that. Our individuals speak only for themselves. It is a mistake to look upon American newspapers as a national press. Even so, the society exerts a profound influence in raising newspaper standards. It inspires a sense of professional pride, of dignity, of respect, and of responsibility. The society's influence comes, not despite the fact that it refuses to regulate our conduct of newspapers, but because it does not do so.[1]

Another former president, Marvin Creager (1936–1937), said that trying to analyze and diagnose journalism is a slippery job, like "trying to nail a custard pie to the wall":

The process is full of intangibles; it just is not finite. But therein is the great charm of journalism. It cannot be run by rules and measures. The fellow who makes toothpicks or

buttons knows exactly what he has to do every day. He has to change his methods only
when a new kind of wood or a different sort of clam shell is found. But men want to be
individuals. We want to be challenged. We want new problems. And so we are or should
be on the alert against standardization and rut-following, whether of our own device or
of outside origin. They are the most insidious foes of the broad and useful press. In fact,
they are foes to the very life of the press.[2]

Notwithstanding such custard pie problems, historians are obligated to assess
for their readers where the historians have been, what they have seen and perhaps even what they think, using a variety of gauges and tools. What follows is
an attempt to assess the success of ASNE by comparing claimed effects or leadership with the six purposes of the society as set forth in the preamble to its constitution and described by Casper Yost in his presidential address at the first
meeting in 1923.

For most of its history, the annual president's message has served as a primary
source of critical evaluation, or as Norman Isaacs said, its purpose is "to inform,
to raise sights or to raise hell in the society."[3] Although the presidential message
has shifted in recent years from a specific evaluation of the society to one of
journalism in general, it helps gauge the accomplishments, leadership and perhaps influence of ASNE on an annual basis. As noted by William Hornby in his
1980 report to members:

We know that the criticisms have been well-taken, and ours is an intensely self-critical
calling. Indeed, one of the rewards of being your president is the opportunity to know in
some depth on their home grounds, a great number and variety of editors. I have yet to
meet that arrogant, all-knowing, power-oriented, commercially obsessed and prurient
editor who would match some popular stereotype of old—a stereotype that may yet lurk
there in the shadows of government and academe.[4]

In addition to evaluations from ASNE presidents and members, this examination
refers to influential observers outside the organization as well as minutes and
financial records.

I. To promote acquaintance among members

Notwithstanding a letter William Allen White received in the 1920s
recommending that he join ASNE but acknowledging, "I cannot say much for
the benefit to be derived from contact with other newspapermen,"[5] ASNE's first
goal, to promote acquaintance among members, appears to have been reached.
By the last decade of the 20th century, the society had grown from five members primarily from the midwest to 877 members in 50 states as well as Puerto
Rico, the Virgin Islands, Canada and France. By 1992, ASNE's annual income

was $662,432.92 with expenses of $654,807.87.[6] ASNE may have dissolved some of the isolation Yost spoke of when he said that an editor functioned "as a monk, as it were, performing his individual orisons within his individual cell with little regard to what others similarly engaged are doing, with no windows on the outer world of journalism."

Yost emphasized the importance of merging individual editors into a collective force to provide leadership. In his four presidential addresses delivered from 1923 to 1926, the usually cautious editorial writer did not hesitate to use the words *effects* and *influence* to describe the impact of the society. Although Yost conceded that the growing interest in journalism in the 1920s was based in part on an "awakening professional consciousness," he believed that ASNE was a powerful force and would continue as such in the future. In his opinion,

Real accomplishment in an undertaking such as ours is not to be found in some definite and great achievement effected speedily and by main strength, but in the gradual and cumulative results of continuing influence and effort, directed along the ground, toward a practicable end, however ideal that end may be. . . . If we expect this society to accomplish any great and immediate reform of, or advance in newspaper conduct, we are likely to be disappointed and discouraged. Such results are rarely brought about save through continuous and cumulative impressions acting upon an increasing consciousness. That consciousness, once made fully alive and active, through the influences we are setting in motion, will gradually effect the primary purposes of our organization.[7]

Creager foresaw the power of individual editors growing through acquaintances that would have been impossible without ASNE and great good coming from "knee-to-knee discussions with men who speak our language and whose opinion we value."[8] Don Sterling of the Oregon *Journal*, president in 1939–1940, noted the growing networks which were being developed by personal contact across the country: "Our newspaper world is rather small numerically and thus through such meetings as these it is possible to know personally men and women who are representative of the best newspaper performance anywhere. And that in itself is an opportunity."[9]

In his unpublished biography, Sterling added: "The society has done much to raise American journalism to what Washington bureaucracy calls 'top level.' It has performed one other tangible and invaluable service. It has created many enduring friendships which in itself is sufficient justification for its being."[10]

In his 1949 presidential address, Erwin Canham assessed the influence of acquaintanceship: "America's newspapers are the principal source of information for the American people. And the American Society of Newspaper Editors is the chief professional forum where the men and women responsible for the thinking that goes into American newspapers meet and take a good look at themselves and their world."[11]

By 1963 Herbert Brucker observed:

Certainly in the past 41 years ASNE has moved to the front and center of American
journalism. And as the recent newspaper strikes have shown once again, the newspaper
remains fundamental to our society despite all that those modern electronic marvels,
radio and TV, can do. Those famous branches of our government, the executive, legislative, and judicial, together could not function without an informed citizenry. And it is the
daily newspaper alone that makes possible an informed citizenry by printing and preserving each day's history as it happens.[12]

ACQUAINTANCE WITH FOREIGN EDITORS AND ISSUES

ASNE has also served as a forum for foreign editors. The society has actively
supported international organizations, including IPI (International Press
Institute), IAPA (Inter-American Press Association) and FIEJ (Federation
Internationale des Editeurs de Journaux et Publications). Concern for foreign
causes did not begin in earnest until shortly before the Japanese attack on Pearl
Harbor, however, when Tom Wallace observed that failure to get involved
beyond U.S. borders had created problems: "This is not the time or place for
extended discussion of our failure to make the best of our opportunities in
Tropical America, but had we done so during our first generation there would
have been no anxiety in the United States at the outbreak of Europe's latest war
about hemispheric solidarity."[13]

Wallace, the society's president in 1940–1941, recommended that ASNE
"pay more attention than we have paid to our economic and political problems
in the other Americas, and that we cultivate acquaintance with them for our
social benefit."[14] Major efforts were made to foster international acquaintanceship and alliances near the end of World War II, when the society sent three
members around the world to promote press freedom. After their return in 1946,
John Knight enthusiastically described the tour "as one of the finest achievements in the history of American journalism."[15] Wilbur Forrest was equally
enthusiastic: "The American Society of Newspaper Editors has, I believe,
attained an international stature. We have also gained the prestige of being
asked to assist in the writing of the provisions of an instrument which may have
vast significance in this postwar world."[16]

Forrest pointed out that world press freedom was being discussed in many
quarters. He also stated that while ASNE had passed many resolutions to sustain
a free press over the years, others had provided similar leadership: "Mr. Kent
Cooper of the Associated Press and Mr. Hugh Baillie of the United Press both
had publicly identified themselves with the movement before the ASNE entered
the picture in an active manner. We find little difference in the objectives

of these gentlemen with those of the ASNE. We are working separately along similar lines."[17]

Knight also heralded efforts by individual members and directors, some of whom appeared before the resolutions committees of the two major political parties. Knight said ASNE had persuaded both Republicans and Democrats to include as part of their platforms support for a free press and unrestricted communications for news throughout the world.[18]

Two years later, in the period before the founding of the United Nations, Canham identified ASNE as a society that "has come of age" internationally. He reminded members,

You will remember the important role ASNE has played in preserving the cause of world freedom of information. The Forrest Committee, which we sent around the world in 1945, the Finnegan draft treaty of 1947, the visit of the Russian editors to this Society in 1947, the support of state governors in 1947, and the steady pressure we kept up on American government to further the free interchange of information, have all in a sense culminated in the situation which now exists at Lake Success.[19]

Despite an unfortunate experience in attempting to shepherd press freedom resolutions through the United Nations, B. M. McKelway felt the society would still provide leadership in the area of press freedom:

As a society of American newspapermen, we should continue to lend encouragement to our fellow newspapermen in other parts of the world whose situation may not be so fortunate as our own. We should continue to strengthen our ties with them, work with them toward the ultimate removal of barriers to free exchange of honest news, remembering always that we can learn just as much from them as they can learn from us.[20]

Further evidence of ASNE's leadership in developing acquaintances around the world is seen in the contributions of Wallace, Knight and Hills, who served as presidents of the IAPA as well as ASNE. ASNE sent delegates of editors to Russia in 1962 and 1969 and to China in 1972, 1975 and 1978. Reciprocal visits from the Chinese to the United States occurred in 1973 and 1978. ASNE also held one of its 12 conferences outside the United States in Montreal, Canada, in 1966. The program agenda has traditionally included foreign speakers, including Konrad Adenauer and Fidel Castro. Primarily, however, the society has remained an American organization with occasional spurts of international interest.

MEMBERSHIP BECOMING TOO LARGE

On the opposite side of the efforts to foster acquaintanceship, however, was the concern that the society would become too large to be effective. In 1924

Yost stressed the value of "the smallness of our organization"; size was controlled by deliberate restrictions upon membership. While Yost regarded the restrictions as wise, he realized that a considerable percentage of the membership could not attend ASNE's annual meetings. Recognizing this problem, he wondered whether the society should change its membership restrictions and yet still enable directing editors to retain full control of the organization and its activities.[21]

After World War II, the large membership became so unwieldy that the board instructed its secretary to limit further membership so as to protect the quality of the society. In his 1948 presidential speech, N. R. Howard of the Cleveland *News* discussed efforts to manage membership, which was then nearing 500:

I disliked the word "purge," but the fact is that the membership rolls have been tightened by an inspection of the present qualifications of members, some of them long-time and most excellent members, whose present work seems to have removed them from the membership qualifications specified in our by-laws. I am only candid when I say that this screening which is done on behalf of our having an active and vigilant membership of editors, will take from the society some of the fraternalism and congeniality of the older days when the size of membership offered no problem.[22]

The following year, McKelway discussed the size of the society, which he said was too large to find accommodations in Washington. Linked closely to the problem of size was the problem of direction of the society; in other words, the direction in which ASNE should move as a professional organization. "For the larger we grow, the more weight we shall be asked to carry, and we wish to be sure that we are carrying that weight in the most desirable direction."[23] Other editors who expressed concern about the size of the society in the 1960s included former presidents Vincent S. Jones and Norman E. Isaacs. Richard Smyser was also concerned about the disadvantages of a large membership. In his 1985 presidential speech, he discussed the changes in membership rules which allowed editors-turned-publishers to stay in the organization. He wondered whether the ASNE membership dilemma were a direct reflection of some very basic changes in the nature of the editor's role:

What is happening, what has already happened to the editor who rather consciously stays apart from the business side and concentrates on being the champion of and watchdog over excellence in the newsroom? Which is not to say that there is anything wrong with the business side or anything especially noble about the role of the editor—just editor. But which is to say there are distinct roles both of which need to be played well and to the hilt if there is to be a proper balance between the separation of news and business sides of the newspaper. I don't know if this statistic means anything, but in 1955, 42 percent of ASNE members had the title of 'editor'—just that one word. Of the current membership, 31 percent have the title of editor—just one word.[24]

II. To develop a stronger and professional esprit de corps

One way in which ASNE members have encouraged devotion, honor and enthusiasm within the society and throughout the newspaper industry is by having their leaders speak to other professional organizations and to editors, reporters and schools of journalism. "It is easy to perceive that in our brief history we have started something," Yost said in 1925.

Directly and indirectly this society has helped materially to arouse a larger degree of interest in journalism, its principles, its methods and its purposes, within the profession and without. It has prompted an increased thought about journalism as a whole as distinguished from journalism as an individual endeavor. It has stimulated discussion of principles and of modes of conduct far beyond our own field or membership. The evidence of this is to be seen in the increased attention given to these matters in numerous gatherings of journalistic organizations outside of our own, in the greater frequency of their discussion in the editorial columns of newspapers, in the larger number of articles on journalism in periodicals, whether commendatory or condemnatory, and in the use of the theme in public discussions similarly varied in views.[25]

ASNE's success in creating an esprit de corps with other journalism organizations can also be seen in its resolutions to cooperate with Sigma Delta Chi[26] and its consideration (but rejection) of a proposal for joint issuance of the SDX *Quill* and *ASNE Bulletin*.[27] The ASNE board of directors also considered a 1948 request by the newly organized National Conference of Editorial Writers for affiliation with ASNE as an associate organization.[28]

JOURNALISM EDUCATION

From its first meeting, when a committee headed by Arthur M. Howe of the Brooklyn *Eagle* was appointed to work with journalism educators to establish standards, ASNE has been a major force in journalism education. One decade after ASNE was organized, Frank Fuller Shedd quoted Willard G. Bleyer of the University of Wisconsin to the effect that a joint committee of professionals and educators was "of as great consequence for the efficient education for journalism and the confirmation of its highest standards, as all that had previously been accomplished in more than 20 years of service."[29] N. H. (Nat) Howard said in 1948 that an interguiding council had "crossed the Rubicon" in a decade-long effort to classify schools of journalism:

I would like the society to understand that this is no mere pleasant junket, but an assertion of our influence in American education for a kind of professional work which may serve as a turning point for the country's schools of journalism. There may be repercussions from disappointed universities which will come to the attention of some of our members. It seemed fitting to have the whole story told on the program, and to have the operation benefitted by the comments of the whole membership. I think it may mean more work and more money by the society in years to come, in the interest of better application of the journalism colleges to the functions which we are in a position to define.[30]

Similar comments about ASNE leadership were made in 1972 by Norval Dean Luxon, former dean of the University of North Carolina School of Journalism: "It is my firm belief that the society through its schools of journalism and education committee, has done more than any other journalistic organization to influence the improvement of professional education for journalism in the nation's colleges and universities."[31]

Such successes did not prevent ASNE from overlooking the subtle changes taking place within journalism education in the 1980s. As suggested by John Seigenthaler in 1989, the diminishing number of journalism students demonstrated the need for higher starting salaries in the newsroom and for "close and constant monitoring" of those salaries by the ASNE Education for Journalism Committee: "The swing is now heavily toward advertising and public relations. In my judgment, if that trend continues, it inevitably will have an impact inside the academy. It is clear to me that communications schools will shift resources—by that I mean faculty and program funding—to meet the changes. It is impossible to predict what this change will mean in the future of journalism education programs."[32]

FAILURE TO PROVIDE FULL-TIME STAFF

From the society's earliest days, ASNE presidents complained about the lack of full-time help; this was probably the chief factor in preventing ASNE from having real influence. The lack of a full-time staff became the most consistent criticism of the society by its leaders.

E. C. Hopwood (1926–1928) was the first president to propose a society office. In 1927 he recommended a fund of $20,000 to $25,000 annually to establish an office and to retain an adequate investigator and necessary legal counsel.[33] Hopwood's pleas were followed by those of Walter Harrison (1928–1930) and Frank Fuller Shedd, Harrison's successor. Shedd urged a program of action by which ASNE would maintain contact with other newspaper associations in order to achieve by "earnestness and effectiveness of its purpose and effort" a position of leadership. He warned that such continuing contact could not be established and maintained without a permanent secretariat.[34] Such presidential pleas were rejected. The only assistance to the growing society was provided by Alice Fox Pitts, who began work in January 1933 as an assistant secretary. Her primary tasks were to publish the *Bulletin* more frequently, to gather material that criticized newspapers, and to aid generally in the work of ASNE. Her salary was $25 per week.[35] After 13 years of service, Mrs. Pitts received the title of assistant secretary and *Bulletin* editor, and her salary increased to $5,000 per year. One other part-time employee, Mrs. DeVee K. Fisher, served as an assistant to the treasurer until the late 1970s.[36]

The need for a permanent staff to function beyond the annual meeting and to assist the president and board was emphasized for the next two decades by such leaders as Marvin Creager. His comments in 1937 hinted at how slowly the society was developing: "We are fifteen years old and in long pants. It is high time for us to decide which school we are going to. And we should make sure that we are not overlooking opportunities of service that may be seized by some other group if the field is left open. I urge that the members of the new board give the matter their close attention."[37]

The frustration of many members over the organization's inability to exert itself as a society and to have an impact on journalism culminated during World War II. President W. S. Gilmore, in his 1943 presidential address, renewed the call for a permanent executive officer who could be a spokesperson throughout the year and provide recognition similar to that of the Associated Press Managing Editors (APME), which he believed was more visible than ASNE:

For twenty-one years we have existed largely to have an annual meeting such as this, at which time we elect new officers. The result is that WE know who is president and secretary and treasurer and so forth, but persons in the government or even in the American Newspaper Publishers Association do not. Therefore, it is natural that the APME has come to be looked upon as the voice of the principal newspapers in the country.[38]

"This is wrong," Gilmore told members.

We who are primarily concerned with reporting the news and commenting editorially thereon; and with the ethics of our business (or profession, if you prefer), are the ones who should be carrying the flag for a free and untrammeled press. We are the society to which the government should have appealed when it wanted the newspapers of the country to clean up the scrap. We are the organization that should take the lead in every movement involving the press as a medium of information.[39]

The call for a full-time secretariat was resumed after World War II by John S. Knight. He said membership had reached a point where it was "virtually impossible for officers located in various parts of the country to conduct the affairs of the society on an efficient and thoroughgoing basis without a Washington office." The following year Wilbur Forrest restated the plea. By the 1950s, President Dwight Young (1950–1951) said the society was approaching the time when the president would have only "a minimum amount" of time to devote to his own newspaper:[40]

I confess that I have no recommendation to make as to how this problem is to be solved. It is too much to ask that an incoming president should request a year's leave of partial absence from his newspaper in order to meet the requirements of the presidential office. At the same time it is too much to expect of any editor that he fulfill his responsibilities to the Society and at the same time carry on normally as editor of his newspaper. There are not enough hours in the day to meet both requirements.

Two years later, Alexander F. (Casey) Jones described ASNE as "the only major society representing a great profession" that did not maintain a secretariat. The most devastating criticism of the weaknesses of the society came in 1960 when Russell Wiggins expressed his concerns in remarks that were generally unreported. Turning his attention to the institution, Wiggins said: "Is the ASNE the proper agency through which such a continuing analysis and appraisal should be going on? If not, who is going to do it? The informal exchange of ideas at meetings such as this is helpful; but no great commercial enterprise would be content with such haphazard and informal inquiry into its future."[41]

Wiggins noted that during the 1950s, members of the press had been analyzed by those outside the profession, and they seemed to be in a cycle where more advice would be offered. But without a technical staff the society was unable to accomplish much. Although not reported in the *ASNE Bulletin*, Wiggins' speech served as a watershed for a change in the tone and approach of presidential addresses from 1960 until the present. In contrast to observations, conclusions and constructive criticism specifically aimed at the society in former speeches, most presidential addresses since that time have focused more generally on the profession and not on ASNE. Wiggins believes that the toning down of the speeches may have resulted in part from the elimination of the heated debates over resolutions on the last day of the convention. In particular, he recalled a debate he had with Jack Knight which became so heated that it had to be stopped.[42] Wiggins found that as the society grew larger and more social, the intellectual and ideological disputes also toned down.

CLOSER AFFILIATION WITH PUBLISHERS

Prompted in part by ASNE's inability (because of a lack of resources) to carry out its goals with other news/editorial-oriented groups and to pursue other issues, the editors of the society began to be more closely associated with their owners in the 1960s. This new ecumenical alliance contrasted with the outlook of founding father E. S. Beck when he wrote to Arthur Krock of the New York *Times* 40 years earlier and expressed his concern over the editors' lack of independence in establishing the society: "At the outset I fell in with the idea but on the whole the organization developed feebly. In a basic sense, it seems to me the whole trouble is that we are employees and are, to a degree, under inhibitions and cannot speak freely for our papers. I do not know that the association as it has evolved is of considerable value, but the acquaintanceship is pleasant and perhaps useful."[43]

Despite such reservations, a closer ASNE affiliation with publishers appears to have started in earnest during World War II when President Marvin announced his plans "to cement, if possible, with the publisher associations of the country, particularly with the ANPA, a relationship of cooperative equality and comradeship." Marvin later described how he had "worked together with the ANPA as a matched team."[44]

The following year, however, President Gilmore questioned the wisdom of a growing alliance with publishers and with the ANPA, noting that the two organizations still had basic ideological differences. "They must be concerned with problems quite different from ours," Gilmore noted, "just as in our daily work there must be a sharp division of interest and duties between business office and editorial department. Let us find a way to carry that same division of interest into the public eye with respect to duties and responsibilities of ANPA and ASNE."[45]

Among the first to attempt to formalize closer relations with the publishers was Kenneth MacDonald (1955–1956), who suggested that ASNE and ANPA participate in joint projects: "During the last year one meeting was held to see whether there were further areas of mutual interest which our organization should explore. Nothing definite has been accomplished as yet, but I hope these efforts will not be abandoned. There are several areas of newspaper operations which should be the joint responsibility of editors and publishers, and I think we might profitably combine our efforts in these areas."[46]

President Hays in 1975 referred to two weaknesses which detracted from ASNE's efforts to influence its members and journalism in general: financial problems and failure to provide ample opportunities for members to participate actively in its affairs. He urged future boards to find ways to obtain additional revenue and to get more than one-sixth of the membership involved in projects. He observed that perhaps these weaknesses did not disturb everyone: "There always used to be members who felt that ASNE does not do very much, that a strong society would, indeed, be dangerous. That may have been a reasonable position at one time; it seems to me an impossible one today. Facing the problems that we do, we need all the strength that we can muster."[47]

Such concerns were also voiced by Michael O'Neill. In the 1977 draft of a memo calling for greater ASNE editorial leadership, O'Neill said that ASNE's purposes had tended to make the society fraternal, insular, and in a sense, somewhat self-protective. He contended that society members were aloof from the big picture while focusing on parochial concerns in the newsroom: "Editors have traditionally kept their distance from the business side of newspapers, fearful of commercial intrusions that could threaten editorial integrity. This has reinforced the idea that they are a breed apart. It has encouraged publishers to lean mainly on other departments for the advice they need to solve their problems."[48]

As a case in point, O'Neill referred to the Newspaper Advertising Bureau. Whereas ASNE limped along with three employees and less than $150,000 a year in the 1970s, the bureau had 112 employees and a budget of nearly $6 million. Understandably, its ideas had a far greater impact on industry thinking. The bureau became the driving force in a National Readership Project, a project that carried it deeply into editorial issues while the ASNE followed slowly.

By the 1970s, with ASNE's assumption of the co-chair of the readership committee, ASNE editors had moved closer to the publishers' orbit. The traditionally financially threadbare editors also received funding for much-needed research projects. Eugene Patterson noted this as

the new posture ASNE has chosen to assume aggressively in preference to the alternative isolation of defensiveness and resistance which would have us believe we can only rattle our chains. When we started rattling the chinaware instead, we were heartened indeed to find ourselves being cheered on by our colleagues in publishing and advertising, whose support shows their relief at finding us ready to manage our news and editorial destiny. We have growing confidence that we can act from a position of strength, among companion groups that depend on our judgment of news and editorial imperatives.[49]

III. To maintain the dignity and rights of the profession

From the very first, the society was anxiously involved in maintaining the dignity and rights of the press. This can be seen to some extent by studying, both qualitatively and quantitatively, the committees which were appointed to carry out the society's work. Among the six standing committees started in 1923—along with the institutional housekeeping committees of program and membership, as well as committees on schools of journalism and ethics—were committees who were to grapple with two major problems of the day: syndicates and press services, and legislation. The former committee has long since died, but the latter has evolved into various other committees relating to freedom of the press and freedom of information. Creed Black, in his 1965 report as chair of the FOI committee, observed: "FOI is not a very sexy subject, and it is sometimes hard to get even our own members interested. But one conclusion I do have after two years on the job is that as bored as even we get with it sometimes, I do think that the only way we are going to get anywhere is for every member, even if it is a chore, to interest himself in the questions."[50]

Eugene S. Pulliam, Jr., of the Indianapolis *News*, chairman of the 1961 Freedom of Information Committee, said the society did not appear to make much progress over the long haul. But he added that it was necessary for ASNE to continue its efforts: "We of the newspaper profession are the only group that is both willing and able to keep up this fight. The bigger government becomes, the more important it is that we are free to keep the American public informed."[51]

Robert C. Notson added to Pulliam's remarks, noting that freedom is not automatic: "Every generation must either rewin or defend it in important ways, or it will surely be lost. Nearly every loss of freedom is inadvertent. The change simply masquerades a cloak of some new and plausible public benefit."[52]

Both Notson and Warren Phillips reminded editors that freedom of the press is not the journalist's alone. According to Phillips, "We need to repeat again and again, first that the First Amendment created a free press for the public's protection and not as a privilege for publishers and editors."[53]

Notson's remarks were similar:

We need to remind ourselves and our readers that freedom of the press is not freedom of newspapers. It is a guarantee of an unfailing access of a free people to report on public affairs. And this includes the administration of justice, which is important in public business, not just the business of attorneys and judges.[54]

It took a while for ASNE to reach this stage, however. During its early years, the society was not seriously involved in the fight for press freedom at home or abroad. Rather than provide leadership, according to Walter Harrison, it was more engaged in "catching up with the caboose." One of the few issues ASNE was involved in during its first four years was the crusade against secrecy in government and against efforts by the bar to curtail court news. Two of the first issues of journalistic rights discussed by Erie Hopwood were attacks on journalists for allegedly violating contempt of court orders, and attacks on newspaper representatives, notably photographers.[55] Two years later Walter Harrison praised the Chicago *Tribune* for assuming the financial obligations in the famous *Near* v. *Minnesota* case involving press freedom. According to Harrison, "If our organization is not the proper medium through which to defend aggressively all such invasions in the future, we have little excuse for existence. We should be so organized that first news of such tyrannical legislation should filter into a headquarters office, where a fight might be planned for the whole fraternity."[56]

At the start of World War II, ASNE became a major participant, along with government, in developing and implementing voluntary censorship. As noted by Dwight Marvin, the problems of war changed the tempo of the times and ASNE had to quicken its pace to keep up. Along with the American Newspaper Publishers Association, ASNE and military officials worked out a plan for voluntary censorship at home that served as a model for the next three years. By 1944, Roy Roberts was able to report that ASNE had succeeded in every possible way to make newspapers' influence felt constructively in regard to the war effort. Despite being criticized by ASNE member Carl Ackerman for serving on government propaganda bodies, Roberts viewed keeping news channels open as "the first duty of this society and its membership."[57]

John Knight reported in 1946 that many times during his stewardship as ASNE president he had been urged by editors to repudiate the voluntary censorship agreements, which one editor said "resulted in ridiculous withholdings of legitimate news from the public." Knight stated that he considered such recommendations ill-advised, even though he had protested to President Truman the suspension of AP filing facilities from Europe after the premature release of the Armistice story.[58]

President Howard reported the next year that ASNE efforts on behalf of world freedom of information were being considered by the Truman administration. "We have never before in peacetime become identified with a national government policy," Howard told members. He said it was no mean compliment to the society that its standing committee chairman, Erwin Canham, was also a delegate to the Geneva session on freedom of world news. Two other members of the society (Sevellon Brown of the Providence *Journal and Bulletin* and Oveta Culp Hobby of the Houston *Post*) were also included in the government delegation.[59]

Canham told members in 1949 that the U.S. effort for world press freedom was a crusade which the ASNE and its members had "a large share in initiating" and which could not be abandoned in midstream. The situation at the time, according to Canham, was hopeful. "For this change in the atmosphere, I am certain the chief credit goes to the editorial attention many American newspapers gave to freedom of information in the last week or ten days."[60]

In a 1973 appraisal of the society's contributions to world press freedom, however, Canham was less optimistic about the results of ASNE efforts:

The treaties were virtually dead. They lived in the half-world of United Nations diplomatic bureaucracy for many years, but have never been of any effect, either good or bad, in the cause of freedom of information. . . . From all the hopes and disappointments of the immediate postwar period have sprung no lasting treaties, no binding commitments, no official guarantees. But a reasonably healthy array of international newspaper organizations does now exist. They are of some value in supporting aspirations for a free press, seeking sometimes to rescue an editor in distress, and whacking away at continuing barriers through private professional action.[61]

THE PUBLIC'S RIGHT TO KNOW

The ASNE is also credited with being a major force in promoting the public's right to know. Although these words did not appear until 1945 in an address by the general manager of the Associated Press, Kent Cooper, the concept was widely promoted by ASNE and its counsel, Harold Cross. According to Herbert Altschull, Cross justified the concept on the basis of a three-century-old demand for the government to open its documents to citizens who needed to use them.[62] In his 1951 report, Dwight Young said Cross and the FOI committee would survey the increasing tendency by both elected and appointed public officials—and various bureaucrats, national, state and local—to restrict the gathering and publishing of thoroughly legitimate news in the United States.[63]

Five years later, President MacDonald was able to report the success of the project: "The society has expended more time and energy on that one project than on any other in the society's history. We arranged for the publication of a book on *The People's Right to Know*, written by a distinguished member of our society, Harold Cross. We inspired similar crusades on the part of other newspaper organizations, so that now freedom of information committees are functioning in almost every state."[64]

More specifically, in 1959, Russell Wiggins said that under the leadership of James Pope's committee, Cross had accomplished a great deal:

Many local governing bodies, hitherto operating behind closed doors, have opened their proceedings to the public. Many state legislatures, under the impetus of state newspaper committees drawing upon the counsel of Dr. Cross, have passed better access laws. Congress has amended the 1789 housekeeping statute (5 USC 2) under which many federal officials were withholding information. Amendments to the Administrative Procedures Act are in committee. Groundwork has been laid for a better federal records statute. Information amendments to the ICA legislation have been approved. In Congress, and in the country, sentiment has been gathering, slowly but surely, behind the principles that Dr. Cross laid out in his book *The People's Right to Know* and that he defended in public addresses and in his frequent appearances before congressional committees.[65]

The general topic of freedom of the press was refocused in 1957 at the San Francisco meeting when members adopted "A Declaration of Principles," which emphasized the right of the American people to know, except where military necessity plainly prevented it.

Although ANPA overshadowed ASNE in the freedom of information struggle during its fledgling years,[66] ASNE later became more involved in a greater variety of legal issues under the direction of Richard Schmidt, its attorney. Society members also received impetus to expand their efforts into broadcasting and commercial speech by presidents such as Michael Gartner.[67] Many ASNE leaders fought for a free press, as evidenced by the number of John Peter Zenger awards awarded to past ASNE members.

IV. To consider and perhaps establish ethical standards of professional conduct

One of the best examples of ASNE leadership and influence is its Statement of Principles or Code of Ethics, first adopted in 1922 and later revised in 1975. The revised code better reflected editors' desire to prevent their professional ideology from being used against them in legal suits. Although lacking the ability to enforce principles, the statement has served as the foundation for ethics codes for other journalists as well as the rhetorical basis of the journalistic ideology. In his 1929 presidential address, Walter Harrison predicted: "Those first members should be signally honored and long remembered. I think the thing started there someday will cast a shadow across the continent as the medium through which journalism will develop the ethical standards of the profession."[68]

Defending the ASNE's lack of enforcement of its ethics code, Casper Yost said,

It has stimulated thought throughout the profession as nothing else has ever done. There has been more discussion of ethical questions since these canons were adopted than, I venture to say, in the whole previous history of journalism. It has been influential in no small degree in causing journalism generally to turn the searchlight upon itself. Many state and regional press associations have followed the examples of this society in formulating codes of ethics. The ethical quality of instruction in the schools of journalism has been strengthened. There has been not only a quickened consciousness of professional responsibilities in the moral sense, but a quickened professional conscience.[69]

Numerous discussions about code enforcement followed. A committee on ethical standards lasted only a few years. B. M. McKelway recalled hearing the report of William Allen White at the 1927 convention: "Mr. Chairman and Fellow Members . . . the Committee cannot report. It has no idea what the ethics of this business is. The subject is too broad. We return for further instructions."[70]

Marvin Creager commented: "The American Society of Newspaper Editors does not and cannot set itself up as the autocrat of journalism." Even in 1937, Creager said the society could not be accused of any aspiration to be "Der Fuehrer of the press."

One of the most significant criticisms of the society and its position on ethics was contained in the Hutchins Commission report on *A Free and a Responsible Press*. Among other complaints was its charge that the society had failed to enforce its code of ethics. In his bitter defense against the charge, Wilbur Forrest overstated the commission's concerns by claiming that the commission saw the society only as

a social organization backed up by a high-sounding code of newspaper ethics about which it does nothing whatsoever. We have utterly failed, says the commission. The commission says that we made a feeble attempt a long time ago to enforce our code against a case of gross malpractice, but after long and painful deliberation we dropped the case. This, the commission says, settled the function of the code which otherwise could or would have made newspapers responsible carriers of news and discussions.[71]

Overly defensive, Forrest claimed that this part of the commission's report seemed to indicate strongly the opinion that newspapers are "not responsible carriers of news and discussions." The point is clearly made that in the opinion of the commission, the public is not getting what it should get. McKelway noted that there had been other attempts to revive the ethics committee so it could answer the harsh characterizations of the press by those so bold as to criticize its performance. He said he had found the same yen for such machinery present in the society during his tenure.[72]

V. To interchange ideas for the advancement of professional ideals and the more effective application of professional labors

Speaking during what he viewed as a long period of "mental unrest, worriment, dissatisfaction and actual discontent" in the Depression, Fred Fuller Shedd saw both an opportunity and a responsibility for newspapers to provide a forum in which changes would be discussed by the people, and public opinion formed, organized and brought into action:

Better that the newspaper should render this service than it be left to the soap box, or even to the radio broadcast, or to the various mouthpieces that range in between. Better in the newspapers than in the magazines of comparatively limited circulation. Better that the discussion shall be before the whole who are newspaper readers, than before groups of the people who may be tuned into partisan messages. Critics of newspapers are prone to say that we have lost our prestige, our influence, that editorial pages are not read, and even that they are not worth being read. And this ought to be our opportunity and answer, as it shall be if we do the part that is given us as moulders of public opinion.[73]

In particular, Basil "Stuffy" Walters saw the function of the society as similar to that of a great university:

It provides a forum for the exchange of the best thinking in our profession but it avoids like poison any effort to regiment. We encourage the dissenters because it is the dissenters who jar us out of ruts. To conventions like this, we come, we speak, we listen and question. Then each of us goes home and fights his own battles, inspired by a desire to do a better job in serving as eyes and ears of the American people and sentinels in the ever-necessary battle to preserve the freedoms which have made this the greatest nation in all history.[74]

As noted by Walters, the best tool for advancing professional ideals and more effectively applying professional labors was the annual ASNE meeting. The meeting proceeded, according to Paul Bellamy, upon the theory that ASNE members are not afraid to tackle "hot pokers" because they are hot. "We have felt that the same policy that makes individual newspapers great, namely, never flinching from a hard decision, would be that followed by this society as a whole," he said. Marvin Creager voiced similar sentiments:

These meetings are the only gatherings of working metropolitan editors where everybody has an opportunity to have his say. It is the only meeting where the only object is the general and free discussion of the common problems and hopes of editors without reference to any organizations or to any interest other than the general interest. . . . Its success depends upon you out there in the chairs. We want to know what is in your minds so that we may profit by it. This is a meeting of articulate editors. It is not a sit-down or shut-up strike.[75]

The following year, A. H. Kirchhofer claimed that the addresses and activities of the conventions were "a moving guide toward better newspaper work." By analyzing the problems of the day, he said, members clearly act more wisely toward achieving the "just aspirations of American journalism" which the founders set forth as the objectives of the society.

ASNE PRINTED WORKS

Next to the interchange at its annual meetings, ASNE became nationally known for its prodigious outpouring of publications. Much changed after Yost's observation in 1923 that "journalism is almost bookless." One of the strongest, most influential areas of ASNE leadership has been publications. The society has produced hundreds of books, pamphlets and printed positions. Its major publication has been *Proceedings of the American Society of Newspaper Editors*, a detailed account of its annual meetings. Originally published as *Problems in Journalism*, the annual volume is distributed to newspapers and journalism schools around the nation, where it serves as an annual record. Making note of this resource in 1937, Creager said, "The printed records of the 14 conventions already held constitute a priceless library and contemporary history of journalism. I have just re-read the 14 volumes. They get down to the brass tacks of newspaper making without losing faith in its ideals. They alone would justify 15 years in the life of any organization."[76]

In 1994 the *Proceedings* became an issue of controversy within ASNE when the board of directors voted to preserve and distribute the record of the annual meeting in a different and more timely manner as well as to save the costs entailed in transcribing and publishing the green book. However, a group of retired ASNE editors led by Creed C. Black, président of the Knight Foundation, intervened to postpone the death of the *Proceedings*. In addition, journalism historians around the nation, led by the American Journalism Historians Association (AJHA), wrote letters and passed resolutions. The ASNE board, at its fall 1994 meeting, voted to continue publication of the *Proceedings* in its green book format.

Since 1925, ASNE has also published the *Bulletin of the American Society of Newspaper Editors* on a monthly and occasionally semimonthly basis for members, journalism schools and others. Despite ongoing criticism that the *Bulletin* lacks credibility and is self-serving, a study of its volumes indicates that it serves as a major forum for voicing all sides of issues. James Kerney, Jr., noted, "The society liked to maul it over before deciding."[77] Much of this mauling is done in the *Bulletin*.

In recent years, ASNE has also published dozens of other pamphlets, books, studies and books from its Reston, Virginia, headquarters. One of the most influential has been Harold Cross' *The Right to Know*, described as a major instrument in the post–World War II freedom of information movement.

In addition to the institutional influence predicted by Casper Yost, ASNE has provided leadership through individual members who have used their identification with ASNE to advance important items on the media agenda. This has been particularly true in the tenures of the society's presidents who have reflected its membership. ASNE presidents have demonstrated their leadership by publishing more than 100 books. Although some of these books are personal or about nonmedia topics, many others touch on major problems of journalism.

Surprisingly, despite the numerous books published individually by ASNE members, little mention is made of ASNE by the writers. As an example, autobiographies by Jack Knight, George W. Healy, Jr., Turner Catledge and Vermont Royster are nearly silent about ASNE's impact. The bulk of references about the society's involvement focus primarily on the ASNE ethics code, the conventions, or a site for their speeches or other activities. Catledge recalls ASNE as the place where he met his second wife. ASNE is not even mentioned in the index to his autobiography.

IMPROVING WRITING AND REPORTING

With varying success, ASNE has also contributed to projects to improve writing in newsrooms across the nation. At least two presidents have argued that poor reporting and poor writing have contributed to a decline in the credibility of the editors and their profession. In one of the more severe scoldings on this subject in 1971, Newbold Noyes said it was obvious that editors are "lazy and superficial in much of our reporting. Often we do not even bother to challenge ourselves with the difficult questions as to what the hell is going on. We rely, instead, on certain stereotypes as to what makes a news story, and we are content when none of these pat, easily-covered happenings is omitted from our news report."[78]

Angrily, Noyes contended that editors were manipulated by various interests —some for change and some against it; some for the system, some seeking to tear it down—but all clever enough to play on the editor's weaknesses, laziness, superficiality and gullibility. "No doubt the Pentagon easily makes suckers of the press—but no more than the New Left does," Noyes charged. He added that he had long ago stopped being amazed at his own inertia and stupidity, but he was truly amazed to find fellow editors "precisely as inert and stupid as I was."[79]

Exactly one decade later, Michael O'Neill again called attention to this reporting failure: He said the investigative reporting of the post-Watergate era had caused the decline of more significant kinds of reporting. If journalists had not been so busy chasing corrupt officials, they might not have missed some of the biggest stories of the century. He cited these examples:

- The great migration of blacks from the South to the industrial cities of the North, "something we didn't discover until there were riots in the streets of Detroit."

- The first mincing steps toward war in Vietnam, "which we did not begin reporting seriously until our troops were involved."

- The women's liberation movement and the massive migration of women to the job market, "a social revolution that we originally dismissed as an outbreak of bra burning."

In trying to grapple with such problems, ASNE has been involved in several projects since its earliest days. On the recommendation of Herbert Bayard Swope, starting in 1925, ASNE named jurors in all newspaper categories for selection of Pulitzer Prize winners. This practice ended in 1950, because, according to Harry Ashmore, "some of the ex-jurors privately voiced the dark (and still recurring suspicion) that the Pulitzer committee engaged in back-scratching politics in passing the prizes around, and that ASNE's good name was being misused as a screen to sanctify the logrolling."[80]

John Seigenthaler pointed to ASNE influence in the area of civil rights reporting. He recalled in 1989 that in the aftermath of the 1954 *Brown* v. *Board of Education* ruling on school desegregation, ASNE editors began to focus on their failure to cover the U.S. Supreme Court adequately: "As a result, newspapers and other news agencies recruited, trained and assigned to that court a new corps of reporters, experts in the law, some of them with legal education. Today there is a cadre of experienced professional journalists, a dozen of them with law degrees, covering the U.S. Supreme Court."[81]

ASNE has also encouraged better writing through its annual writing awards. This program has had a significant impact on the profession.

VI. To work collectively for the solution of common problems

Success in this last area, relating to the society's achievements in working together to solve common problems, is probably the hardest to determine. One difficulty is the growing number of issues ASNE has become involved in since its inception. In its early years the society concerned itself primarily with problems that had an immediate and innate relationship to the print media. Later the society expanded its concerns to problems on the perimeter of print and to those involving the nonprint media. This broadened agenda has generated debate as to which of the many issues ASNE should choose to pursue.

In his first presidential address Yost foresaw the dangers of entering a field whose boundaries were beyond the horizon. "Yet, there are boundaries, or ought to be, that should confine us to the field of our profession." He continued:

We should make it a fixed principle of this society that public questions that do not involve the rights or obligations of journalism specifically are not to be discussed by the society, and that no officer of the society may commit it to any opinion or course of action relating to such questions. It is essential to the mainstream and progress of this organization that it is to limit itself to the consideration of professional interests, that there be no attempt to encroach upon the individual independence of its members.[82]

Nevertheless, a few of Yost's early colleagues used their presidential platforms to urge united action against major economic and political changes which they perceived as harmful to newspapers in the 1930s. During the early years of the Depression, Shedd criticized those who were content to "let George do it and betray our form of government and entire scheme of prosperity." On the other hand, Paul Bellamy, in his 1933 address after the inauguration of Franklin Delano Roosevelt, urged that the editorial mind be an open one.

New problems require new cures. I pray daily to be preserved from crystallized thinking, in short, from the assumption that everything old is good and everything new is bad. At the same time, I pray to be preserved from the other extreme of assuming that everything which is currently proposed is correct and all the fine achievements of the past should be thrown into the discard. I wish for my paper that it should take a balanced view of these matters, inclining toward the liberal side.[83]

Members, and particularly presidents, have been careful to avoid turning ASNE into a lobbyist group: they have also avoided speaking out on their own without board approval. This practice has been referred to by several presidents. In 1944, Roy A. Roberts observed that ASNE had received many requests to endorse various movements: "Most of these, doubtless, were worthy and useful causes. But your president and your board felt emphatically that the society should stick to its knitting and act only on problems immediately involving the newspaper profession from its editorial aspects. So most of these letters made a generous contribution to the waste paper salvage campaign."[84]

Wilbur Forrest voiced similar concern about the danger of the society's becoming involved in too many peripheral issues. He observed: "A defender of press freedom has the right to go on the record publicly in this respect. No president, however, feels authorized to issue statements either in the name of the society, its board or its membership unless or until a sober study of the issues has taken place."[85]

Also noting the concern was Basil Walters as he prepared to relinquish his presidency in 1954:

As you know, I have interpreted it to be your wish that I carefully preserve the society from all efforts, mostly from outside organizations, to make it another pressure group. I have taken the stand that no one has the authority to speak for you, that you reserve the right to voice your own views on your own editorial pages. Therefore, come midnight Saturday, and I shall resume my freedom to pop off any subject on any occasion.[86]

As stated by James S. Pope,

We do not enter into any activities that do not seem innately connected with our basic common interests and free from any trespass whatever upon the rights of individual members to use their own opinions and their own judgments. Although we fight the concept of professionalism in the sense that we don't want to be licensed, we do consider ourselves a professional society, and I would like to say we are still not an action group, political or any other kind of action. We are not even an editorial action group except on a few fundamental principles which really find us united.[87]

Notwithstanding such caveats, ASNE has increasingly become involved in "common problems," as can be seen by contrasting the number of ASNE committees in 1923 (6), with those in 1990 (16) and by examining the range of topics ASNE is involved in during the 1990s.

In addition to those problems already mentioned, ASNE members have become increasingly involved in such issues as the history of newspapers, human resources, international communications, literacy, minorities, disabilities, ownership, press, bar and public affairs, prison journalism and readership.

Although successful in interchanging ideas with other journalists and in providing leadership for journalism schools, ASNE has lagged significantly behind in two major areas—equal opportunities for women and minorities. Progress was made in 1987 when Katherine Fanning was elected as the society's first female president. Loren Ghiglione also notes that the percentage of women on the ASNE board has been markedly better than at such institutions as ANPA and AP. The election of Mrs. Fanning, however, did not completely eliminate the long-standing reluctance of editors to encourage female membership and leadership.

The minority issue was highlighted in the decade following the 1968 Kerner Commission Report. Thomas Winship addressed the topic in 1981. While chastising the leadership of the print media for its casual attitude toward the critical moral issue, Winship congratulated ASNE for its leadership and made some recommendations:

Among newspaper organizations, the nation's editors have been in front of others in expressing concerns over minority hiring. Only ASNE has a standing committee on minorities, thanks to the wisdom of Eugene Patterson of St. Petersburg, who set up this committee three years ago during his presidency. Since then, this committee, especially under the leadership of chairman Richard Smyser, has been the most active group in ASNE.[88]

Winship cited the Newspaper Readership Project as a structural model to bring all elements of the newspaper industry together (including advertising directors, circulation managers and publishers) to address the most crucial moral and economic issues. "I urge the hierarchy of ANPA, ASNE and ANPE to consider the proposal. Tear it apart, come up with a substitute approach, if you will. But, please at least address seriously this overriding problem," Winship pleaded. His request was followed by a Task Force on Minorities in the Newspaper Business, which was backed by ANPA.

Norman E. Isaacs also continued to serve as a gadfly for the society in speeches and in *Bulletin* articles. As noted in Chapter 1, Isaacs was a major force in resurrecting the ethics debate and in seeking outside solutions such as the National News Council to serve as catalysts for change in journalism as well as in the expanding society. He argued for a smaller rather than larger society. Unlike many editors who preferred to make their charges about the press in general, Isaacs was specific in occasionally focusing on the society in such books as *Untended Gates: The Mismanaged Press*.

Even among the major addresses of the 1980s, no ASNE president appeared to "take on" the society in public. Presidential speeches focused on the media in general, both print and broadcast. One of the most critical speeches was Michael J. O'Neill's nine-page discussion of "The Power of the Press: A Problem for the Republic—a Challenge for Editors." Although not discussing ASNE specifically, O'Neill gave an indication of the influence of the media as a whole and what he perceived as a lack of responsibility:

The extraordinary powers of the media, most convincingly displayed by network television and the national press, have been mobilized to influence the major public issues and national elections, to help diffuse the authority of Congress and to disassemble the political parties—even to make presidents or break them. Indeed, the media now weigh so heavily on the scales of power, that some political scientists claim we are upsetting the historic checks and balances invented by our forefathers.[89]

To illustrate his thesis of irresponsible power, O'Neill quoted Samuel P. Huntington of Harvard, who said that during the '60s and '70s, "the media were the institutions whose power expanded most significantly and that posed the most serious challenges to governmental authority." Max M. Kampelman had warned that "relatively unrestrained power of the media may well represent an even greater challenge to democracy than the publicized abuses of power by the Executive Branch and Congress." And Senator Daniel P. Moynihan, who conceded that the press already had the upper hand in Washington, stated that if the balance should tip too far in its direction, "our capacity for effective democratic government will be seriously and dangerously weakened."

Creed Black added to such criticism of the power of the media, which lumped print and broadcast together. In 1990, Loren Ghiglione urged editors to become more active as frontline fighters. To change, he said, "We need to stop making pronouncements like this. Resolutions and rhetoric must give way to plans and programs. 'Make no little plans,' wrote Daniel Burnham, 'they have no magic to stir men's blood and probably themselves will not be realized.' What we can accomplish is limited only by our vision."[90]

CONCLUSION

As seen in the annual speeches of the presidents and in other records, the American Society of Newspaper Editors has not always achieved its lofty goals and ambitions. This has not been because of a lack of desire. Much of it has been due to the transitory devotion of the members of professional organizations, who, though coming together for annual or committee meetings, must devote most of their time and talent to their newspapers and communities. Despite accusations that journalists are liberal and out of touch with the people, this study of ASNE presidents indicates that few of them are the "Prolicons" Jack Knight believed they were. Instead, in the process of moving closer to the corporate culture, many have adopted the protective, conservative coloring of the middle-road, individually and institutionally. Like the value systems they reflect, they are outer-directed and follow safe trends, including the cues of publishers who have attracted the editors into their economic orbits. They remain, as first president Casper Yost suggested, as "Gods within the newspaper machine." This is seen particularly during times of war, when the members become defenders of the faith, no matter what the faith may be. Such an outlook contributed to the society's major failure to adapt mechanisms to promote and encourage greater gender and racial diversity in newspaper offices around the country. The issue was finally forced upon Americans in the decade after the Kerner Commission report declared the press had contributed to racism. Adding to this cautious approach was the limited staff and resources that inhibited ASNE from carrying out its responsibilities for the fourth estate with the same vigor as the publishing and advertising professional groups to which ASNE is moving, as editors begin to look upon themselves as potential publishers, editor-businessmen.

Such inevitable consequences of change and adaptation to the economic and social facts of life need not detract from ASNE's limited leadership and positive influence on American journalism. In addition to providing one of the first major models for an ethics code; scholarly, legal leadership in the right to know movement; direction for journalism education and research and publications; ASNE has served as a major forum and agenda setter for its American members as well as those in countries where the society was frustrated in its efforts to "put Mother Hubbards on the heathen." In the words of Russell Wiggins, ASNE has been able to succeed despite the fact that "if [it] were any looser it would fall apart" and "if it was more effectively organized it would be a menace." Although institutionally incapable of carrying out all its desires, the American Society of Newspaper Editors has provided honorable, albeit ordinary, leadership during its extraordinary first seven decades of existence.

NOTES

1. Lee Hills, "The State of the Society," *ASNE Bulletin*, April 1962, 1.
2. ASNE *Proceedings*, 1937, 15.
3. ASNE *Proceedings*, 1970, 201.
4. ASNE *Proceedings*, 1980, 81.
5. ASNE *Proceedings*, 1990, 58.
6. *ASNE Bulletin*, November 1992, 31.
7. ASNE *Proceedings*, 1925, 21.
8. ASNE *Proceedings*, 1937, 19.
9. ASNE *Proceedings*, 1940, 16–17.
10. Donald J. Sterling, *A Sterling Story*, Portland: Arcady Press, 1952, 143.
11. ASNE *Proceedings*, 1949, 12.
12. Herbert Brucker, "Our Next Forty Years," *ASNE Bulletin*, February 1964, 7.
13. ASNE *Proceedings*, 1941, 17.
14. Ibid., 19.
15. ASNE *Proceedings*, 1946, 13.
16. Ibid., 118.

17. Ibid., 131.

18. Ibid., 11.

19. ASNE *Proceedings*, 1949, 12.

20. ASNE *Proceedings*, 1950, 34.

21. ASNE *Proceedings*, 1924, 59.

22. ASNE *Proceedings*, 1948, 21.

23. ASNE *Proceedings*, 1950, 31.

24. ASNE *Proceedings*, 1985, 13.

25. ASNE *Proceedings*, 1925, 20.

26. ASNE minutes, January 13, 1927, 39.

27. ASNE minutes, October 14, 1928, 49.

28. ASNE minutes, April 14, 1948, 278.

29. ASNE *Proceedings*, 1932, 26.

30. ASNE *Proceedings*, 1948, 18.

31. Pitts, *Read All About It! 50 Years of ASNE*, Reston, Va.: ASNE, 1974, 120.

32. ASNE *Proceedings*, 1989, 8–9.

33. ASNE *Proceedings*, 1927, 17.

34. ASNE *Proceedings*, 1931, 17.

35. ASNE minutes, December 10, 1932, 71–72.

36. ASNE minutes, April 23, 1949, 297.

37. ASNE *Proceedings*, 1937, 20.

38. ASNE *Proceedings*, 1943, 18.

39. Ibid.

40. ASNE *Proceedings*, 1951, 17.

41. ASNE *Proceedings*, 1960, 28.

42. Russell Wiggins, telephone interview with author, January 29, 1991.

43. Pitts, 7.

44. ASNE *Proceedings*, 1942, 19.

45. ASNE *Proceedings*, 1943, 18.

46. ASNE *Proceedings*, 1956, 22.

47. ASNE *Proceedings*, 1975, 43.

48. Michael J. O'Neill, draft, "Editorial Leadership Program: A New Direction for the ASNE," March 28, 1977, 3.

49. ASNE *Proceedings*, 1978, 86.

50. ASNE *Proceedings*, 1965, 25.

51. ASNE *Proceedings*, 1961, 19.

52. ASNE *Proceedings*, 1967, 64.

53. ASNE *Proceedings*, 1976, 21.

54. ASNE *Proceedings*, 1967, 64.

55. ASNE *Proceedings*, 1927, 17.

56. ASNE *Proceedings*, 1930, 19.

57. ASNE *Proceedings*, 1944, 13.

58. ASNE *Proceedings*, 1946, 15.

59. ASNE *Proceedings*, 1948, 20.

60. ASNE *Proceedings*, 1949, 16.

61. Pitts, 185.

62. J. Herbert Altschull, *From Milton to McLuhan: The Ideas behind American Journalism*, New York: Longman, 1990, 250.

63. ASNE *Proceedings*, 1951, 12–13.

64. ASNE *Proceedings*, 1956, 21.

65. ASNE *Proceedings*, 1960, 251.

66. Pitts, 171.

67. ASNE *Proceedings*, 1987, 10–12.

68. ASNE *Proceedings*, 1929, 19.

69. ASNE *Proceedings*, 1926, 21.

70. ASNE *Proceedings*, 1950, 31.

71. ASNE *Proceedings*, 1947, 20.

72. ASNE *Proceedings*, 1950, 32.

73. ASNE *Proceedings*, 1931, 17.

74. ASNE *Proceedings*, 1954, 10.

75. ASNE *Proceedings*, 1937, 18–19.

76. ASNE *Proceedings*, 1939, 16.

77. Pitts, 124.

78. ASNE *Proceedings*, 1971, 18.

79. Ibid., 19.

80. Pitts, 125.

81. ASNE *Proceedings*, 1989, 10.

82. ASNE *Proceedings*, 1923, 20.

83. ASNE *Proceedings*, 1933, 13.

84. ASNE *Proceedings*, 1943, 16.

85. ASNE *Proceedings*, 1947, 18.

86. ASNE *Proceedings*, 1954, 9.

87. ASNE *Proceedings*, 1955, 11.

88. ASNE *Proceedings*, 1981, 337.

89. ASNE *Proceedings*, 1982, 11–12.

90. ASNE *Proceedings*, 1990.

Appendix A

Past Presidents of ASNE

YEAR	EDITOR	NEWSPAPER
1922–1926	Casper S. Yost*	St. Louis *Globe-Democrat*
1926–1928	E. C. Hopwood*	Cleveland *Plain Dealer*
1928–1930	Walter M. Harrison*	Oklahoma City *Oklahoman*
1930–1933	Fred Fuller Shedd*	Philadelphia *Evening Bulletin*
1933–1934	Paul Bellamy*	Cleveland *Plain Dealer*
1934–1936	Grove Patterson*	Toledo (Ohio) *Blade*
1936–1937	Marvin H. Creager*	Milwaukee *Journal*
1937–1938	A. H. Kirchhofer*	Buffalo *Evening News*
1938–1939	William Allen White*	Emporia (Kans.) *Gazette*
1939–1940	Donald J. Sterling*	Oregon *Journal*
1940–1941	Tom Wallace*	Louisville (Ky.) *Times*
1941–1942	Dwight Marvin*	Troy (N.Y.) *Record*
1942–1943	W. S. Gilmore*	Detroit *News*
1943–1944	Roy A. Roberts*	Kansas City (Mo.) *Star*
1944–1946	John S. Knight*	Knight Newspapers
1946–1947	Wilbur Forrest*	New York *Herald Tribune*
1947–1948	N. R. Howard*	Cleveland *News*
1948–1949	Erwin D. Canham	*Christian Science Monitor*
1949–1950	B. M. McElway*	Washington *Star*
1950–1951	Dwight Young*	Dayton *Journal-Herald*
1951–1952	Alexander F. Jones*	Syracuse (N.Y.) *Herald-Journal*
1952–1953	Wright Bryan*	Atlanta *Journal*
1953–1954	Basil L. Walters*	Knight Newspapers
1954–1955	James S. Pope*	*Courier-Journal* and Louisville (Ky.) *Times*

* Deceased

1955–1956	Kenneth MacDonald	Des Moines *Register and Tribune*
1956–1957	Jenkin Lloyd Jones	Tulsa (Okla.) *Tribune*
1957–1958	Virginius Dabney	Richmond (Va.) *Times-Dispatch*
1958–1959	George W. Healy, Jr.*	New Orleans *Times-Picayune*
1959–1960	J. R. Wiggins	Washington *Post*
1960–1961	Turner Catledge*	New York *Times*
1961–1962	Felix R. McKnight	Dallas *Times Herald*
1962–1963	Lee Hills	Knight Newspapers
1963–1964	Herbert Brucker*	Hartford (Conn.) *Courant*
1964–1965	Miles H. Wolff*	Greensboro (N.C.) *Daily News*
1965–1966	Vermont Royster	*Wall Street Journal*
1966–1967	Robert C. Notson	Portland *Oregonian*
1967–1968	Michael J. Ogden	Providence (R.I.) *Journal and Bulletin*
1968–1969	Vincent S. Jones	Gannett Newspapers
1969–1970	Norman E. Isaacs	*Courier-Journal* and Louisville (Ky.) *Times*
1970–1971	Newbold Noyes	Washington *Star*
1971–1972	C. A. McKnight*	Charlotte (N.C.) *Observer*
1972–1973	J. Edward Murray	Detroit *Free Press*
1973–1974	Arthur C. Deck*	Salt Lake *Tribune*
1974–1975	Howard H. Hays, Jr.	Riverside (Calif.) *Press-Enterprise*
1975–1976	Warren H. Phillips	*Wall Street Journal*
1976–1977	George Chaplin	Honolulu *Advertiser*
1977–1978	Eugene C. Patterson	St. Petersburg (Fla.) *Times*
1978–1979	John Hughes	*Christian Science Monitor*
1979–1980	William H. Hornby	Denver *Post*
1980–1981	Thomas Winship	Boston *Globe*
1981–1982	Michael J. O'Neill	New York *Daily News*
1982–1983	John C. Quinn	Gannett Newspapers
1983–1984	Creed C. Black	Lexington (Ky.) *Herald-Leader*
1984–1985	Richard D. Smyser	Oak Ridge (Tenn.) *Oak Ridger*
1985–1986	Robert P. Clark	Harte-Hanks Newspapers
1986–1987	Michael G. Gartner	Louisville (Ky.) *Courier-Journal*
1987–1988	Katherine W. Fanning	*Christian Science Monitor*
1988	Edward R. Cony	*Wall Street Journal*
1988–1989	John Siegenthaler	*USA Today* and Nashville *Tennessean*
1989–1990	Loren Ghiglione	Southbridge (Mass.) *News*
1990–1991	Burl Osborne	Dallas *Morning News*
1991–1992	David Lawrence, Jr.	Miami *Herald*
1992–1993	Seymour Topping	New York *Times*
1993–1994	William A. Hilliard	Portland *Oregonian*
1994–1995	Gregory Favre	Sacramento *Bee*

Appendix B

ASNE Code of Ethics

Code of Ethics
or Canons of Journalism

The American Society of Newspaper Editors

The primary function of newspapers is to communicate to the human race what its members do, feel and think. Journalism, therefore, demands of its practitioners the widest range of intelligence, or knowledge, and of experience, as well as natural and trained powers of observation and reasoning. To its opportunities as a chronicle are indissolubly linked its obligations as teacher and interpreter.

To the end of finding some means of codifying sound practice and just aspirations of American journalism, these canons are set forth:

I.

RESPONSIBILITY—The right of a newspaper to attract and hold readers is restricted by nothing but considerations of public welfare. The use a newspaper makes of the share of public attention it gains serves to determine its sense of responsibility, which it shares with every member of its staff. A journalist who uses his power for any selfish or otherwise unworthy purpose is faithless to a high trust.

II.

FREEDOM OF THE PRESS—Freedom of the press is to be guarded as a vital right of mankind. It is the unquestionable right to discuss whatever is not explicitly forbidden by law, including the wisdom of any restrictive statute.

III.

INDEPENDENCE—Freedom from all obligations except that of fidelity to the public interest is vital.

1. Promotion of any private interest contrary to the general welfare, for whatever reason, is not compatible with honest journalism. So-called news communications from private sources should not be published without public notice of their source or else substantiation of their claims to value as news, both in form and substance.

2. Partisanship, in editorial comment which knowingly departs from the truth, does violence to the best spirit of American journalism; in the news columns it is subversive of a fundamental principle of the profession.

IV.

SINCERITY, TRUTHFULNESS, ACCURACY—Good faith with the reader is the foundation of all journalism worthy of the name.

1. By every consideration of good faith a newspaper is constrained to be truthful. It is not to be excused for lack of thoroughness or accuracy within its control, or failure to obtain command of these essential qualities.

2. Headlines should be fully warranted by the contents of the articles which they surmount.

V.

IMPARTIALITY—Sound practice makes clear distinction between news reports and expressions of opinion. News reports should be free from opinion or bias of any kind.

1. This rule does not apply to so-called special articles unmistakably devoted to advocacy or characterized by a signature authorizing the writer's own conclusions and interpretation.

VI.

FAIR PLAY—A newspaper should not publish unofficial charges affecting reputation or moral character without opportunity given to the accused to be heard; right practice demands the giving of such opportunity in all cases of serious accusation outside judicial proceedings.

1. A newspaper should not invade private rights or feeling without sure warrant of public right as distinguished from public curiosity.

2. It is the privilege, as it is the duty, of a newspaper to make prompt and complete correction of its own serious mistakes of fact or opinion, whatever their origin.

DECENCY—A newspaper cannot escape conviction of insincerity if while professing high moral purpose it supplies incentives to base conduct, such as are to be found in details of crime and vice, publication of which is not demonstrably for the general good. Lacking authority to enforce its canons the journalism here presented can but express the hope that deliberate pandering to vicious instincts will encounter effective public disapproval or yield to the influence of a preponderant professional condemnation.

Appendix C

ASNE Statement of Principles

PREAMBLE

The First Amendment, protecting freedom of expression from abridgment by any law, guarantees to the people through their press a constitutional right, and thereby places on newspaper people a particular responsibility.

Thus journalism demands of its practitioners not only industry and knowledge but also the pursuit of a standard of integrity proportionate to the journalist's singular obligation.

To this end the American Society of Newspaper Editors sets forth this Statement of Principles as a standard encouraging the highest ethical and professional performance.

ARTICLE I - Responsibility

The primary purpose of gathering and distributing news and opinion is to serve the general welfare by informing the people and enabling them to make judgments on the issues of the time. Newspapermen and women who abuse the power of their professional role for selfish motives or unworthy purposes are faithless to that public trust.

The American press was made free not just to inform or just to serve as a forum for debate but also to bring an independent scrutiny to bear on the forces of power in the society, including the conduct of official power at all levels of government.

ARTICLE II - Freedom of the Press

Freedom of the press belongs to the people. It must be defended against encroachment or assault from any quarter, public or private.

Journalists must be constantly alert to see that the public's business is conducted in public. They must be vigilant against all who would exploit the press for selfish purposes.

ARTICLE III - Independence

Journalists must avoid impropriety and the appearance of impropriety as well as any conflict of interest or the appearance of conflict. They should neither accept anything nor pursue any activity that might compromise or seem to compromise their integrity.

ARTICLE IV - Truth and Accuracy

Good faith with the reader is the foundation of good journalism. Every effort must be made to assure that the news content is accurate, free from bias and in context, and that all sides are presented fairly. Editorials, analytical articles and commentary should be held to the same standards of accuracy with respect to facts as news reports.

Significant errors of fact, as well as errors of omission, should be corrected promptly and prominently.

ARTICLE V - Impartiality

To be impartial does not require the press to be unquestioning or to refrain from editorial expression. Sound practice, however, demands a clear distinction for the reader between news reports and opinion. Articles that contain opinion or personal interpretation should be clearly identified.

ARTICLE VI - Fair Play

Journalists should respect the rights of people involved in the news, observe the common standards of decency and stand accountable to the public for the fairness and accuracy of their news reports.

Persons publicly accused should be given the earliest opportunity to respond.

Pledges of confidentiality to news sources must be honored at all costs, and therefore should not be given lightly. Unless there is clear and pressing need to maintain confidences, sources of information should be identified.

These principles are intended to preserve, protect and strengthen the bond of trust and respect between American journalists and the American people, a bond that is essential to sustain the grant of freedom entrusted to both by the nation's founders.

This Statement of Principles was adopted by the ASNE board of directors, October 23, 1975; it supplants the 1922 Code of Ethics ("Canons of Journalism").

Appendix D

Political Leanings of ASNE Presidents

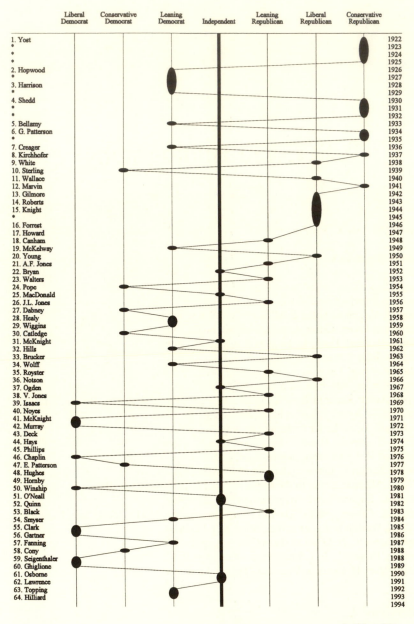

	Liberal Democrat	Conservative Democrat	Leaning Democrat	Independent	Leaning Republican	Liberal Republican	Conservative Republican	
1. Yost								1922
•								1923
•								1924
•								1925
2. Hopwood								1926
•								1927
3. Harrison								1928
•								1929
4. Shedd								1930
•								1931
•								1932
5. Bellamy								1933
6. G. Patterson								1934
•								1935
7. Creager								1936
8. Kirchhofer								1937
9. White								1938
10. Sterling								1939
11. Wallace								1940
12. Marvin								1941
13. Gilmore								1942
14. Roberts								1943
15. Knight								1944
•								1945
16. Forrest								1946
17. Howard								1947
18. Canham								1948
19. McKelway								1949
20. Young								1950
21. A.F. Jones								1951
22. Bryan								1952
23. Walters								1953
24. Pope								1954
25. MacDonald								1955
26. J.L. Jones								1956
27. Dabney								1957
28. Healy								1958
29. Wiggins								1959
30. Catledge								1960
31. McKnight								1961
32. Hills								1962
33. Brucker								1963
34. Wolff								1964
35. Royster								1965
36. Notson								1966
37. Ogden								1967
38. V. Jones								1968
39. Isaacs								1969
40. Noyes								1970
41. McKnight								1971
42. Murray								1972
43. Deck								1973
44. Hays								1974
45. Phillips								1975
46. Chaplin								1976
47. E. Patterson								1977
48. Hughes								1978
49. Hornby								1979
50. Winship								1980
51. O'Neall								1981
52. Quinn								1982
53. Black								1983
54. Smyser								1984
55. Clark								1985
56. Gartner								1986
57. Fanning								1987
58. Cony								1988
59. Seigenthaler								1988
60. Ghiglione								1989
61. Osborne								1990
62. Lawrence								1991
63. Topping								1992
64. Hilliard								1993
								1994

David Jensen, 1991

212

Selected Bibliography

PRIMARY SOURCES

Correspondence

Black, Creed C. Letter to the author, July 29, 1992.
Creager, Marvin. Letter to David Lawrence, August 2, 1952. (ASNE files, Reston, Va.).
Dabney, Virginius. Letter to Miles H. Wolff, July 14, 1972.
Ghiglione, Loren. Letter to the author, August 28, 1990.
Giancarlo, Gene. Letter to the author, August 31, 1990.
Hughes, John. Letter to the author, August 20, 1990.
Isaacs, Norman. Letter to the author, March 12, 1992.
Jones, Vincent. Letter to the author, July 24, 1990.
Krock, Arthur. Letter to David Lawrence, June 23, 1951. (ASNE files, Reston, Va.).
MacDonald, Kenneth. Letter to the author, July 30, 1990.
McKnight, Felix. Letter to the author, July 21, 1990.
Murray, J. Edward. Letter to the author, June 29, 1992.
Natt, Ted M. Letter to the author, April 12, 1990.
Notson, Robert C. Letter to the author, July 18, 1990.
O'Neill, Michael. Letter to the author, August 3, 1990; July 17, 1992.
Patterson, Eugene. Letter to the author, July 20, 1990.
Patterson, Grove. Letter to David Lawrence, August 7, 1951. (ASNE files, Reston, Va.).
Phillips, Warren H. Letter to the author, July 12, 1990.
Pope, James S., Jr. Letter to the author, August 2, 1990.
Sterling, Donald J., Jr. Letters to the author, July 9, 12, 1990.
Wolff, Miles H. Letter to Virginius Dabney, September 6, 1972.

Interviews

Chaplin, George. Cambridge, Mass., April 9–12, 1991.
Clark, Robert P. Telephone interview. July 25, 1990.

Dennis, Everette. Washington, D.C., April 5, 1990.
Giancarlo, Gene. Washington, D.C., Boston, April 1990, 1991.
Hills, Lee. Telephone interviews. 1990–1994.
Isaacs, Norman. Telephone interviews. 1990, 1991, 1992.
Osborne, Burl. Dallas, Texas, July 15, 1992.
Pease, Ted. Washington, D.C., April 5, 1990.
Pope, James S., Jr. Telephone interview. January 2, 1991.
Schmidt, Richard. April 1990, 1991.
Sterling, Donald J., Jr. Telephone interviews. July 5 and 9, 1990.
Stinnett, Lee. April 1990, 1991, 1992.
Wiggins, Russell. Telephone interviews. December 5, 1990; January 29, 1991.
Wolff, Miles, Jr. Telephone interviews.

Minutes

The Board of Directors, American Society of Newspaper Editors, April 25, 1922, to
    April 1993.

Proceedings

Proceedings of the American Society of Newspaper Editors, 1923–93.

ASNE Periodicals and Publications

Aarons, Leroy F. "Gay and Lesbian Journalists Report Most Newsrooms Are Good
    Places to Work." *ASNE Bulletin,* May–June 1990.
————. "Membership Is Approaching 500 in New Association for Gay and Lesbian
    Journalists." *ASNE Bulletin,* January–February 1992.
Beck, Edward. "Fate of Newspaper Hangs on Character." *ASNE Bulletin,* February 1,
    1943.
"Bingay Traces Growth of Society from Founder's Dream to '46 Meeting." *ASNE
    Bulletin,* June 1, 1946.
Block, Randy. "How Effective Is Our Code of Ethics?" *ASNE Bulletin,* July
    1968.
"He Wore His Honor as a Badge as if to Encourage Honor in All He Met." *ASNE
    Bulletin,* May 1956.
"Illicit Representation Abroad." *ASNE Bulletin,* October 1933.
McVea, Denise. "Marriott Ready for Puttin' on the Ritz." *ASNE Reporter,* April 3,
    1990.
"Magazine Belittles News Yardstick." *ASNE Bulletin,* February 1933.
"Mr. Harrison Corrects *Time.*" *ASNE Bulletin,* May 1933.
Seymour, Gideon. "Reflections on Atrocities." *ASNE Bulletin,* July 1945.

Speeches

Jones, Vincent. Paper for the Humdrum Club, March 2, 1970.

SECONDARY SOURCES

Articles

Armstrong, O. K. "Kansas City's Boss-Busting Editor." *Progressive,* January 27, 1947.
Cobb, Frank I. "The Press and Public Opinion." *New Republic,* December 31, 1919.
Harwood, Richard. "Poor Editors." *Washington Post National Weekly Edition,* April 16–22, 1990.
Jones, Alex S. "Newspaper Talk: Reappraisal and the 60s." *New York Times,* April 6, 1990.
Lippmann, Walter and Charles Merz. "A Test of the News." *New Republic,* August 4, 1920.
"Roy Roberts Refuses to Resign from OWI Group." *Editor & Publisher,* July 17, 1943.

Scholarly Journals

Bukro, Casey. "The SPJ's Double-Edged Sword: Accountability, Credibility." *Journal of Mass Media Ethics* (Fall–Winter 1985–86).
Gould, Lewis. "First Ladies and the Press: Bess Truman to Lady Bird Johnson." *American Journalism* (Summer 1983).
Kennerly, Evelyn. "Mass Media Ethics and Mass Murder: American Coverage of the Holocaust." *Journal of Mass Media Ethics* (Fall–Winter 1986–87).
Lipstadt, Deborah E. "Pious Sympathies and Sincere Regrets: The American News Media and the Holocaust from Krystlnacht to Bermuda 1938–1943." *Modern Judaism* (1982).
Logan, Robert A. "Jefferson's and Madison's Legacy: The Death of the National News Council." *Journal of Mass Media Ethics* (Fall–Winter 1985–86).
Mankiewicz, Frank. "From Lippmann to Letterman: The Ten Most Powerful Voices." *Gannett Center Journal* (Spring 1989).
Ohrn, Karin Becker. "What You See Is What You Get: Dorothea Lange and Ansel Adams at Manzanar." *Journalism History* (Spring 1977).
Pollard, James E. "The Kennedy Administration and the Press." *Journalism Quarterly* (Winter 1964).
Pratte, Alf. "A Tortuous Route Growing Up: The Rise of Women in the American Society of Newspaper Editors." *Journal of Women's History* (Spring 1994).
————. "Going Along for the Ride on the Prosperity Bandwagon: Peaceful Annexation Not War between the Editors and Radio, 1923–1941." *Journal of Radio Studies* 2 (1993–94).
Shedd, Frank Fuller. "The Newspaper Heritage." *Journalism Quarterly* (Spring 1931).

Teel, Leonard C. "The Shaping of a Southern Opinion Leader: Ralph McGill and Freedom of Information." *American Journalism* 5.1 (1988).

Washburn, Patrick S. "The Office of Censorship's Attempt to Control Press Coverage of the Atomic Bomb duringWorld War II." *Journalism Monographs* (April 1990).

Winfield, Betty H. "FDR's Pictorial Image, Rules and Boundaries." *Journalism History* (Winter 1978–79).

Books

Allen, Frederick Lewis. *Only Yesterday.* New York: Harper & Row, 1931.

Ashley, Perry J., ed. *Dictionary of Literary Biography.* Vols. 23, 25, 29, 43. Detroit: A Bruccoli Clark Layman Book, Gale Research, 1983, 1984, 1986.

Bird, Caroline. *The Invisible Scar.* New York: Pocket Books, 1966.

Blanchard, Margaret. *Exporting the First Amendment: The Press Government Crusade of 1945–1952.* New York: Longman, 1986.

Bogart, Leo. *Preserving the Press: How Daily Newspapers Mobilized to Keep Their Readers.* New York: Columbia University Press, 1991.

Brucker, Herbert. *Communication Is Power: Unchanging Values in Changing Journalism.* New York: Oxford Press, 1973.

Canham, Erwin. *Commitment to Freedom.* Boston: Houghton Mifflin, 1958.

Catledge, Turner. *My Life and the Times.* New York: Harper & Row, 1971.

Chamberlin, Joseph Edgar. *The Boston Transcript: A History of the First Hundred Years.* Boston: Houghton Mifflin, 1930.

Clabes, Judith G., ed. *New Guardians of the Press: Selected Profiles of America's Women Newspaper Editors.* Indianapolis: R. J. Berg, 1983.

Claiborne, Jack. *The Charlotte Observer: Its Time and Place, 1869–1986.* Chapel Hill: University of North Carolina Press, 1987.

Commission on Freedom of the Press. *A Free and Responsible Press.* Chicago: University of Chicago Press, 1947.

Conrad, Will C., Kathleen F. Wilson and Dale Wilson. *The Milwaukee* Journal: *The First Eighty Years.* Madison: University of Wisconsin Press, 1964.

Emery, Edwin. *History of the American Newspaper Publishers Association.* Minneapolis: University of Minnesota Press, 1950.

Folkerts, Jean and Dwight L. Teeter, Jr. *Voices of a Nation.* New York: Macmillan, 1989.

Fowler, Gene. *Timberline: A Story of Bonfils and Tammen.* Garden City, N.Y.: Blue Ribbon Books, 1940.

Ghiglione, Loren, ed. *The Buying and the Selling of America's Newspapers.* Indianapolis: R. J. Berg, 1984.

————, ed. *Gentlemen of the Press.* Indianapolis: R. J. Berg, 1984.

Hart, Jim A. *A History of the St. Louis* Globe–Democrat. Columbia: University of Missouri Press, 1961.

Healy, George. *A Lifetime on Deadline: Self-Portrait of a Southern Journalist.* Gretna: Pelican Publishing Co., 1976.

Hecht, Ben. *A Child of the Century.* New York: Donald I. Fine, 1954.

Hosokawa, Bill. *Thunder in the Rockies: The Incredible Denver Post.* New York: William Morrow, 1976.

Irons, Peter. *Justice at War: The Story of the Japanese Internment Camps.* New York: Oxford University Press, 1983.

Isaacs, Norman. *Untended Gates: The Mismanaged Press.* New York: Columbia University Press, 1986.

Kaltenborn, H. V. "The Role of Radio." In *Journalism in Wartime.* Washington, D.C.: American Council on Public Affairs, 1943.

Kluger, Richard. *The Paper: The Life and Death of the New York* Herald Tribune. New York: Alfred A. Knopf, 1986.

Kneebone, John T. *Southern Liberal Journalists and the Issue of Race, 1920–1944.* Chapel Hill: University of North Carolina Press, 1985.

Knightley, Philip. *The First Casualty.* New York: Harcourt Brace Jovanovich, 1975.

Leab, Daniel J. *A Union of Individuals: The Formation of the American Newspaper Guild 1933–36.* New York: Columbia University Press, 1970.

Lowery, Shearon and Melvin DeFleur. *Milestones in Mass Communication Research: Media Effects.* New York: Longman, 1983.

Lutz, William. *The News of Detroit: How a Newspaper and a City Grew Together.* Boston: Little, Brown and Co., 1973.

McKerns, Joseph P., ed. *Biographical Dictionary of American Journalism.* New York: Greenwood Press, 1989.

Mills, George. *Things Just Don't Happen.* Ames: Iowa State University Press, 1977.

Morrison, Joseph L. *Josephus Daniels: The Small-d Democrat.* Chapel Hill: University of North Carolina Press, 1966.

Moscowitz, Raymond. *"Stuffy": The Life of Newspaper Pioneer Basil "Stuffy" Walters.* Ames: University of Iowa Press, 1983.

Patterson, Grove. *I Like People: The Autobiography of Grove Patterson.* New York: Random House, 1948.

Phillips, Cabell. *From the Crash to the Blitz, 1929–39.* New York: Macmillan, 1969.

Pitts, Alice Fox. *Read All About It! 50 Years of ASNE.* Reston, Va.: ASNE, 1974.

Postman, Neil. *Amusing Ourselves to Death: Public Discourse in the Age of Show Business.* New York: Penguin Books, 1986.

Roberts, Chalmers M. *The Washington* Post: *The First 100 Years.* Boston: Houghton Mifflin, 1977.

Salisbury, Harrison. *Without Fear or Favor.* New York: Ballantyne Books, 1980.

Schramm, Wilbur. *Responsibility in Mass Communication.* New York: Harper & Brothers, 1957.

Seldes, George. *Freedom of the Press.* Garden City, N.Y.: Garden City Publishing, 1935.

—————. *Lords of the Press.* New York: Julian Messner, 1938.

Shaw, Archer H. *The* Plain Dealer: *One Hundred Years in Cleveland.* New York: Alfred A. Knopf, 1942.

Sloan, David. *The Media in America: A History.* Worthington, Ohio: Publishing Horizons, 1989.

Smiley, Nixon. *Knights of the Fourth Estate: The Story of the* Miami Herald. Miami: Seemann Publishing, 1974.

Snyder, Louis L. and Richard B. Morris. *A Treasury of Great Reporting.* New York: Simon and Schuster, 1962.

Steffens, Lincoln. *The Autobiography of Lincoln Steffens.* New York: Harcourt, Brace and Co., 1931.

Sterling, Donald. *A Sterling Story.* Portland: Arcady Press, 1952.

Villard, Oswald Garrison. *The Disappearing Daily: Chapters in American Newspaper Evolution.* New York: Alfred A. Knopf, 1944.

Washburn, Patrick. *A Question of Sedition: The Federal Government's Investigation of the Black Press during World War II.* New York: Oxford University, 1986.

Wendt, Lloyd. *Chicago* Tribune: *The Rise of a Great American Newspaper.* Chicago: Rand McNally, 1979.

Weschler, James. *Reflections of an Angry Middle-Aged Editor.* New York: Random House, 1960.

White, Charles. *Knight: A Publisher in the Tumultuous Century.* New York: E. P. Dutton, 1988.

Williams, Harold A. *The Baltimore* Sun, *1837–1987.* Baltimore: Johns Hopkins University Press, 1987.

Index

About the Author

PAUL ALFRED PRATTE is Professor of Communication at Brigham Young University where he specializes in media history, opinion writing, news reporting, and mass media and society. A former reporter for the Honolulu *Star-Bulletin*, Lethbridge (Alberta) *Herald*, Salt Lake *Tribune*, and Salt Lake *Desert News*, he is a founder and 1994 president of the American Journalism Historians Association.

ISBN 0-275-94976-1

90000>

EAN

9 780275 949761

HARDCOVER BAR CODE